International and Development Education

The *International and Development Education Series* focuses on the complementary areas of comparative, international, and development education. Books emphasize a number of topics ranging from key international education issues, trends, and reforms to examinations of national education systems, social theories, and development education initiatives. Local, national, regional, and global volumes (single authored and edited collections) constitute the breadth of the series and offer potential contributors a great deal of latitude based on interests and cutting edge research. The series is supported by a strong network of international scholars and development professionals who serve on the International and Development Education Advisory Board and participate in the selection and review process for manuscript development.

SERIES EDITORS
John N. Hawkins
Professor Emeritus, University of California, Los Angeles
Senior Consultant, IFE 2020 East West Center

W. James Jacob
Assistant Professor, University of Pittsburgh
Director, Institute for International Studies in Education

PRODUCTION EDITOR
Heejin Park
Project Associate, Institute for International Studies in Education

INTERNATIONAL EDITORIAL ADVISORY BOARD
Clementina Acedo, *UNESCO's International Bureau of Education, Switzerland*
Philip G. Altbach, *Boston University, USA*
Carlos E. Blanco, *Universidad Central de Venezuela*
Sheng Yao Cheng, *National Chung Cheng University, Taiwan*
Ruth Hayhoe, *University of Toronto, Canada*
Wanhua Ma, *Peking University, China*
Ka-Ho Mok, *University of Hong Kong, China*
Christine Musselin, *Sciences Po, France*
Yusuf K. Nsubuga, *Ministry of Education and Sports, Uganda*
Namgi Park, *Gwangju National University of Education, Republic of Korea*
Val D. Rust, *University of California, Los Angeles, USA*
Suparno, *State University of Malang, Indonesia*
John C. Weidman, *University of Pittsburgh, USA*
Husam Zaman, *Taibah University, Saudi Arabia*

Institute for International Studies in Education
School of Education, University of Pittsburgh
5714 Wesley W. Posvar Hall, Pittsburgh, PA 15260 USA

Center for International and Development Education
Graduate School of Education & Information Studies, University of California, Los Angeles
Box 951521, Moore Hall, Los Angeles, CA 90095 USA

Titles:

Higher Education in Asia/Pacific: Quality and the Public Good
Edited by Terance W. Bigalke and Deane E. Neubauer

Affirmative Action in China and the U.S.: A Dialogue on Inequality and Minority Education
Edited by Minglang Zhou and Ann Maxwell Hill

Critical Approaches to Comparative Education: Vertical Case Studies from Africa, Europe, the Middle East, and the Americas
Edited by Frances Vavrus and Lesley Bartlett

Curriculum Studies in South Africa: Intellectual Histories & Present Circumstances
Edited by William F. Pinar

Higher Education, Policy, and the Global Competition Phenomenon
Edited by Laura M. Portnoi, Val D. Rust, and Sylvia S. Bagley

The Search for New Governance of Higher Education in Asia
Edited by Ka-Ho Mok

International Students and Global Mobility in Higher Education: National Trends and New Directions
Edited by Rajika Bhandari and Peggy Blumenthal

Curriculum Studies in Brazil: Intellectual Histories, Present Circumstances
Edited by William F. Pinar

Access, Equity, and Capacity in Asia Pacific Higher Education
Edited by Deane Neubauer and Yoshiro Tanaka

Policy Debates in Comparative, International, and Development Education
Edited by John N. Hawkins and W. James Jacob

Increasing Effectiveness of the Community College Financial Model: A Global Perspective for the Global Economy
Edited by Stewart E. Sutin, Daniel Derrico, Rosalind Latiner Raby, and Edward J. Valeau

Curriculum Studies in Mexico: Intellectual Histories, Present Circumstances
William F. Pinar

Internationalization of East Asian Higher Education: Globalization's Impact
Edited by John D. Palmer, Amy Roberts, Young Ha Cho, and Gregory S. Ching

Taiwan Education at the Crossroad: When Globalization Meets Localization
Chuing Prudence Chou and Gregory S. Ching

Mobility and Migration in Asian Pacific Higher Education
Edited by Deane E. Neubauer and Kazuo Kuroda

University Governance and Reform: Policy, Fads, and Experience in International Perspective
Edited by Hans G. Schuetze, William Bruneau, and Garnet Grosjean

University Governance and Reform

Policy, Fads, and Experience in International Perspective

Edited by
Hans G. Schuetze, William Bruneau, and Garnet Grosjean

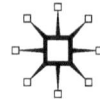

UNIVERSITY GOVERNANCE AND REFORM
Copyright © Hans G. Schuetze, William Bruneau, and Garnet Grosjean, 2012.

All rights reserved.

First published in 2012 by
PALGRAVE MACMILLAN®
in the United States—a division of St. Martin's Press LLC,
175 Fifth Avenue, New York, NY 10010.

Where this book is distributed in the UK, Europe and the rest of the world, this is by Palgrave Macmillan, a division of Macmillan Publishers Limited, registered in England, company number 785998, of Houndmills, Basingstoke, Hampshire RG21 6XS.

Palgrave Macmillan is the global academic imprint of the above companies and has companies and representatives throughout the world.

Palgrave® and Macmillan® are registered trademarks in the United States, the United Kingdom, Europe and other countries.

ISBN: 978–0–230–34012–1

Library of Congress Cataloging-in-Publication Data

   University governance and reform : policy, fads, and experience in international perspective / Edited by Hans G. Schuetze, William Bruneau, and Garnet Grosjean.
      pages cm.—(International and development education)
      ISBN 978–0–230–34012–1 (hardback)
     1. Universities and colleges—Administration. I. Schuetze, Hans Georg. II. Bruneau, William A., 1944– III. Grosjean, Garnet.

LB2341.U568 2012
378.1'01—dc23   2011051533

A catalogue record of the book is available from the British Library.

Design by Newgen Imaging Systems (P) Ltd., Chennai, India.

First edition: July 2012

Contents

Series Editors' Preface   vii

Foreword   xi
Hans G. Schuetze, William Bruneau, and Garnet Grosjean

List of Abbreviations and Acronyms   xiii

Part I: Premises and Problems

1. University Governance Reform: The Drivers and the Driven   3
   Hans G. Schuetze

2. Reconsidering University Autonomy and Governance: From Academic Freedom to Institutional Autonomy   11
   Pavel Zgaga

Part II: North America

3. The Provost Office as Key Decision-Maker in the Contemporary US University: Toward a Theory of Institutional Change   25
   Nelly P. Stromquist

4. Professors in Their Places: Governance in Canadian Higher Education   47
   William Bruneau

5. University Governance and Institutional Culture: A Canadian President's Perspective   63
   Ross Paul

6. The Politics of Policy Making in Postsecondary Education in Canada and in the Province of Ontario: Implications for Governance   77
   Paul Axelrod, Theresa Shanahan, Richard Wellen, and Roopa Desai-Trilokekar

7. Liberality and Collaborative Governance in a New Private University: The Experience of Quest University Canada   95
James Cohn

Part III: Latin America

8. International Forces Shaping Latin American Higher Education Governance   109
Alma Maldonado-Maldonado

9. Reforms of University Governance in Mexico: Inducements for or Impediments to Change?   125
Wietse de Vries and Germán Álvarez-Mendiola

10. Federal Policies and Governance of Universities in Mexico, 1990–2010   147
Adrián Acosta Silva

11. Higher Education Reform in Ecuador and Its Effect on University Governance   161
F. Mauricio Saavedra

Part IV: East Asia and Australia

12. Incorporation of National Universities in Japan: An Evaluation Six Years On   179
Motohisa Kaneko

13. Current Challenges Facing Japanese Universities and Future Perspectives   197
Masao Homma

14. Intellectuals, Academic Freedom, and University Autonomy in China   209
Qiang Zha

15. Higher Education Reform in Indonesia: University Governance and Autonomy   225
W. James Jacob, Yuanyuan Wang, Tracy Lynn Pelkowski, Ravik Karsidi, and Agus D. Priyanto

16. "Transforming Australia's Higher Education System": New Accountability Policies for a Global Era?   241
Lesley Vidovich

Contributors   257

Index   261

Series Editors' Preface

We are pleased to welcome this important volume on higher education reform, governance, and transformation to our series on comparative and development education. This topic has only gotten more critical as the world economy moves into uncharted waters and the demand for higher education has only gotten greater. It is difficult to go anywhere in the world where higher education demand has not placed enormous stress on national capacity, and this has in turn led to a transformation of public and private institutions, to issues of quality assurance, various accreditation schemes, educational borrowing, centralization, decentralization, and recentralization of the governance process and so on. Much of this frenzy in the academy can be traced to the rise of neoliberalism developed out of Reagan-Thatcherism, which has spread widely with countries borrowing selectively from it to suit their needs. The various chapters in this volume all illuminate numerous features of how neoliberalism has impacted higher education in a global context. What are some of the tenets of neoliberalism with direct relevance for higher education governance, reform, and change? One is the belief (easily recognized in most of our universities) that market solutions are superior to public sector planning and support. University deregulation followed by heightened quality assurance regimes quickly followed this belief. Public-private debates on higher education governance provided a context of the reorganization of universities and colleges in most international settings and were recognizable in such areas as the alignment issue (does the institution adequately prepare students for the world of work?), the cost of higher education (transferred from society to the individual), the rise of managerialism (loss of tenure-track faculty, dependence on business and government for finance, and decline of academic freedom), pressures to vocationalize the curriculum, the shorting of noneconomic aligned disciplines, and the list could go on.

Based on papers presented at the 7th International Workshop on Higher Education Reform held at the University of British Columbia (UBC) from October 6–8, 2010, the editors of this volume have done an exceptional job of choosing authors that illuminate these critical issues and ground these discussions in specific regional settings. The choice of focusing on Asia, Latin America, and North America is important as those regions in many ways are setting trends for the transformations that are taking place in higher education. The authors of the chapters are at the cutting edge in their fields having both theoretical and practical experience on the topics and in the regions. We believe that this volume will become one of the standards in the ongoing quest to understand the rapidly changing world of university governance.

While each year the International Workshop on Higher Education Reform is organized at a university in a different country, the workshop secretariat is maintained at UBC's Centre for Policy Studies in Higher Education and Training (CHET). Hans Schuetze and Garnet Grosjean, both of UBC, served as the 2010 workshop cochairs. Members of the International Advisory Committee include Germán Alvarez Mendiola, Center of Educational Research and Studies, Mexico City, Mexico; W. James Jacob, University of Pittsburgh, United States of America; Mei Li, East China Normal University, China; Hans G. Schuetze, UBC, Canada; Maria Slowey, Centre for Higher Education Research and Development, Dublin City University, Ireland; Andrä Wolter, Humboldt University, Germany; and Shinichi Yamamoto, Research Institute for Higher Education, Hiroshima University, Japan.

The 7th International Workshop on Higher Education Reform met many of the relatively high expectations Schuetze and his UBC colleagues established at the beginning of the workshop: "To provide a venue for mingling, networking, and academic partnerships." The annual workshops are cosponsored by the Higher Education Special Interest Group of the Comparative and International Education Society. The most recent workshop was held in October 2011 at Humboldt University in Berlin, Germany.

Four major themes were identified at the 2010 UBC Workshop: (1) institutional and social responsibilities; (2) tighter fiscal constraints and increased accountability (especially in the aftermath of the global financial crisis and recovery period); (3) identification and establishment of four principles of good governance: *coordination, information flow, transparency,* and *accountability*; and (4) quality assurance as a major component of governance in higher education (Jacob and Rust 2010).

The emergence of an emphasis on higher education good governance is not new but received a societal call to revisit and reemphasize the importance of including it in higher education curricula in the aftermath of the Enron scandal in the United States in October 2001 and more recently in the wake of the global financial crisis that began in 2007. Governance issues remain at the forefront of higher education reform efforts worldwide.

JOHN N. HAWKINS
University of California,
Los Angeles

W. JAMES JACOB
University of Pittsburgh

REFERENCE

Jacob, W. James, and Val D. Rust. 2010. "Principles of Good Governance: A Review of Key Themes Identified at the 7th International Workshop on Higher Education Reform." *Comparative and International Higher Education* 2 (2): 31-32.

Foreword

Hans G. Schuetze, William Bruneau, and Garnet Grosjean

In autumn 2010, the University of British Columbia at Vancouver welcomed the 7th annual International Workshop on Higher Education Reform. Like the six preceding meetings, the workshop drew together an international community of researchers, writers, and practitioners, keenly interested in the history, sociology, economics, politics, and general theory of higher education. After its founding meeting in Vancouver (2003), the annual gathering moved to Vienna, thence to Tokyo, Dublin, Shanghai, Mexico City, and once again to Vancouver. In each case, the meetings have generated significant and pointed debate and argument—and much publication.

The workshop is reminiscent of the "invisible college," the informal, but sustained community of mind that lay at the origins of the Royal Society in the seventeenth century. Like that "college," the workshop is the expression of the commitment of a great many individuals, rather than the automatic product of a formal association. The workshop is constantly renewed by a core and network of writer-researcher-practitioners whose commitment is evident in every aspect of the book you are about to read.

The quality of research presentations at the workshops motivated the organizers to find a regular publishing "home" for dissemination of this information to a broader audience. This volume helps to fulfill that ambition, and will, we think, stimulate even more research and debate on the central problems of the university.

The theme of our essays—university governance—has attracted unusually great interest since about 1985. Mind you, it has an awfully long pedigree. Since the late Middle Ages, university teachers have claimed to be natural governors of their institutions. But other groups and agents, especially the state, the church, students, and staff and the rising commercial classes, have sometimes claimed their own rights and roles. Since the Industrial Revolution, these competing claims have been discussed in the agora, in legislatures and cabinets, and in the university itself. Now pressure is rising to find a way of resolving, however temporarily, the tensions between and among the claimants. In some ways, the workshop offers a valuable framework for arriving at that resolution.

The questions we ask are pressing ones. Have the traditional forms of university self-governance been rendered irrelevant and impotent at the beginning of the twenty-first century? If they have, what are the consequences? What, if anything, should be done to remedy the situation? What were the roots and reasons, and what are the effects of this collegial form of governance? Does the emphasis on research and external resources and the quest for greater accessibility and accountability require business-like forms and processes of management? If so, which of these management techniques are appropriate for the particular mission, culture, and environment of universities, and which ones are "fads" that are inadequate, inefficient, and even counterproductive?

In the pages that follow, several comparative studies of university governance and control shed light on the new challenges and responses. They sit cheek by jowl with historical, philosophical, and work on the political economy of the individual university systems in Asia, Australia, and the Americas.

To help readers make their way through the book, the opening chapter offers a preview of the big questions being asked in higher education studies—in universities and in government—this century. The title of our introduction is "the drivers and the driven," and as we go to press, we see no reason to tone down its rhetorical emphasis.

The book is organized to show how continental groupings view the question of governance. It begins in North America with an overview of the problems of a Canadian university president, a Canadian faculty union leader, an American advisor to government, then moves through Latin America, Asia, and Australia.

We have said enough about the point of the book and recommend only that anyone wanting more guidance spend a little time with the opening chapters. We thank all the participants who contributed ideas, comments, and questions to the workshop, not just the authors. They are the energizing network without whom this book would not exist. It is they who will continue this effort and produce future discussions.

Above all, we thank the authors of this volume, who have written original essays for a book that is needed because it fills a void. But then, a book on the problem of university governance is *always* a good idea.

Abbreviations and Acronyms

AALE	American Academy of Liberal Education
AAU	Association of American Universities
AUCC	Association of Universities and Colleges of Canada
AHELO	Assessment of Higher Education Learning Outcomes
AIHEPS	Alliance for International Higher Education Policy Studies (USA)
AIUM	Association for Innovative University Management (Japan)
ALFA-ACRO	Accreditation for Official Recognition
ANUIES	National Association of Universities and Institutions of Higher Education (Mexico)
BAN-PT	National Accreditation Board for Higher Education (Indonesia)
BHMN	State Owned Legal Entity Universities (Indonesia)
BUAP	Benemérita Universidad Autónoma de Puebla (Mexico)
CAE	Content Area Expert
CAO	Chief Academic Officer
CAUT	Canadian Association of University Teachers
CEO	Chief Executive Officer
CERI	Centre for Educational Research and Innovation (France)
CFHSS	Canadian Federation for the Humanities and Social Sciences
CFI	Canada Foundation for Innovation
CHET	Center for Policy Studies in Higher Education and Training, University of British Columbia (Canada)
CHST	Canada Health and Social Transfer
CLA	Collegiate Learning Assessment (Australia)
CONACYT	National Council on Science and Technology (Mexico)
CONEA	Consejo Nacional de Evaluación y Acreditación (Ecuador)
CONESUP	Consejo Nacional de Educación Superior (Ecuador)
CSR	Common Sense Revolution (Canada)
DGHE	Director General of Higher Education (Indonesia)
DPT	Board of Higher Education (Indonesia)
DQAB	Degree Quality Assessment Board (Canada)
EUA	European University Association

FOMES	Fund for the Modernization of Higher Education (Mexico)
FPRC	Faculty Performance Review Committee
FTE	Full-Time Equivalent
G 8	Group of representatives from each of the eight major economies (Canada, France, Germany, Italy, Japan, Russia, UK, and USA).
G-10	Group of 10 Research-Intensive Universities (Canada)
G-13	Group of 13 Research-Intensive Universities (Canada)
G 20	Group of 20 Finance Ministers and Central Bank Governors
GDP	Gross Domestic Product
GPA	Grade Point Average
H1N1	A subtype of influenza A virus that was the most common cause of human influenza (flu) in 2009
HEI	Higher Education Institution
HRD	Human Resources Development
IAA	Independent Administrative Agency (Japan)
ICCPR	International Covenant on Civil and Political Rights
ICESCR	International Covenant on Economic, Social and Cultural Rights
ICR	Income-contingent [loan] repayment (Canada)
ICT	Information and communication technology
IDLN	Indonesian Distance Learning Network
IMF	International Monetary Fund
IMHERE	Managing Higher Education for Relevance and Efficiency (Indonesia)
IRB	Institutional Review Board
ISGUG	Independent Study Group on University Governance (Canada)
ISO	International Organization for Standardization
IT	Information technology
JMA	Japanese Management Association
JUAM	Japanese University Administrators Association
KPTIP	Consortium of Indonesian Universities-Pittsburgh
LU	Lakehead University (Canada)
MDG/s	Millennium Development Goal/s
MERCOSUR	Customs union of four Southern-cone countries (Argentina, Brazil, Paraguay, and Uruguay) established under the 1991 Treaty of Asunción
METI	Ministry of Economy, Trade and Industry (Japan)
MEXT	Ministry of Education, Culture, Sports, Science, and Technology (Japan)
MONE	Ministry of National Education (Indonesia)
MORA	Ministry of Religious Affairs (Indonesia)

Abbreviations and Acronyms

NAFTA	North American Free Trade Agreement
NIAD	National Institute for University Evaluation and Academic Degrees (Japan)
NSERC	Natural Sciences and Engineering Research Council (Canada)
NUC	National University Corporation (Japan)
OECD	Organisation for Economic Co-operation and Development
OREALC	Regional Bureau of Education for Latin America and the Caribbean (Chile)
PAGSE	Partnership Group for Science and Engineering (Canada)
PDCA	Plan, Do, Check, Act
PIAAC	Program for the International Assessment of Adult Competencies
PIFI	Integral Program for Institutional Development (Mexico)
PISA	Program for International Student Assessment
PQAB	Postsecondary Education Quality Assessment Board (Canada)
PRI	Institutional Revolutionary Party
PROMEP	Programa de Mejoramiento del Personal Académico (Mexico)
PSE	Postsecondary education
QA	Quality assurance
QI	Quality improvement
QUE	Quality for Undergraduate Education (Indonesia)
RIACES	Ibero-American Network for Higher Education Accreditation
SEAMEO	Southeast Asian Ministers of Education Organization
SENESCYT	Secretaría Nacional de Educación Superior, Ciencia, Tecnología e Innovación (Ecuador)
SENPLADES	Secretaría Nacional de Planificación y Desarrollo (Ecuador)
SEP	Secretaría de Educación Pública (Mexico)
SES	Undersecretary for Higher Education (Mexico)
SINAPPES	National Permanent Planning System of Higher education (Mexico)
SNI	National System of Researchers (Mexico)
SSHRCC	Social Sciences and Humanities Research Council of Canada
SSRI	Selective Serotonin Reuptake Inhibitor
STEM	Science, technology, engineering, and mathematics
TEQSA	Tertiary Education Quality and Standards Agency (Australia)
UACJ	Universidad Autónoma de Ciudad Juárez (Mexico)
UBC	University of British Columbia (Canada)

UG	Universidad de Guadalajara (Mexico)
UK	United Kingdom
UN	United Nations
UNAM	National Autonomous University of Mexico
UNDP	United Nations Development Programme
UNESCO	United Nations Educational, Scientific and Cultural Organization
UOIT	University of Ontario Institute of Technology (Canada)
U of T	University of Toronto (Canada)
UQAM	Université du Québec à Montréal (Canada)
US	United States
USAID	United States Agency for International Development
USON	Universidad de Sonora (Mexico)
UTFA	University of Toronto Faculty Association (Canada)
UV	Universidad Veracruzana (Mexico)
WHO	World Health Organization

Part I

Premises and Problems

Chapter 1

University Governance Reform: The Drivers and the Driven

Hans G. Schuetze

Although rational models of planning suggest otherwise, higher education reforms are not always isolated developments, even if they appear to be country- or context-specific. Despite idiosyncratic features and practices, universities and other academic institutions all over the world have models that come from somewhere else, sometimes explicitly acknowledged and, more often, not. Most reforms in modern times are products of such "mimetic isomorphism" or emulation. They travel from one jurisdiction to another by various means. Historically speaking, travel has not always been voluntary as models, structures, and traditions were imposed by an occupying country or by colonial powers. More recently, mimetic isomorphism occurs either through regional integration, as the Bologna Process in the European Union (EU), or through developments and forces external to higher education, including marketization of services and functions previously rooted in the public domain.

Since 1945, higher education systems across the world have changed remarkably and irrevocably. Reform has been continuous—in organization, management, accessibility, curriculum, and finance. Emphasis has moved to policy and programs that raise university profiles, relying on institutional entrepreneurialism and competitive behavior to attract outside funding, to lure international fee-paying students, and to acquire "star" faculty members. The older ideal of the university—liberal, enlightening, accessible, and embodying the public interest—is barely recognizable in the contemporary "reformed" institution.

The question arises, who runs and governs this reformed university? Can it still be considered an autonomous actor in the world? Or has it become a passive interpreter of narratives and scripts written in think-tanks, cabinet rooms, and corporate board rooms? If the university maintains autonomy, on what mechanisms, particular forms, and procedures of university governance does it rest? Does power lie with faculty, as in the past, or has it shifted to managers and technicians? Are these questions even relevant at a time when public institutions and the public sector are themselves put in question?

As pressure mounts on universities, the matter of their internal and external governance has become an irresistible topic of discussion, not only among faculty and students, but also in the pages of newspapers and other news media, and in other forums with no prior interest in such matters.

Manifestations of Change

The signs and portents of change are everywhere. Scientific research moves from being "curiosity-driven" to "application-driven" and does so on an unprecedented scale and at unprecedented speeds. In the classroom, teaching must respond to "consumer" expectations in ways that were unthinkable in earlier times. Exceptions to these generalizations—for instance, Quest University in Canada, discussed in this volume by James Cohn—simply prove the rule.

In one way, none of this is surprising: industrial innovation and modern society rely on science-and-technology-based research and development. At the same time, labor-market demand for better-qualified workers—the backbone of the "knowledge-based" economy—remains vigorous and apparently boundless. Most important, social demand for advanced education continuously intensifies in populations that see and seek skill and knowledge not just as a foundation for solid employment and income, but also as a means of social mobility.

In an era of reduced public funding, universities compete for money from nonpublic sources. They engage in commercial activities, cooperate with industry in joint research, protect and market the results of academic research as intellectual property rights (i.e., patents and copyrights), and "recruit" foreign students who pay "full-cost" or "market-based" tuition fees. They also outsource services such as food, parking, travel, housing, and rental of university facilities. Commercialization does not end there: continuing university education in North America, once a community service and a feature of the university's core mission, has become a "cost-recovery" activity and a revenue source.

The Changing Role of the State

The "hollowing-out" of the welfare state, or its transformation to a "faciliatory" or "enabling" state, has significantly changed the relationship between higher education and government in some countries. In Canada, for example, as Paul Axelrod and his colleagues (Chapter 2) suggest in their history of higher education policy in Ontario, the universities have survived intact, but bruised under the new relationship.

By contrast, in Mexico, Ecuador, and Latin America more generally, the new academy-state nexus has turned universities into sometimes unwilling laboratories for the restructuring of higher education—as suggested by the chapters in this volume by Alma Maldonado (Chapter 8), Wietse de Vries and Germán Álvarez Mendiola (Chapter 9), Adrián Acosta Silva (Chapter 10), and Mauricio Saavedra (Chapter 11).

Meanwhile public universities in Japan, Germany, and Austria are undergoing dramatic changes, having been freed from the yoke of direct government interference and control and made legally autonomous (see Motohisa Kaneko's Chapter 12). Paradoxically, the loosening or severance of tight connections between ministries of (higher) education and universities may be a staging point after which the state will have as much or more control than before. Performance-based indicators and funding and various external quality control schemes are examples for these new instruments of external (state) control.

In countries with an Anglo-Saxon tradition, such as Canada, reforms of higher education have been less dramatic. Although universities in these countries have enjoyed a greater degree of institutional autonomy than elsewhere (consider the Chinese case, described by Qiang Zha in Chapter 14), a contrary pattern of reform is discernable over the past 30 years. In Canada, too, performance indicators have been introduced to increase institutional accountability (William Bruneau's Chapter 4), while targeted performance-based funding and higher enrollments have been imposed under the flag of "productivity improvement."

If "government" is a change agent, there are several "governments," not just one great governing agency at the origin of university reforms. This is obviously the case where higher education is vested in regional governments as in Canada, the United States, and Germany; even here, national governments can still play important roles in setting the legal framework for regional policies, as until recently in Germany. In Europe, there is now a third level of government whose impact is indirect, but in some respect immediate and substantial. A prime case is the European Union (EU), whose influence on higher education in member countries is mostly indirect, since education as such remains outside the realm of the EU's regulatory powers (see Pavel Zgaga's Chapter 2). The Bologna Process provides another example of a dynamic reform process. Originally limited to "harmonizing" the structure of degrees and studies to enhance student and graduate mobility, the Bologna Process now includes a much broader palette of policies, such as university access, quality control, and public resources and responsibilities (see Hackl 2012). Fifty years ago, the main challenge for higher education reform in industrialized countries was to open access to postsecondary education (PSE) beyond that available to a privileged élite. The transition to a mass system of higher education required creation of student places in universities and new nonuniversity institutions such as community colleges (in the United States and in Canada), polytechnics (in the UK), and *Fachhochschulen* (in Germany). Enrollment ratios in higher education in nearly all Organisation for Economic Co-operation and Development (OECD) countries now exceeds 30 percent. In countries such as the United States, Canada, and Japan, more than half of the typical college-age population is enrolled in some kind of PSE.

Such developments have lengthy pedigrees, despite claims by proponents that current large-scale, comprehensive reforms are unprecedented in university history. Some reforms are clearly fundamental, planned, and intended for the long term. Examples include Humboldt's creation of a "research university" in Berlin in the first half of the nineteenth century, and the later appearance of industry-oriented, land grant universities in the United States and *Technische Hochschulen* (technical universities) in Germany. In the middle of the twentieth century, Vannevar Bush's master plan to promote scientific research during the Cold War, linked academic science to industrial development of modern technologies and weapons. More recently, the list would include California's "Master Plan," Japan's reforms to eliminate barriers to university-industry collaborations and massive structural changes in Austria and Germany at the opening of the twenty-first century that, as mentioned already, freed universities from direct interference and control by the government.

External Forces and Factors of Change

Important factors and forces of university reform are external. Globalization in its various manifestations is one, providing a larger context of reform. Globalization can have paradoxical effects. On one hand, it supports transnational *convergence* around fashions, cultural events, and shared values and understandings. On the other hand, because of its stress on competition and efficiency, globalization promotes *divergence* in the form of increasing inequality and heterogeneity.

Comparison between countries illustrates the differing effects of global dynamics, including the influence of "world models," international rankings of so-called world-class universities, the influence of institutional isomorphism, and policy-driven strategic change. Global forces affect not only teaching and learning, but also curriculum, pedagogy, and the very organization of education. Lesley Vidovich (Chapter 16) explores the Australian experience, showing the most notable effects in the area of university governance, as much as in cultural or pedagogical reform.

Economic drivers resulting from globalization are perhaps the most commonly noted influence on higher education policy. For example, preparing the workforce for changing market and technical conditions has become a mantra for policy makers and educational institutions. Robert Reich (1992) observed that capital and technology are mobile and available worldwide, and that competitive advantage lies in a nation's workforce. Ministers of economic affairs and industry leaders have since taken an active interest in "human resource development." Social mobility and individual welfare, which dominated the policy agenda in the 1960s and 1970s, have moved further down in the political agenda. Human resources have become even more important in the "knowledge-based economy," a metaphor that makes "knowledge" the most important factor of production, and learning the motor of economic development.

Writers on higher education have been inclined to summarize external effects under the singular label of "privatization" (Levin 1997). The trend to privatization, corporatization, or marketization—called academic capitalism (Slaughter and Leslie 1997)—has been especially influential in driving recent university reforms. Governments have decoupled reform from increased public funding; many reforms come with sharp cuts in educational budgets and general-purpose institutional grants are now the norm. Meanwhile governments promote "targeted," "incentive-based," and competitive funding that reshape how institutions plan and operate (St. John and Parsons 2004; Rhoads and Torres 2006).

University-Specific Factors of Change

Internationalization is in part a phenomenon of globalization. In the search for additional revenues from nonstate sources, universities have exploited a global market demand for tuition from foreign (international) students, estimated to be worth about US$30 billion per annum. Universities compete to attract such students, while exporting their "education-ware" to other countries. Revenues may be the dominant motivation, but not the only reason why higher education institutions work to attract foreign students. It was characteristic of the medieval university to welcome migrant students and scholars. Now, there is recognition that long-term cultural and economic benefits may result from student migrations. Internationalization is therefore bound to grow, despite occasional concerns about the quality of academic programs, modified to accommodate foreign learners.

Consumerism means, among other things, that students are treated as consumers. This attitude is partly a consequence of the "massification" of higher education and the growing diversification of institutions and programs. Further, student choice has been enhanced, as students assume part or all of the costs of their own education. Students have thus become more autonomous and individualistic. Programs are tailored to their needs and universities offer improved student services and financial assistance. However, students may choose programs with less rigorous requirements. Universities find themselves choosing between maintaining high academic standards and attracting enough students to generate the necessary revenue (Geiger 1993).

As a consequence of rising government expectations and investments in research, the traditional research paradigm has shifted, with several consequences. One is that the traditional distinction between research and development—the division of labor between universities (which do "basic" or "pure," basically "curiosity-driven" research) and industry (which engages in "development" from research results to a marketable product)—has weakened. The trajectory from university laboratory to innovative industrial products or processes is no longer linear, but occurs in more circular and collaborative fashion (Nowotny et al. 2003; Mowery et al. 2004; Nelson 2005). The traditional code of research ethics, openness, accessibility to findings, and the absence of direct monetary rewards for research (Merton 1973) have been displaced by a system of private ownership by academic researchers and institutions of intellectual property rights (IPR), legally protected, tradable, and competitive goods.

Some Reform Outcomes

The effects of reforms—both intended and unintended—are many. But, in the present volume, the overarching concern is with governance. The question is: How can a university president hope to combine the traditional and novel elements at work in the life of the university in a time of upheaval and reform? (Ross Paul in Chapter 5 deals with this very point.) Faculty, administration, and state roles in university governance have rarely been so open to reconceptualization and reworking as they are now (see Nelly P. Stromquist's cogent case study in Chapter 3).

Consider how many features of university governance have been altered in such a relatively short period; for example, commercialization of university functions, competitiveness, and managerialism to name only three. These features cannot always be kept distinct. Commercialization, for instance, has produced new forms of management in universities (Birnbaum 2001; Bok 2003; Washburn 2005). Adoption of strategic planning and marketing, the quest for greater efficiency and enhanced productivity, and the introduction of accountability measures suggest loss of faculty autonomy and control over research, teaching, and service. Managerial personnel have expanded, often at the expense of faculty numbers and with concomitant loss of influence of collegial bodies and the university-wide academic senate.

Some argue that the emergence of the "managerial" or "entrepreneurial" university is the natural consequence of the developments discussed so far (see Clark 1998). Universities find themselves closely engaged in regional economic development, actively competing with other institutions for talent, money, and market niche, and building alliances with industry and other external partners. They strengthen their competitive profile by strategic marketing and positioning themselves in national and international league tables and rankings, to appeal to a wide variety of actual and potential stakeholders: consumers, students, faculty, granting agencies, industry, alumni, and other potential funders, sponsors, and benefactors.

From Here to Where?

Summarizing the directions and effects of higher education reform, one may be tempted to conclude that universities in the industrialized world are converging, but are largely independent of the traditions and idiosyncrasies of national systems (Schofer and Meyer 2005). Yet the sheer diversity of higher education systems suggests otherwise.

The old isolated, stand-alone ivory-tower-type university is outmoded as universities are driven in new directions. The trend toward networks of research and learning; internationalization with its unfinished agenda; the information and communication technologies with their potential, still largely untapped; competitiveness and the attempt to create market niches; and commercialization have, or will have, effects that are difficult to capture by one single uniform model. This much can be assumed—despite influences that push universities toward a rational, Western-type model of the university.

References

Bok, Derek. 2003. *Universities in the Marketplace: The Commercialization of Higher Education*. Princeton, NJ and Oxford: Princeton University Press.

Birnbaum, Robert. 2001. *Management Fads in Higher Education: Where They Come From, What They Do, Why They Fail*. San Francisco, CA: Jossey-Bass.

Clark, Burton. 1998. *Creating Entrepreneurial Universities: Organizational Pathways of Transformation*. Oxford: Pergamon Press.

Geiger, Roger. 1993. *Research and Relevant Knowledge: American Research Universities since World War II*. New York and Oxford: Oxford University Press.

Hackl, Elsa. 2012. "Reconceptualizing Public Responsibility and Public Good in the European Higher Education Area." In *State and Market in Higher Education: Reforms, Trends, Policies and Experiences in Comparative Perspective*, ed. Hans

G. Schuetze and Germán Álvarez Mendiola. Rotterdam, The Netherlands: Sense Publishers.

Levin, Ben. 1997. "The Lessons of International Education Reform." *Journal of Educational Policy* 12 (4): 253–266.

Merton, Robert K. 1973. *The Sociology of Science: Theoretical and Empirical Investigations.* Chicago and London: The University of Chicago Press.

Mowery, David C., Richard R. Nelson, Bhaven N. Sampat, and Arvids A. Ziedonis. 2004. *Ivory Tower and Industrial Innovation: University-Industry Technology Transfer Before and After the Bayh-Dole Act in the United States.* Palo Alto, CA: Stanford University Press.

Nelson, Richard R., ed. 2005. *The Limits of Market Organization.* New York: Russell Sage.

Nowotny, Helga, Peter Scott, and Michael Gibbons. 2003. "'Mode 2' Revisited: The New Production of Knowledge." *Minerva* 41 (3): 179–194.

Reich, Robert B. 1992. *The Work of Nations.* New York: Vintage Books/Random House.

Rhoads, Robert A., and Carlos A. Torres, eds. 2006. *The University, State, and Market: The Political Economy of Globalization in the Americas.* Palo Alto, CA: Stanford University Press.

Schofer, Evan, and John W. Meyer. 2005. *The Worldwide Expansion of Higher Education in the Twentieth Century* Palo Alto, CA: Center on Democracy, Development, and The Rule of Law, Stanford Institute on International Studies, Stanford University.

Slaughter, Sheila, and Larry L. Leslie. 1997. *Academic Capitalism: Politics, Policies and the Entrepreneurial University.* Baltimore, MD: Johns Hopkins University Press.

St. John, Edward P., and Michael D. Parsons, eds. 2004. *Public Funding of Higher Education: Changing Contexts and New Rationales.* Baltimore, MD: Johns Hopkins University Press.

Washburn, Jennifer. 2005. *University, Inc.: The Corporate Corruption of Higher Education.* New York: Basic Books.

Chapter 2

Reconsidering University Autonomy and Governance: From Academic Freedom to Institutional Autonomy

Pavel Zgaga

Introduction

Although concepts such as "academic freedom" and "institutional autonomy" look simple and clear, they ought not to be treated as the "last station" of a long and winding historical journey. Rather, we should think of these concepts as under continuous negotiation.

In Europe and around the world, the concept of academic autonomy has passed through turbulent times over the last half-century. Between the 1960s and 1980s, the universities grew into a mass system. Among the consequences of that development were renewed ideas of university autonomy. In the 1960s and immediately afterward, academic freedom remained in the forefront of debates, although differently in the East than in the West. Still, between 1980 and 2000, institutional autonomy was increasingly central to debate. Today, academic freedom is a primary concern only in rare cases (as in Belarus, the last country in the European region outside the Bologna Process) where democracy is still not characteristic of public life.

I argue that the shift in understanding of the relationship between academic freedom and institutional autonomy deserves far more attention.

Autonomy: Between "Philosophical" and "Managerial" Discourses

The transition from the 1960s to the 1970s in most of Europe was characterized by mass student protest movements and reconsideration of the universities' critical potential. Academic freedom was at the forefront of debates. University autonomy was predominantly understood as a guardian of that freedom ("academic autonomy"). Financial or managerial aspects of autonomy, popular in twenty-first century discussion, were almost absent. Academic freedom was thought to be an integral feature of the fight for freedom and democracy in various parts of the world, whereas institutional autonomy was understood simply in opposition to state interference in academic affairs.

There is now wide consensus in published writings on higher education that the 1980s brought a sea-change in higher education. Governance of higher education in Europe changed (Veld et al. 1996; Wolff 1997; Eurydice 2000; Kwiek 2003; Marga 2005; Kehm and Lanzendorf 2006; Zgaga 2007; Neave 2009) mainly as a result of ongoing and apparently irresistible social, economic, and political development. Despite important differences, the sea change was felt strongly in the West and the East. Especially in continental Europe, the state had formerly controlled important features of national systems, but now withdrew from direct institutional governance and restricted itself to setting general objectives (structures, degrees, and qualifications). This was a conceptual turn—a move away from traditional intervention toward the "facilitatory state" (Neave and Vught 1991). Higher education institutions acquired more autonomy but faced a strong parallel demand for accountability. In the East during *perestroika*, this change was not immediately noticeable; but everything changed radically and definitely after the 1989-1990 political earthquakes.

Political and economic changes of the 1980s in the West and "the transition" of the 1990s in the East led to legislative reforms that gradually transformed the traditional relationship between the state and higher education institutions. In a Council of Europe monograph on higher education governance reforms in the early 1990s, one finds a concise description of those challenging times: "Since 1981, discussions in higher education in western Europe have been and are dominated by three topics: budget cuts, quality assessment and institutional autonomy. The political changes in 1990 in central and eastern Europe gave those discussions a completely new dimension" (Veld et al. 1996, 7).

In assessing this period, the Eurydice study on "two decades of reform in higher education in Europe" made a similar point: "One of the most significant reforms observed has been the increased autonomy given to higher education institutions, especially universities, in most European countries." Further, "The main focus was on reforms in institutional management linked to the increase in autonomy granted to higher education institutions and to the reinforcement of links with the economic environment during the period under consideration" (Eurydice 2000, 19, 24-25).

In Europe after the fall of the Berlin Wall, academic freedom seemed better protected than ever. Besides the provision on academic freedom in national legislation, United Nations Educational, Scientific and Cultural Organization (UNESCO) (1997) adopted its *Recommendation Concerning the Status of Higher-Education Teaching Personnel.* Legislative reform removed state control over various aspects of academic life and the autonomy-accountability dichotomy appeared. Autonomy has increased, but numerous tasks—administrative, managerial, and financial—have been given to higher education and research institutions. Thus, along with the traditional academic autonomy (related mainly to teaching and research), financial, organizational, and staffing autonomy entered institutions. The internationalization and in this case, Europeanization of higher education is evident in a strategic paper published much later by the European University Association (EUA) (2007, 2):

> For universities, the adaptability and flexibility required to respond to a changing society and to changing demands relies above all on increased autonomy and adequate funding, giving them the space in which to find their place. The common purpose of contributing to Europe's development is not opposed to diversity; instead, it requires that each university should define and pursue its mission, and thus collectively provide for the needs of individual countries and Europe as a whole. Autonomy implies control of major assets such as estates, and of staff; it also implies a readiness to be accountable both to the internal university community—both staff and students—and to society as a whole.

Institutions had not been much involved in these tasks, at least not on the Continent. The new arrangements have thus been not entirely easy to accommodate. Earlier experience of state control over the management and financing of institutions (in the West and the East, despite the two substantially different modes of appearance) was a strong reason why autonomy was understood as "independence," that is, self-governance and protection from "external interference" in academia.

In the late twentieth century these ideas have significantly mutated, and autonomy is no longer an exclusively "*philosophical*" concept. Instead it is often treated as an "instrumental," "managerial" concept. Despite the general European trend, Europe's regions, countries, and institutions display variant understandings of autonomy. Unsurprisingly a recent exploratory study found that autonomy is "understood differently across Europe" (Estermann and Nokkala 2009, 9). In other continents (Anderson and Johnson 1998) and in other times, institutional autonomy meant other things again.

Still, at a general level we typically see it as a universal value, rather as we understand human rights, democracy, and the rule of law. But at a concrete level, the application of the idea of autonomy implies a changing relation between the state and higher education institutions. That relationship rests on national contexts, circumstances, academic, and political cultures. It is not an "ideal" to which countries and/or institutions will move closer, but rather a set of agreed and recognized basic principles or values.

Over this past decade, a broad consensus among European politicians and academics (European Higher Education Area 1999; Salamanca Convention of European Higher Education Institutions 2001) has grown up, embodied comprehensively in the *Magna Charta Universitatum* (1988). That charter's impact has reached well beyond Europe (721 signatory institutions from 79 countries to date). Its external stimulus was preparations for the ninth centenary of the Bologna University (1987) while, on the content side, this was an opportunity "to relaunch the traditional concept of higher education, underlining the decisive role it has played in European history and in the development of Europe" and to diminish "a degree of risk involved for universities, in the sense that higher education policy might be determined by others, beyond universities" (Observatory 2009, 45).

On the occasion of the twentieth anniversary of the *Magna Charta*, its main proponents recalled that "the initiative was intended to promote the role of the universities in the service of society as a whole" and, on the other side, to respond to "a need to proclaim the principles of certain universal truths" (Observatory 2009, 46-47). The core of these "truths" is contained in four "fundamental principles":

1. The university is an autonomous institution at the heart of societies.
2. Teaching and research in universities must be inseparable.
3. Freedom in research and training is the fundamental principle of university life.
4. A university is the trustee of the European humanist tradition. (*Magna Charta* 1988, 2)

Although the values of the *Magna Charta* have been recognized broadly and reconfirmed in political documents again and again there are clear differences in European discourse. Thus, in a high-impact EU policy document of the last decade the concept of autonomy was put this way: "In an open, competitive and moving environment, autonomy is a pre-condition for universities to be able to respond to society's changing needs and to take full account for those responses." In short, the issues "universities should be responsible for" are as follows:

1. "setting specific medium-term priorities";
2. "managing and developing their human resources";
3. "defining their curricula—subject to internal QA and in accordance with the common principles of the European Higher Education Area"; and

4. "professionally managing their facilities." (European Commission 2005, point 3.2.2)

In academic circles these two discourses often produce disputes about university autonomy. In their report on autonomous universities, knowledge societies, and their impacts on research, Ulrike Felt and Michaela Glanz (2004, 24–26) distinguish three "basic myths":

1. the university is an institutional space free of politics and power relations;
2. universities once lived in a "golden age" of basic research; and
3. the university professor embodies in its ideal form the unity of research and teaching.

The most common academic myth is the idea of university autonomy as "ideal," "absolute autonomy." It is true that that more could be done if ossified, inherited state procedures were loosened and set free. Thus, universities' leaders and staff complain that they need "more autonomy" or "full autonomy."

These complaints may be well grounded, and "more autonomy" might have positive results. But university autonomy would be simplified and endangered if placed in a continuum with "full state control and no autonomy" on one end and "full autonomy and no more state control" on the other. Autonomy is relative. "It is won; and not once and for all" (Henkel 2007, 96). It is "to be understood as a continuous negotiation redefining academic positioning, a procedure rather than a status for universities to enjoy" (Felt and Glanz 2004, 39).

"Epistemic Roots" of Autonomy and the Need for a Contract with Authority and Society

Theories of knowledge have strong implications for academic autonomy. In the industrial period, however, knowledge has separated from or even opposed values. Yet knowledge is a value, a specific human value. Knowledge production (if we may use the modern term and extend it to the history of the university) in knowledge societies does not necessarily follow on the expectations, wishes, or demands of rulers or peoples. Indeed, the drive to knowledge may conflict with particular interests.

At the dawn of the modern era, Immanuel Kant noted that "parents care for the home, rulers for the state," adding that "neither has as its aim the universal good and the perfection to which man is destined." One of his findings was that progress "depends, then, mainly upon private effort, and not so much on the help of rulers...; they have not the universal good so much in view, as the well-being of the state." He concluded: "So it is with everything which concerns the perfection of man's intellect and the widening of his knowledge. Influence and money alone cannot do it; they can only lighten the task" (Kant 1900, 15–17).

Only a few years later, his junior compatriot Wilhelm von Humboldt—preparing to establish the University of Berlin—stressed that "the state must understand that intellectual work will go on infinitely better if it does not intrude." In knowledge production two elements are open to dispute, "the selection of persons and the assurance of freedom in their intellectual activities." However,

> this intellectual freedom can be threatened not only by the state, but also by the intellectual institutions themselves which tend to develop, at their birth, a certain outlook and which will therefore readily resist the emergence of another outlook. The state must seek to avert the harm which can possibly arise from this source. (Humboldt 1970, 244, 246)

Relying on more traditional vocabulary, the pursuit of the truth or disinterested research may be said to follow its own law, its own rules (that is, *auto-nomia*). For Socratics, the search for the truth could only be successful if pursued through persistent questioning, and in the past millennium it was thought essential that the search go on "without listening either to the bishop or to the king," as Umberto Eco's (2003, 51–62) medieval literary hero *Baudolino* put it.[1] The authority of an argument instead of the argument of authority: this was the basis of "true" knowledge. This initial point I call "epistemic autonomy." It reminds us of academic freedom, often regarded as derivative of other basic rights. But academic freedom as an expression of epistemic autonomy is *sui generis*. As exemplified by the freedom of education, academic freedom is "an independent fundamental right" (Veld et al. 1996, 56).

However, university autonomy understood as institutional autonomy is not entailed by freedom or basic rights. Rather, it is "an institutional and procedural implementation of the educational freedom," its "protection vis-à-vis the State" (57). Institutional autonomy is functional. External authority's interference in "academic business" would harm both authority and academia. This argument has always provided bases for negotiating the "contract" between society (represented by public authorities) and the university. Traditionally, it created a demarcation between "external powers" and "university towers." Even so the relation between society and the university has never been interrupted (except in modern myths about ivory towers). The university cannot live on its thoughts only and society needs knowledge to survive and progress.

Joseph Bricall and Fabio Roversi Monaco, two of the distinguished founders of the *Magna Charta Universitatum*, recently noted that "the traditional 'contract' between society and the University was based on separation, but today there is a need for interaction" (Observatory 2009, 48). We would do well to read the first sentence of the "Fundamental principles" of the *Magna Charta*: "The university is an autonomous institution at the heart of societies differently organized because of geography and historical heritage." Here, the concept of autonomy does not exclude the university from society; on the contrary, autonomy should be understood as a cohesive capacity: "it produces, examines, appraises and hands down culture by research and teaching." This is still more necessary today, in the so-called knowledge society. "To meet the needs of the world around it, its research and teaching must be morally and intellectually independent of all political authority and economic power" (*Magna Charta* 1988). "At the heart of societies" and to "serve society's needs," the university relies on the privilege of being "independent" from "external forces." It is important, even crucial, that autonomy is not confused with *autarchy* (Zgaga 2007, 95–96).

Autonomy should not be confused with sovereignty. Autonomy allows universities to fulfill their basic mission—"producing, examining, appraising and handing down culture by research and teaching," if we use the *Magna Charta* definition from above—without any external interference. As a concept, autonomy does not impose or oblige universities to govern (i.e., to organize social subsectors, and so on). On the contrary, university autonomy remains a pure *idea* up until the point it is not recognized by (public) authorities: it is "an important part of the higher education framework and can only exist if public authorities make adequate provisions for autonomy in the legal and practical framework for higher education" (Bergan 2009, 48).

Autonomous universities do not organize social subsectors but rather influence society. The knowledge produced, examined, and transmitted by universities is important in one respect or another for all parts of society. Students come from the "outside" and graduates return with their higher education qualifications to the "external world" and take up roles in the economy, culture, and politics. If every single university interfered with society in its own "autonomous" (autarchic?) way there would be trouble for all. Analogously, there would be trouble if "external" authorities were to interfere in academic affairs without restraint. The university cannot be responsible for "internal" knowledge production only; the production and dissemination of new knowledge have an obvious "external" dimension.

The traditional continuum of knowledge production has come to a breaking point. Despite contests over detail, there is consensus that universities are no longer monopolistic scientific knowledge producers. The shift of the mode of knowledge production—for example from "mode 1" to "mode 2" (Gibbons et al. 1994)—has important consequences for understanding academic autonomy. Mary Henkel argues that these changes "undermine the idea of academe as a well-defined territory, dedicated to its own specialized goals, and thus present a major challenge to academic rights of self-governance and non-intervention." In these processes, "self-governance has become shared governance, and not only between the state and academe": today, "the governance of knowledge and knowledge-based institutions is shared and often contested between the state, the market and academic institutions" (Henkel 2007, 91, 98).

We come then to public responsibility, shared responsibility *for* as well as *of* higher education and research (Weber and Bergan 2005). The right to higher education—encompassing the academic freedom as argued above—is not only a fundamental right. In the democratic order, it is also a legal obligation and public authorities have a duty to assure conditions that enable everyone to fulfill their rights without violating the equal rights of others. The university as an institution cannot fulfill this task alone. Furthermore, authorities must preserve the legal order. In other words, they are responsible for the legal and practical framework for higher education:

> The state's legitimate sphere of action must be adapted to the following circumstances: in view of the fact that in the real world an organizational framework and resources are needed for any widely practiced activity, the state must supply the organizational framework and the resources necessary for the practice of science and scholarship. (Humboldt 1970, 244)

A broadly accepted principle today is that authorities should ensure access to quality education for all and, in the case of higher education, for specific reasons, access on equal terms for all qualified candidates. Education and higher education in particular are too important to be left as a private business. The idea that public higher education institutions might accommodate more "private business," or even itself privatized, has produced sharp disputes. This was certainly the case in parts of Europe where the previously "hairy hand" of the state has ceased to exist. In this sense, higher education is—or should be—treated as a public good: open access to knowledge requires public responsibility. The systemic framework (qualification framework, quality assurance, and so on) lies within the responsibility of public authorities (Bergan 2009, 45–47). Yet it does not diminish the responsibility of higher education institutions.

"Shared Governance": The Role of Institutional Autonomy and Academic Freedom

Thus, academic freedom, institutional autonomy, and public responsibility form a triangle; its corners are interdependent but give the field its dynamism. Public authorities have a responsibility to set the basic rules and regulations of society; however, some stipulations could conflict with the principles and needs of specific sectors—but not necessarily conflict with the law. Rule-setting is not enough. The question how to deal with a potential collision in practice deserves an answer. While some collisions are real, others exist in theory. University laboratories have to observe general safety regulations, and this duty may theoretically be in contradiction with institutional autonomy. Yet, few would argue that universities should not be bound by general obligations to ensure the safe operations of their laboratories.

As certain responsibilities move gradually from public authorities to higher education institutions, academic freedom could be endangered. Even if the rationale for institutional autonomy were specifically to ensure academic freedom, one does not produce the other. Members of academic staff may enjoy a high degree of academic freedom even if their institutions have a low degree of autonomy and, conversely, a highly autonomous institution may offer its members only a limited degree of academic freedom. In other words, in today's relationship between university autonomy and the state, university autonomy does not subsume academic freedom. As argued above, academic freedom is a right *sui generis*. The problem cannot be presented on a straight line with two ends only; it requires the drawing of a triangle.

Yet, the triangle composed of academic freedom, institutional autonomy, and public responsibility allows for "twilight zones" (Bergan 2009, 50). For example, it is taken for granted in liberal democracies that, although there is no monopoly on the definition of the truth, not all possible views are acceptable. It is definitely the case in the wider society. In academia, this matter can be treated "liberally" as disputes and *advocatus diaboli* traditionally lie at the heart of the search for truth. Still, it is an open secret that not all possible ways are acceptable in "academic tribes."

From human cloning to history teaching (issues related in different ways to both institutional autonomy and academic freedom), there is pressure on the university rapidly to provide answers. But research and scholarly discussions take time. External pressures to speed them up may harm all. The *Baudolino* principle of the Middle Ages has not changed. Autonomy cannot be an excuse to exclude abuses of autonomy (for instance, corruption in institutions) from critical discussion or prosecution.

A major (dis)harmony in the triangle of academic freedom, institutional autonomy, and public responsibility arises when the university is organized and understood as an entrepreneurial institution. This arrangement is best described by a square instead of a triangle—a square delineated by university autonomy, academic freedom, state, and market forces. The expanding higher education and research sectors have encountered a serious limitation: public funds that drove both sectors in the past are no longer sufficient. Institutions have to search for other sources. Market forces have entered the game.

Policy documents claim that institutions should develop more intensive and richer contacts with society beyond the ivory towers. It is claimed for instance that "universities will not become innovative and responsive to change unless they are given real autonomy and accountability" and that "the public mission and overall social and cultural remit of European universities must be preserved," but it is also strongly expected that—as part of their commitment to serving the public interest—"they should increasingly become significant players in the economy, able to respond better and faster to the demands of the market and to develop partnerships which harness scientific and technological knowledge" (European Commission 2006, 5, 6). But "research findings are increasingly transformed into intellectual property that can be turned into marketable commodities, thus contributing to economic development in a rather visible way. Industry, on the other hand, contributes more and more to the education of 'knowledge workers,' thus taking a role long considered to be a university monopoly" (Felt and Glanz 2004, 33). Thus, the traditional roles of different actors and their relations are blurred as self-governance has become shared governance.

Is traditional university autonomy necessary to an entrepreneurial university? Should it be? Can enterprises take over traditional roles of universities? What might be the consequences? Entrepreneurialism is impossible if certain autonomy is not granted; however, is academic autonomy in this case a necessary condition? Is it perhaps superfluous? And what is the role of academic freedom in this context?

Along with growing entrepreneurialism in higher education, there are more claims that institutions should be given more autonomy. This is no paradox: the shift from the "traditional" to the "new" governance model is not possible until the definition of institutional autonomy is widened to include organizational, financial, and staffing autonomy, as in any contemporary enterprise. Here university modernization is walking a razor's edge. United in the classical idea of the university, higher education and research must resolve a dilemma: either join the movement for economic prosperity and development, or retain their cultural identity and traditions. Higher education and research have always had to serve both—prosperity and development as well as identities and traditions—but they now find themselves in a situation of uneasiness previously unknown: either prosperity or tradition.

Conclusion

The turn of the millennium came at the peak of "the greatest economic boom in history." Deregulation, privatization, and markets became sacred words with no ready alternative—at least no alternative when the public sector was under discussion. Deregulation has been promoted as a path to prosperity, which everyone deserves. Practically everywhere, the provision of public higher education is under question, accused of inefficiency and poor quality. "Values" have become an explicitly economic term, their ethical connotations lost in the shadows.

Yet, innumerable authors warn against extreme applications of the theory of the invisible hand to higher education. The belief that it coordinates human actions best and that free enterprise will make a life better for everyone, even for those who now look disadvantaged, has not been taken seriously by most analysts for decade. Yet, it is widely agreed in the political classes that the invisible hand, when applied to all social life, makes polity, public space, public care, and public good redundant. Higher education as a public good could be found redundant in this general way, with enormous consequences for academic autonomy and academic freedom. This is why "the struggle for the redefinition and sustenance of academic autonomy" is so crucially important. Mary Henkel aptly concludes: "Key issues in this struggle are the definition of 'socially useful' universities and the place of academic autonomy in that definition" (Henkel 2007, 98).

Note

1. A fragment of the novel gives an excellent though literary explanation of the origin of the University of Bologna.

References

Anderson, Don, and Richard Johnson. 1998. *University Autonomy in Twenty Countries*. Canberra: Centre for Continuing Education, Department of Employment, Education, Training and Youth Affairs, Australian National University.

Bergan, Sjur. 2009. "Higher Education 'As a Public Good and Public Responsibility': What Does It Mean?" In *Public Responsibility for Higher Education*, ed. Sjur Bergan, Rafael Guarga, Eva Egron Polák, José Dias Sobrinho, Rajesh Tandon, and Jandhyala B. G. Tilak. Paris: UNESCO.

Eco, Umberto. 2003. *Baudolino*. London: Vintage.

Estermann, Thomas, and Terhi Nokkala. 2009. *University Autonomy in Europe I: Exploratory Study*. Brussels, Belgium: European University Association.

European Commission. 2005. *Communication from the Commission: Mobilising the Brainpower of Europe: Enabling Universities to Make Their Full Contribution to the Lisbon Strategy*. Brussels, Belgium: European Commission.

European Commission. 2006. *Communication from the Commission: Delivering on the Modernisation Agenda for Universities: Education, Research and Innovation*. Brussels, Belgium: European Commission.

European University Association. 2007. *Europe's Universities Beyond 2010: Diversity with a Common Purpose*. Brussels, Belgium: EUA.

Ministers of Education, European Higher Education Area. 1999. *Bologna Declaration: Joint Declaration of the European Ministers of Education*. Bologna, Italy: Ministers of Education, European Higher Education Area.

Eurydice. 2000. *Two Decades of Reform in Higher Education in Europe: 1980s Onwards*. Brussels, Belgium: Eurydice, the Information Network on Education in Europe.

Felt, Ulrike, and Michaela Glanz. 2004. "University Autonomy in Europe: Shifting Paradigms in University Research." In *Managing University Autonomy. Shifting Paradigms in University Research*, ed. Magna Charta Universitatum Observatory (pp. 15–99). Proceedings of the Seminar of the Magna Charta Observatory, September 15, 2003. Bologna, Italy: Bononia University Press.

Gibbons, Michael, Camille Limoges, Helga Nowotny, Simon Schwartzman, Peter Scott, and Martin Trow. 1994. *The New Production of Knowledge: The Dynamics of Science and Research*. London: Sage.

Henkel, Mary. 2007. "Can Academic Autonomy Survive in the Knowledge Society? A Perspective from Britain." *Higher Education Research & Development* 26 (1): 87–99.

Humboldt, Wilhelm von. 1970/1810. "On the Spirit and the Organisational Framework of Intellectual Institutions in Berlin." *Minerva* 8 (1–4): 242–267.

Kant, Immanuel. 1900/1803. *On Education*. Boston, MA: D.C. Heath.

Kehm, Barbara M., and Ulrike Lanzendorf, eds. 2006. *Reforming University Governance. Changing Conditions for Research in Four European Countries*. Bonn, Germany: Lemmens.

Kwiek, Marek, ed. 2003. *The University, Globalization, Central Europe*. Frankfurt, Germany: Peter Lang.

Magna Charta Universitatum. 1988. Bologna, September 18, 1988. http://www.aic.lv.

Marga, Andrei. 2005. *University Reform Today*. 4th ed. Cluj, Romania: Cluj University Press.

Neave, Guy. 2009. "Institutional Autonomy 2010–2020. A Tale of Elan—Two Steps Back to Make One Very Large Leap Forward." In *The European Higher Education Area: Perspectives on a Moving Target*, ed. Barbara M. Kehm, Jeroen. Huisman, and Bjørn Stensaker (pp. 3–22). Rotterdam, The Netherlands: Sense Publishers.

Neave, Guy, and Franz van Vught, eds. 1991. *Prometheus Bound. The Changing Relationship between Government and Higher Education in Western Europe*. Buckingham, UK: Pergamon Press. Observatory for Fundamental University Values and Rights. 2009. "Past, Present and Future of the Magna Charta Universitatum." Proceedings of the Conference of the Magna Charta Observatory, September 18–20, 2008. Bologna, Italy: Bononia University Press.

Salamanca Convention of European Higher Education Institutions. 2001. *Message from the Salamanca Convention of European Higher Education Institutions: Shaping the European Higher Education Area*. Salamanca, Spain, March 29–30, 2001.

United Nations Educational, Scientific and Cultural Organization (UNESCO). 1997. *Recommendation Concerning the Status of Higher-Education Teaching Personnel*. Paris: UNESCO.

Veld, Roel in 't, Hans-Peter Füssel, and Guy Neave, eds. 1996. *Relations between State and Higher Education*. The Hague, The Netherlands: Kluwer Law International.

Weber, Luc, and Sjur Bergan, eds. 2005. *The Public Responsibility for Higher Education and Research*. Strasbourg, France: Council of Europe Publishing.

Wolff, Klaus Dieter, ed. 1997. *Autonomy and External Control: The University in Search of the Golden Mean*. Erfurter Beiträge zur Hochschulforschung und Wissenschaftspolitik, 2nd ed. München, Germany: Iudicium.

Zgaga, Pavel. 2007. *Higher Education in Transition. Reconsiderations on Higher Education in Europe at the Turn of the Millennium*. Umeå, Sweden: Umeå University.

Part II

North America

Chapter 3

The Provost Office as Key Decision-Maker in the Contemporary US University: Toward a Theory of Institutional Change

Nelly P. Stromquist

Introduction

Higher education is at the fore of most educational efforts in contemporary globalization. With the advent of the "knowledge society," much attention is given to the importance of higher education, especially graduate education, as a means to sustainable development, international economic competitiveness, and the expansion of democratic ideals (World Bank 2002; EUA 2005).

There is consensus on the exogenous nature of the forces affecting the university (Cowen 1996; Honan and Teferra 2001; Altbach 2002; Schugurensky 2007; Enders and de Weert 2009; Wolhuter et al. 2010). Among these forces four are salient:

First, the massive expansion of higher education (in part as a result of the push toward the "knowledge society"), leading to larger and more complex institutions as well as new institutions. Human capital has greater salience in the labor market of today than 50 years ago (Acemoglu and Robinson 2006). As sophisticated skills and knowledge come into greater demand for the high-paying salaries, individuals are investing more in themselves. Since most financial rewards will accrue to a highly skilled and mobile force, job seekers need advanced degrees so that they may gain a competitive edge. As universities have moved from elite to mass institutions and must attend to larger numbers of students, they must also increase their levels of efficiency.

Second, the widespread competition for resources in the form of students and research funds. In the case of public universities, the decrease of state support for education has resulted in constant search for new profit-generating initiatives. In the case of private universities, these efforts, always present, have become discernibly paramount.

Third, the deregulation of higher education. This has introduced new players into the arena. For-profit institutions of higher education, which force established universities to respond to stay ahead of the game. These efforts are taking place not only in industrialized countries but also in the developing countries. The World Bank Group's International Finance Corporation has emerged as an increasingly strong investor in private education since 2000 (World Bank 2010). New providers have broken the monopoly of conventional higher education institutions and placed them in a mode of constant search for innovation.

And fourth, improvements in the range of information and communication technologies (ICTs). These include very user-friendly technologies for the application of online education programs.[1] Because of their ability to affect time and space, online degrees are expanding and attracting nonconventional students (older, homebound, and working full time); again, this increases the competition for students among universities.[2]

Today, universities must struggle to get ahead of their competitors, from setting up a wide array of short-term certificates to establishing enduring relationships with industrial firms. The exogenous factors at work create internal shocks, which then open opportunities for new internal actors. It is my contention that shared governance, one of the most precious traits of academic life, is being affected by the array of exogenous factors and that research universities, sites of traditional academic power, are not exempt from these dynamics.

To be sure, universities have "mixed methods of authority—a combination of bureaucratic structure, medieval tradition, and scholarly charisma" (Labaree 2010, 2). Forty years ago they were found to be "organized anarchies" (Cohen and March 1974; March and Olsen 1976; Weick 1976), characterized by their loosely coupled procedures. In my view, this may have been the case in the 1970s and 1980s, but since the 1990s a much tighter system has been emerging.

In this chapter, I explore the mechanisms through which the research university has responded to exogenous threats and opportunities, and in so doing has reduced the influence of academics in governing their institutions.

General University Responses

Universities have four revenue markets: student enrollments, research funding, public financial support, and philanthropic giving (Brewer et al. 2002).

The two most highly sought are (1) Recruitment of students, preferably full-tuition students or students who can pay even higher tuition (out-of-state and international students). Except in the case of the very elite universities, the tendency is toward enrollment growth. (2) Funding of research. Competition for this resource gives salience to science and technology and often takes the form of partnerships with industry and the search for international contacts.

The search for fee-paying students has generated a search for international students and contacts with pertinent educational and business groups abroad. These efforts, collectively known as "internationalization," include an element of increasing one's cultural awareness, which is pursued through study-abroad programs for undergraduates. But the bulk of the effort is in attracting international students to US universities. Not surprisingly, the numbers of students in higher education studying outside their country has risen greatly, from 600,000 in 1975 to 2.7 million in 2005, of whom 2.3 million study in OECD countries (Centre for Educational Research and Innovation [CERI] 2008).

The Impact of Recent University Responses on their Functioning and Structures

Universities are becoming increasingly massive and complex organizations serving numerous clients: governments at all levels, students, community, banks/lending institutions, and donors. With multiple clients come multiple functions, beyond knowledge creation and provision: fund-raising, student services, and strategic decision making. The multiple structures include the growing administrative offices: institutional development (fund-raising), legal offices (counsel regarding contracts, patents, and labor rights), student affairs (by far the largest unit, involving the management of dorms, health and food services, and extracurricular activities), international offices (study abroad, faculty exchanges, and interuniversity agreements), admissions, undergraduate and graduate offices, academic affairs, security (to protect not only people on campus, but also the increasingly expensive equipment), and physical planning departments (architects, landscape specialists, and maintenance crews to oversee the expansion and upkeep of the university facilities).

In light of all this, we ask: What mechanisms account for rapid institutional response? What changes are happening in university governance structures and procedures? How do they affect the university on an everyday basis? This chapter is an effort to flesh out specific mechanisms in place at the university today. Figure 3.1 presents in concise form my proposed theoretical model.

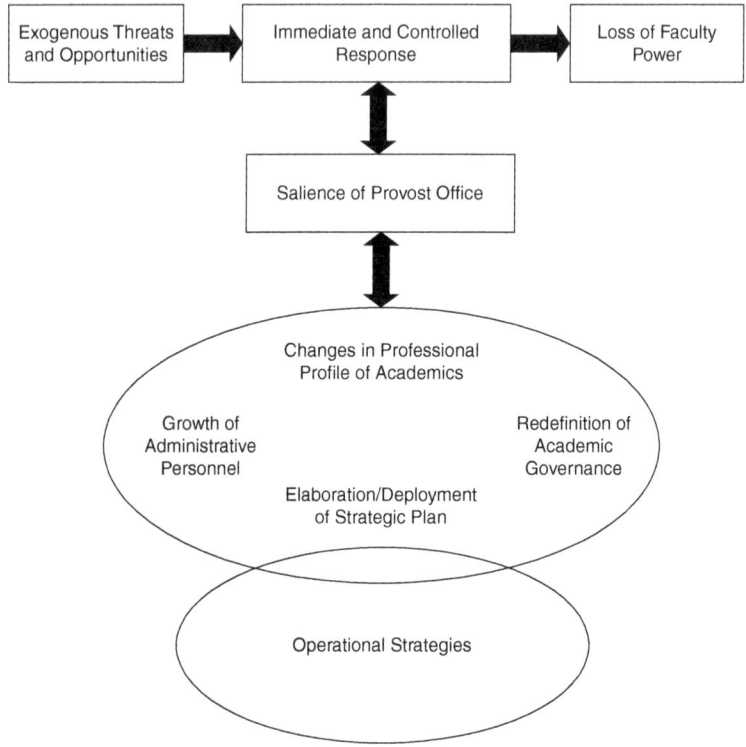

Figure 3.1 The Twenty-First Century University: Explaining Effects on Faculty Governance.

Data Sources

The data for this study are drawn from two universities: one private, the other public. Both are research universities with similar student enrollment, similar annual budgets (about US$1.5 billion), and about the same amount of research revenues per year (about US$500 million). I collected the data as a participant observer, having worked 20 years in the private university and three years in the public university. I have played an active role in academic politics as chair of faculty council in a private university's college of education for three years and chair-elect for one year in a public university, where I served also in a university-wide committee advising the provost on academic matters. In both universities, I served in the campus-wide faculty senate.

The private university claims a very productive financial performance during the past 20 years, in which the "most successful fundraising campaign ever" was conducted, raising US$2.85 billion in the campaign's first nine years, enlarging its endowment fund from US$460 million to US$3.7 billion, and "complet[ing] two comprehensive university-wide strategic planning processes." It also rose in academic ranks. The public university engaged in a fund-raising campaign as well, raising US$645 million toward a projected US$1 billion in about 12 years; it was less successful in raising funds than the private university, but it also faced the less favorable economic climate of the past decade.

I present, therefore, two institutional studies using case study methods to provide a link between mere description and some generalized ideas embedded in a conceptual framework. My study examines the two universities but focuses particularly on their colleges of education. For reasons of space, the presentation of evidence will be reduced to a few instances.

Key Consequences for Governance

While several mechanisms are pervasive and tangible, five can be detected as having a direct impact on faculty governance: (1) growth of administrative personnel as full-time employees, with concomitant growth of administrative structures; (2) elaboration and deployment of strategic plans at the institutional level; (3) changes in the professional profile of academics; (4) redefinition of shared governance; and (5) selective use of operational strategies.

Expansion of Administrative Positions and Structures

A well-established principle of organizational theory is that organizational growth is accompanied by differentiation (Blau 1970). As complex organizations, universities require a division of labor as well as specialized knowledge for many of its operations. There is increasing recognition that central administrators play a strong role in the setting of university objectives and modes of working, and that there are now structures parallel to the conventional organization of deans, heads of department, and professors (Kogan and Bleiklie 2007). Evidence of changes in the university structure is the increase in the number of administrators. During the 1977-1989 period, the number of administrators increased almost twice the number of faculty (Rhoades 1998). Based on the Integrated Postsecondary Education Data System (sponsored by the US Department of Education) for 197 leading American universities, Jay Greene (2010) found that between 1993 and 2007, the number of full-time administrators per one hundred students had increased by 39 percent in contrast with the number of those in teaching, research, and service, which had grown only by 18 percent. And, administrators are not averse to giving themselves generous salary increases (Rhoades 1998). Whereas in previous decades it was possible for faculty members to assume administrative positions, today faculty comprise a minority of such positions (Rhoades 1998).

In the private university, there are 34 senior administrators (mostly as vice provosts and vice presidents, and not including deans) in the areas of administration, university relations, academic planning and budget, finance, development, government and community relations, student affairs, general counsel, continuing education, and summer programs. The provost has directly under him four vice provosts: undergraduate programs, planning and budget, research advancement, and institute for innovations. Student Affairs is the largest administrative unit, comprising 40 subunits and covering such issues as health, counseling, career advice, personal counseling, student associations, alumni groups, orientation, residential education, student judicial affairs, IT, student government, and university publications. In its college of education, there is also a growing layer of administrators. In the past three years, three assistant deans have been appointed to help the associate dean for research. The associate dean for academic affairs has now one assistant dean. There is also an assistant dean for communications (to handle all publicity and news about the college), with two writers and a half-time webmaster.

In the public university, administrators have different titles. There are no vice provosts but there are vice presidents (six), one of whom deals exclusively with Institutional Research, Planning, and Assessment, thus reflecting the importance given to internal functioning and monitoring. There are 11 "major academic administrative offices," with a total of 32 senior administrators. The Student Affairs unit here is also the largest, with a staff of some 1,400 persons, many of them in minor supportive positions. The public university has a Center for Leadership and Organizational Change within the Provost Office as a "consulting department" to "provide advice to deans and department heads" to develop their specific strategic plans. To promote the speedy administrative deployment in the creation of new structures dealing with distance education, there is a Center on Learning, which includes in turn a Center for Distance Learning and a Center for Pedagogical Technology, both under the direction of a vice president for Educational Innovation. The number of administrators in the college of education has remained stable, except for new positions as director and assistant director for the Office of International Initiatives.

Effect on Governance: In many research universities today, most provosts simultaneously occupy positions as vice presidents for academic affairs (Lombardi et al. 2002). There is an invariable leakage of functions; consequently, administrative decisions affect academic programs, which in turn have consequences for faculty engagement and deployment.

In the private university, a major decision to develop a distance education master's in teaching came as a result of the provost's call for the expansion of online programs. Consultation with faculty was minimal. The dean, who openly states that he "responds to the provost," has proceeded to make numerous decisions about faculty hiring for this program with little faculty input. In the public university, the provost has reduced PhD admissions across all programs for the university to be more selective and thus move up in rank. This decision, which seriously affects the nature of doctoral programs, was made with minimal consultation with the faculty and argued as merely implementing the strategic plan. In this sense, decisions tend to be seen as primarily technical and financial.

The growing presence of administrators is creating a vertical structure, characterized by values of compliance with commands from higher-level administrators. While university-wide senates and college-level senates continue to exist, their agenda is becoming increasingly reactive and often to give postfacto legitimacy to administrative initiatives.

The Elaboration and Deployment of Strategic Plans

Michael D. Cohen and James G. March (1974), referring to universities as "organized anarchies," found them to possess three key properties: problematic preferences—having unclear goals and displaying inconsistent preferences; unclear technology—unsure of what is being done by other people in the organization and learning by trial and error; and fluid participation—characterized by participants drifting in and out of decision making. At the time of their study on the American college president, Cohen and March saw little evidence of planning and, if any, these plans were primarily for physical construction; moreover, plans were used as "symbols," "advertisement," and "games" (1974, 115). A decade ago, a former president of Harvard University stated, "Presidents and deans have little coercive authority; they cannot order professors to teach better courses, or pay more attention to students, or labor longer at their research... They can succeed only through persuasion" (Bok 2003, 114). These observations may have applied to universities in the past, in the times before globalization. Not so much now.

In recent years, strategic plans have emerged as central command mechanisms in universities. These plans are long-term instruments committing the institution to specific actions. Strategic plans function as major agenda-setting devices, but might serve primarily to enforce the vision of administrators. Frank Gaffikin and David Perry (2009, 129) call the strategic plan "the most important brand statement of the research university that embraces its full range of institutional/structural activities." Strategic plans both confer legitimacy and exert pressure upon institutional members (Bourgeois and Nizet 1993). Almost all US universities by now have a strategic plan. Gaffikin and Perry (2009) found that 73 percent of all major US research universities had made such formal plans available on the Internet and that this access was more common among public universities.[3]

All strategic plans are described as having been developed with broad faculty participation. However, most of the work is done by provost-appointed committees and these committees are usually under the close supervision of administrators.[4] Invariably, these plans serve to enforce the vision of the highest-level administrators, usually the provost and sometimes the president.[5] One key property of strategic plans is that they are invoked to draft subsequent policies without discussion with faculty either before or after implementation.

"Branding" is becoming as important to the university as it has been for commerce and industry. In the private university, a crucial element of its strategic plan was the development of a "new image," including a new slogan. This necessitated the investment of US$1 million to an outside marketing firm. A similar objective was sought by the public university. Its campus newspaper reported that the university "was investing more than a US$1 million over a three-year period to come up with a fresh image for the university, possibly including a new slogan," but a year later the administrators maintained that only US$250,000 had been spent on the new slogan and that the funds had been paid entirely by an anonymous donor. While this was good news, for the faculty there was no way of ascertaining the truth, let alone having influence in the selection of the slogan.

The private university started its first strategic plan in 1996 and is now preparing its fourth strategic plan. Its current one seeks three main objectives: meeting societal needs; expanding the university's international presence; and promoting lifelong, learner-centered education. Underneath the appealing language lie very competitive "strategic capabilities," defined as those that will enable the private university "to secure its place among the world's greatest universities." For instance, "learner-centered" is described as "greater flexibility and individual responsiveness in the way we structure and deliver education and student services." One of the strategic capabilities along this line has involved persistent efforts to move into distance education. The public university began working on its strategic plan in 1994 and is now implementing its third plan. Four objectives were identified in the current document: undergraduate education; graduate education; research, scholarship, and the creative and performing arts; and partnerships, outreach, and engagement. These objectives are to be implemented through 74 strategic actions. Not immediately visible is that the improvement of undergraduate education implies increasing the admission requirements, and that programs of excellence in the PhD programs will be subject to "right sizing," meaning the development of much more exclusive doctoral programs. Reflecting a strong interest in internationalization, the term "international" appears 73 times in the strategic plan.

The Provost Office as Key Decision-Maker 33

In the case of the private university, special mention must be made of the online master's in education degree, established in 2009. Under pressure from the provost and the strategic plan to move into offering online programs, the dean of the college of education contacted an entrepreneur to negotiate their provision. This arrangement was done entirely between the dean and the entrepreneur; faculty were told after the fact, and the details are still not completely known. The entrepreneur is in charge of student recruitment and advisement and providing and maintaining the technological system. The provision and assessment of the students' internship experience, an important aspect of this online master's in teaching program, is in the hands of the business partner (2tor 2008); faculty members attached to this program do not have a clear sense of what happens in the internship. There is supposed to be an associate director of the online master's in education program, but none has yet been appointed. Professors serving as leaders for the online courses that have been designed know little about how this supervision is working. However, it is widely known that the online master's is generating substantial revenues. One estimate puts it at US$36 million a year, which is divided between 2tor and the university, rumored to be a 60–40 split.

The online master's program is rapidly expanding and efforts have begun to recruit 30 clinical faculty members. These faculty are being hired on 12-month contracts and will teach 36 units a year, including during the summer, and they will be "hired exclusively to give online instruction" (Brewer and Tierney 2010). The online program has attracted about eight hundred students per year, making it as large as the on-campus enrollment of the entire college of education. Tenure faculty has been asked to participate in the design and provision of courses, but the enrollment targets are set by the dean and the hiring of the faculty to serve in the program is also in his hands. Internet announcements by the private entrepreneur indicate that the enrollment will reach "thousands" in future years and the program has all the features of a regular master's program "minus the stringent curriculum of the school's on-campus program." Responsibilities by the entrepreneur focus on advertising, recruitment, placement and coordination of field experience of future teachers, advice, and provision of technical support. It can be observed that two critical functions of academic governance—placement and coordination of field experience (or internship) and the provision of advice—are now in the hands of administrators. The "success" of the college of education has prompted a similar initiative in the school of social work, which will be using the technological platform developed by the same entrepreneur.

In the public university, expansion through distance education programs is less intensive. Considerable efforts are being directed toward increasing the university's reputation in rankings and toward internationalization, for which a prestigious PhD is seen as critical. The strategic plan makes the point that the university's doctoral programs are too many and too large, so the provost announced in his annual presentation to the faculty that he will "set target sizes." He explained that "the point is not to downsize PhD programs but to increase the quality of our students" (Provost of Public University 2009). In the same public meeting, the provost expressed great satisfaction with the increase in Scholastic Aptitude Test (SAT) scores, referring to them as the only measure of quality of the incoming undergraduate class. A few weeks later, it became known that, in a state with a large Black population, the university's fall 2009 admissions had experienced a 28 percent drop in Afro-American freshman admissions compared to the previous year. While administrators expressed "surprise" at this finding in separate statements, they also boasted that the entering class had an average SAT score of 1285 and Grade Point Average (GPA) of 3.93.

In both universities, internationalization is identified as a priority in their strategic plans. This has meant a substantial deployment of administrators in the development of executive degree programs in several fields, particularly business administration, public policy, and education.[6] These initiatives are led by administrators and decisions about course offerings, assignment of faculty to teach them, and the nature of the certificate courses (online vs. on-campus) are often determined by them.

Effect on Governance: The strategic plan in both universities functions as a key leverage for imposing change. Once approved, these plans are difficult to change; rather, they move quickly into an implementation mode. Far from dealing only with institutional decisions, strategic plans deeply affect substantive decisions dealing with the nature of the academic programs.

Changes in the Profile of Academic Employment

A decline in the full-time tenure-track faculty has been observed since the 1970s, although the decline accelerated in the 1990s. Full-time faculty decreased from 78 percent in 1970 to 51 percent in 2007. Moreover, faculty in nontenure appointments has risen from 19 percent in 1975 to 38 percent in 2007 (Ehrenberg 2010). According to other statistics, 3.3 percent of the appointments of full-time faculty in 1969 were off the tenure track, and by the 1990s over half of the new full-time appointments were off the tenure track (Bradley 2004). The twin forces of part-time and nontenure track academics are creating an internal professional stratification. In respect to these forces, Gary Rhoades (2009) argues that academics in nontenured tracks are becoming "salaried employees" rather than central members of a learning institution.

Reasons commonly given for having part-time, off-tenure track professors are the need for a flexible labor force and for greater accountability in faculty performance. Certainly it costs much less to hire an adjunct professor or a lecturer than a tenure-track faculty member at any rank. From the perspective of those who favor off-tenure track positions, this is part of a much needed "rethinking of labor strategies," which will provide a "greater differentiation of job roles, create compensation and retention strategies, and use less permanent workers" (Brewer and Tierney 2010, 8).

For the changing profiles of academics, the primary source in this study is the private institution. The private university had to increase its prestige and generate a reasonable profit, thus it opted for an exclusive PhD program to which only a handful of students (five to seven per year) would be admitted and then offered full stipends for four years—for prestige—coupled with multiple sources of revenue through other degrees—for revenue. Translated into practice at the college of education, this meant a highly selective PhD (only five to seven admissions per year for the entire college)[7] and a massive EdD program in which admission would be lax, students would pay their entire tuition, and large numbers of students would be accepted (about 150-180 admissions per year). The EdD program unambiguously became a profit-producing program involving a large number of clinical professors. As noted earlier, another profit-producing program has been the online master's in teaching. Many of the courses are centrally designed and given to clinical/adjunct faculty to work in their assigned groups, leaving little room for intellectual autonomy. Further, the clinical faculty, whether they want to or not, will, because of demands on their time, be unable to produce research, thus making themselves poorly marketable for better academic positions.

In both universities, the search for a larger number of fee-paying students has led to the creation of a wide array of certificate and executive degree programs. The latter are for persons in high-level positions who have experience in the field, and also for those who can pay a high tuition for accelerated programs. These programs tend to be labor intensive, thus affecting the research productivity of the professors (usually adjuncts) assigned to teach in them. In both universities also there is a strong tendency to equate small programs with inefficiency, which implies that small classes—especially those in the humanities that are not linked to large external contracts—are coming under persistent attack.

Effect on Governance: Faculty who work as adjuncts, even those in full-time positions, face an uncertain work environment. Given their tenuous link to the university, they tend to be outside structures of academic governance and, when included, they seldom raise oppositional points of view, fearful that this will have repercussions on their rehiring. Since academic programs are the core aspect of the university enterprise, as administrators gain more power it is inevitable that their decisions will increasingly involve academic matters.

It is likely that future generations of clinical and adjunct professors, who have a more limited understanding of what the academy is and should be, will come to accept existing conditions as normal and will be more beholden to the dean and other administrators than in the past. Compounding this loss of faculty governance is that professors who work on large research grants—and who therefore have prestige and leverage—devote most of their time to their own projects, thus distancing themselves from teaching (as they buy out courses to concentrate on research activities), and decreasing their engagement in governance concerns.

Redefinition of Academic Governance

The formal site for faculty participation in university and college decision making is their respective college senates. Although these entities continue to exist, their function has become increasingly reduced to weak advisory status (Lazerson 2010). Since deans are not elected but appointed by the provost, they are accountable to his/her authority and, often, do not hesitate to remind their faculty that they "respond to the provost."

In times characterized by institutional competition, universities are being challenged by the private sector and international agencies. From the private entrepreneur perspective, shared governance is characterized as inefficient because it requires "deliberations that produce slow responses to a fast changing environment" (Brewer and Tierney 2010). From the perspective of the World Bank, an influential institution in developing countries, the election of university leaders "often results in weak leadership and a consequent prejudice in favor of the status quo," whereas "appointed leaders are less likely to allow their program to be stalled by a lack of consensus and better placed to make unpopular decisions when required" (World Bank 2000, 65).

In both universities in this study, the deans of their respective colleges of education are extremely compliant to the provost, even though they have different leadership styles—one authoritarian and the other much more inclined to a participatory process. Efforts to reorganize the college of education in these universities provide important insights. In the private university, the dean succeeded in changing the faculty handbook (identifying governance procedures) and met regularly with a small group of senior faculty of his selection. Even so, this "executive team" was confronted with a number of postfacto decisions. The dean eliminated all departments and instead set up a structure by degree program (i.e., master's program, EdD program, and PhD program).[8] Each of these programs was given an executive director and an academic chair, both appointed by the dean. Consultations do occur; yet, it is unlikely that recommendations not accepted by the dean will be followed. Conversely, his recommendations are always obeyed. There is an elected college-wide faculty council that meets twice a year; it has a mostly postdecision informational function.

In the public university, at the directive of the provost, the college of education (as all other colleges) was told to reduce its number of departments and programs. The reduction process was prolonged, lasting about two years. Although the reduction made little sense from a disciplinary perspective, such a compression was not negotiable. There were several faculty meetings at which multiple counterarguments were debated. Exhausted by the debate, the faculty senate appointed a faculty team to produce postfacto a rationale for moving the departments from seven to three. The more contentious part of the process, the fusion and elimination of some programs, will "bite" in the 2011–2012 academic year. In this university, unlike the private one, program chairs are elected by their respective faculty. Its college-wide faculty senate (along with students and staff) meets in the college assembly. As in the case of the private university, this body meets twice during the academic year. There is wider debate than in the private university; measures that are clearly unpopular have been modified by the dean. Also in the public university, there is a large campus-wide senate (which, again, includes faculty, student, and staff representation). It votes on a number of recommendations. So far, it has accepted all recommendations brought to it, except for one dealing with post-tenure review procedures.[9] The senate of the public university, according to its prerogatives, provides "advice to the president" on "virtually all campus policy matters." It has 15 standing committees dealing with such issues as curriculum, campus, and student affairs. Issues involving institutional directions, such as initiatives to elevate the university rankings in prestige or to increase the university's presence abroad, and the allocation of institutional resources are not among them.

Effect on Governance: In the private university, the dean has surrounded himself with a nucleus of highly compliant faculty who share his view of the entrepreneurial university and who find acceptable the bifurcation between a highly selective PhD program and a very-accessible EdD program and the increasing reliance on nontenure faculty. In the public university there is more debate and consultation than in the private university, but the outcomes are surprisingly similar: all are in convergence with the strategic plan and the provost's mandates.

Operational Strategies

Having full-time positions and being present in many academic committees, administrators engage in a number of strategies to which academics, being able to devote only a small fragment of their time to governance procedures, cannot respond. Three such strategies can be detected.

Central Taxation

It is not clear when this strategy started and how widespread it might be, but it can be observed in both universities. It consists of demanding a tax from their various schools and colleges, resources that go to the provost to fund his own initiatives as well as for subsequent distribution among colleges, if they propose plans that further advance implementation of the strategic plan.

In the private university, the taxation varies according to the revenues generated by a given college. In the college of education this taxation has oscillated in recent years between 20 percent and 25 percent of its budget. In the public university, the taxation is only 2 percent, but even so it has affected college response to the strategic plan. For instance, the college of education now has an initiative dealing with Science, technology, engineering, and mathematics (STEM) programs and has initiated the development of online programs, both explicitly identified as priority areas in the strategic plan.

Use of Deadlines

The presentation of proposals to which faculty members have a short time to respond is a common practice. Often, this involves the distribution of a report within a week or less of a scheduled faculty meeting, at which time a vote will be taken on its recommendations. While quick decision making is one of the advantages of a strong administration, the deadlines are frequently arbitrary inasmuch as no clear reason for the urgency is given. As observed by March and Johan P. Olsen (2009), tight deadlines are likely to promote rule compliance rather than consideration of alternatives or reflection on the proposed actions. Deadlines affect the pace of deliberation and might exclude some actors from participation in the decisions. Summertime is increasingly employed for such decision making, taking advantage of the reduced numbers of faculty members available and the absence of regular meetings during that period. During the academic year, another strategy is the use of emergency meetings. Also included among these time-related strategies is the distribution of important announcements shortly before the end of the academic year, when professors are correcting final student papers or arranging for dissertation defenses. In all, the frequent and seemingly calculated use of the time dimension serves to move ahead with programs that might have been modified or delayed through faculty input.

Committee Participation

Administrators participate as ex-officio members in most university committees. While faculty participate in committees in term lengths of one to three years (most often a single year), administrators have permanent access to them and are consequently able to accumulate much greater information than that gained by faculty members and are able to orient discussions in directions more agreeable to their own priorities. The situation in both the private and public universities is similar to that reported by Geoffrey Walford (1987) in his case study of Aston University in the UK. He observed that the power of the provost derives from chairship of key committees, a position that allows him to manage the pace and timing of the meetings, including what become agenda items and in what order they should appear.

Effect on Governance: The three operational strategies strengthen administrative advantages in shaping actions of significant institutional importance. Many of these proposed actions carry implications for the functioning of colleges and disciplinary programs, precisely where sound faculty input is crucial. It is clear that academic governance becomes reduced through the application of these strategies.

Insights from the Case Studies

Comparing the two universities, it can be seen that a central command, operating through compliance with the strategic plan, is at work. Also present in both sites is the growth of the Provost Office and administrative personnel, a growth both in numerical terms and in access to crucial decisions shaping the nature of the institution and the academics in them. Because administrators work within a line of command, they develop cohesion or what John W. Kingdon (1984, 55) calls the "ability to speak with one voice." The differences observed between the private and the public university in this aspect are minimal; perhaps the greatest distinction occurs in the time taken for decisions, with the public university taking longer than the private. My study offers some useful insights, but more systematic research, particularly qualitative research shadowing for several months the Provost Office, is needed.

Two Competing Accounts of Organizational Change

Having examined the main mechanisms of change in the governance of universities, one may ask if they constitute an inexorable process or are a conscious takeover.

Arguing in favor of an *inexorable process*, it may be said that research universities must respond to national and global competition with strategic reasoning. These universities have to engage simultaneously in client-seeking and status-seeking behaviors (Shavit et al. 2007). They are increasingly complex organizations; as a result they require a division of labor as well as specialized knowledge for many of their operations. It may also be said that the ubiquitous presence of ICTs has generated changes in the provision of education, particularly through the creation of online programs. This in turn has favored the emergence of new providers of higher education, who are not only competing for alternative modes of education delivery but also challenging traditional curricula and course organizations, including faculty autonomy. Although the elite universities at the top of the prestige hierarchy are not responding (nor will they) by expansion, most other universities are expanding. Moving from select-few admissions into a mass institution dramatically increases the size and structure of the university and requires an explicit division of labor. The increase in size both results from and leads to an increase in the range of functions. The multiplicity of functions depends increasingly on constant attention, which fosters managerial practices, which in turn challenge professoriate autonomy.

Internationalization—a priority in many strategic plans—has been described as a complex political affair, one that consequently requires specialized expertise and new structures for managing international activities (Bond and Lemasson 1999). It is also best conducted at the institutional level, as it requires coordination of various internal colleges and administrative units.

Universities today rely on personnel with ICT skills. Many student services take place via the web: admissions, registration, billing, financial aid, advising, tutoring, library, placement, counseling, information technology, grades, degree audits, and transcripts (Twigg 2002). This is creating demands for a new breed of administrator. While at first sight it would seem that these administrators do not impinge on academic governance, it should be noted that the ICTs have intensified the annual evaluation of academic performance, producing detailed questionnaires that measure research, teaching, and service activities of professors and which can be easily aggregated to produce individual, program, college, and institutional profiles. These profiles serve to monitor compliance with strategic plans, thus giving administrators yet another tool for running a tight ship.

Arguments in favor of a *conscious takeover* are multiple. Essentially, they attempt to show that administrators seek to strengthen their own positions and roles in shaping university priorities. The new internal players engage in gradual inroads that show deliberation to assert greater power. Evidence in this respect is the much greater rate of growth of administrative compared to faculty positions, the appointment of new faculty members to unstable positions with little institutional identification, and the greater role of administrators in academic program design and implementation. Moreover, following corporate models of leadership in the business world, university leaders are receiving bonuses based on performance, defined as moving their university up in rankings (Rhoades 2009). Academics in one major public university are still resentful that its president gave himself a bonus of half a million dollars and considerable bonuses for his senior administrative team and then announced a few months later university-wide budget cuts in the amount of US$1 million. In the same university, some cuts have been petty, such as telling the faculty to bring their office garbage to a receptacle down the hall.

The continuous presence of administrators in university committees in their ex-officio capacity serves to keep them informed; yet, it also serves to influence committee deliberations. This, added to the operational strategies involving central taxation and use of time, gives a definite impression of deliberate action.

The changes in the academic profile—the increase of contingent faculty, or "knowledge workers," and the reduction of tenure appointments—produces a pliable faculty with less job protection and less questioning of administrative decision making. There is evidence that some contingent faculty have not been renewed for reason of grading "too harshly" (Rhoades 2009), clearly an infringement upon academic judgment and autonomy. As does Rhoades, Jon Nixon (2007) holds that professors are indeed becoming an atomized profession, increasingly managed by administrators and nonacademic personnel.

Final Considerations

Institutional change in universities is moving at a fast rate. This change amounts to a shift in power, with a much greater role for administrators in crucial decision making. Changes in administrative offices and in the appointment of faculty members are producing significant structural transformations. The full-time feature of most administrative positions results in the administrators' greater knowledge of institutional functioning and the building of an asymmetry of information vis-à-vis faculty members. I would argue that we are not witnessing merely managerialism as a style of decision making but also the embodiment of academic decision making in nonacademic actors.

The entrepreneurial competition places universities in the path of narrow self-interest in which such issues as social justice, equity, and other social concerns might receive inadequate attention. We already have evidence of the growing importance of science and technology—areas that produce patents and royalties—over those that are less able to produce material goods such as the humanities and the social sciences but are nevertheless critical to social development. Deploring the weakening of the value of the public good, several observers and leaders of major universities (Neave 1988; Gale 2007; Faust 2009) argue that universities must be seen as society's critical voice and that they should embody values beyond their own self-interests. Academics certainly do not have a monopoly over moral values, but as a whole they do have a tradition of promoting societal concerns, acting to some extent as a social conscience.

A final question that can be raised is whether these observed changes are irreversible. The new state of affairs has not stabilized and my prediction is that it will intensify. The only potential variable in these developments could be a proactive response by the faculty. Such a response, regrettably, does not seem visible at present.

Notes

1. The push for greater use of technology for program provision comes accompanied by the argument that conventional teaching is outmoded. Paul Maeder, founder and general partner at Highland Capital Partners, one of the main investors who raised the money for 2tor, Inc., states: "Education is an enormous market still being delivered by and large the way it was by Socrates. It's a mediocre educational experience that locks people in a room and talks at them for an hour and a half" (2tor 2010).
2. The possibility for gain through distance education is well recognized by private entrepreneurs; at present, 42 percent of the online programs are offered by for-profit institutions (Osterman 2010). The market share of the for-profits in higher education is still small, but they represent the sector with the largest growth in the past four decades, having moved from 0.3 percent of the market in 1967 to 6.5 percent in 2007, or a growth rate of 215 times the original percentage (Hentschke 2010).
3. Strategic plans are spreading throughout the developing world. The World Bank (2002) reports having provided assistance for the preparation of such documents to 25 countries between 1995 and 2001.
4. I participated in the International Committee that worked in the strategic plan in the private university. The final text was not discussed with committee members, much less vetted in the university community.
5. Another indication of the changes affecting the university is that the title "provost" does not even appear in the influential 1974 Cohen and March study.
6. Countries with people who can pay for the executive programs, such as China, Korea, and Vietnam, are usually targeted. The private university offers such programs, which usually last two years of part-time study, for a total of US$150,000. It is also true that 70 percent of the international demand for higher education in the United States is coming from Asia (Knight 2009). The public university also engages in the provision of executive programs.
7. In 2010–2011, the College of Education of the private university moved to accept 20 PhD students. As these students will receive full funding for four years

(about US$25,000/yr.), it is clear that massive programs such as the Management Aptitude Test (MAT) and the EdD are subsidizing the PhD program.
8. A growing trend among colleges of education is the placement of EdD degrees and executive certificate programs under the dean's office. This shelters such programs from demanding requirements while administrators make decisions with limited consultation with faculty in regular programs.
9. The recommendations from the committee working on posttenure review were judged extreme, as they required a salary cut for "low-performing" faculty.

REFERENCES

Acemoglu, Daron, and James A. Robinson. 2006. *Economic Origins of Dictatorship and Democracy*. Cambridge: Cambridge University Press.
Altbach, Philip G. 2002. *The Decline of the Guru: The Academic Profession in Developing and Middle-Income Countries*. Boston, MA: Boston College Center for International Higher Education and Palgrave Macmillan.
Blau, Peter M. 1970. "A Formal Theory of Differentiation in Organizations." *American Sociological Review* 35 (2): 201–218.
Bok, Derek. 2003. *Universities in the Marketplace: The Commercialization of Higher Education*. Princeton, NJ: Princeton University Press.
Bond, Sheryl, and Jean-Pierre Lemasson, eds. 1999. *A New World of Knowledge: Canadian Universities and Globalization*. Ottawa, ON: International Development Research Centre.
Bourgeois, Etienne, and Jean Nizet. 1993. "Influence on Academic Decision-Making: Towards a Typology of Strategies." *Higher Education* 26 (4): 387–409.
Bradley, Gwendolyn. 2004. "Contingent Faculty and the New Academic Labor System." *Academe Online*. http://www.aaup.org/AAUP/pubsres/academe/2004/JF/Feat/brad.htm
Brewer, Dominic J., Susan M. Gates, and Charles A. Goldman. 2002. *In Pursuit of Prestige. Strategy and Competition in US Higher Education*. New Brunswick, Canada: Transaction Publishers.
Brewer, Dominic, and William G. Tierney. 2010. "Barriers to Innovation in Higher Education." Paper commissioned by the American Enterprise Institute and presented at the conference on Reinventing the American University: The Promise of Innovation in Higher Education, American Enterprise Institute, Washington, DC, June 3, 2010.
Centre for Educational Research and Innovation (CERI). 2008. *Trends Shaping Education. 2008 Edition*. Paris: OECD, CERI.
Cohen, Michael D., and James G. March. 1974. *Leadership and Ambiguity: The American College President*. New York: McGraw-Hill.
Cowen, Robert. 1996. "Performativity, Post-Modernity and the University." *Comparative Education* 32 (2): 245–258.
Ehrenberg, Ronald. 2010. "Rethinking the Professoriate." Paper commissioned by the American Enterprise Institute and presented at the conference on

Reinventing the American University: The Promise of Innovation in Higher Education, American Enterprise Institute, Washington, DC, June 3, 2010.

Enders, Jurgen, and Egbert de Weert. 2009. "Introduction." In *The Changing Face of Academic Life: Analytical and Comparative Perspectives*, ed. Jurgen Enders and Egbert de Weert (pp. 1–12). London: Palgrave Macmillan.

European University Association. 2005. *Glasgow Declaration: Strong Universities for a Strong Europe*. Brussels, Belgium: EUA.

Faust, Drew Gilpin. 2009. "The University's Crisis of Purpose." *The New York Times*, September 6, BR19.

Gaffikin, Frank, and David C. Perry. 2009. "Discourses and Strategic Visions: The U.S. Research University as an Institutional Manifestation of Neoliberalism in a Global Era." *American Educational Research Journal* 46 (1): 115–144.

Gale, Richard. 2007. "Braided Practice: The Place of Scholarly Inquiry in Teaching Excellence." In *International Perspective on Teaching Excellence in Higher Education: Improving Knowledge and Practice*, ed. Alan Skelton (pp. 32–47). London: Routledge.

Greene, Jay. 2010. *Administrative Bloat at American Universities: The Real Reason for High Costs in Higher Education*. Policy Report No. 239. Phoenix, AZ: Goldwater Institute. http://goldwaterinstitute.org.

Hentschke, Guilbert. 2010. "Innovations in Business Models and Organizational Cultures: The For-Profit Sector." Paper commissioned by the American Enterprise Institute and presented at the conference on Reinventing the American University: The Promise of Innovation in Higher Education, American Enterprise Institute, Washington, DC, June 3, 2010.

Honan, James, and Damtew Teferra. 2001. "The US Academic Profession: Key Policy Challenges." *Higher Education* 41 (1/2): 183–203.

Kingdon, John W. 1984. *Agendas, Alternatives and Public Policies*. Boston, MA: Little, Brown and Company.

Knight, Jane. 2009. "Peril or Promise? Crossborder Higher Education and Access." Annual Fulbright Conference organized by the Council for International Exchange of Scholars, Washington, DC, April 20, 2009.

Kogan, Maurice, and Ivar Bleiklie. 2007. *Organization and Governance of Universities*. Paris: UNESCO.

Labaree, David F. 2010. "Understanding the Rise of American Higher Education: How Complexity Breeds Autonomy." *Peking University Education Review* 31 (3): 23–39.

Lazerson, Marvin. 2010. *Higher Education and the American Dream: Success and Its Discontents*. Budapest, Hungary: Central European University Press.

Lombardi, John, Diane Craig, Elizabeth Capaldi, and Denise Gater. 2002. *University Organization, Governance, and Competitiveness: An Annual Report for the Lombardi Program on Measuring University Performance*. Tempe: Center for Measuring University Performance, Arizona State University.

March, James G., and Johan P. Olsen. 1976. *Ambiguity and Choice in Organizations*. Bergen, Norway: Universitietsforlaget.

March, James G., and Johan P. Olsen. 2009. "Elaborating the 'New Institutionalism.'" In *The Oxford Handbook of Political Science*, ed. Robert Goodin (pp. 159–175). Oxford: Oxford University Press.

Neave, Guy. 1988. "Education and Social Policy: Demise of an Ethic or Change in Values?" *Oxford Review of Education* 14 (3): 341–351.
Nixon, Jon. 2007. "Excellence and the Good Society." In *International Perspective on Teaching Excellence in Higher Education: Improving Knowledge and Practice*, ed. Alan Skelton (pp. 15–31). London: Routledge.
Osterman, Paul. 2010. "Community Colleges: Promise, Performance and Policy." Paper commissioned by the American Enterprise Institute and presented at the conference on Reinventing the American University: The Promise of Innovation in Higher Education, American Enterprise Institute, Washington, DC, June 3, 2010.
Provost of Public University. 2009. "Dialogue with the Provost." Public University, College Park, MD, May 12, 2009.
Rhoades, Gary. 1998. *Managed Professionals. Unionized Faculty and Restructuring Academic Labor.* Albany: State University of New York.
Rhoades, Garry. 2009. "What's Going with Faculty? Why Does it Matter?" Bag lunch presentation at the College of Education, University of Maryland, College Park, MD, April 28, 2009.
Schugurensky, Daniel. 2007. "Higher Education Restructuring in the Era of Globalization: Toward a Heteronomous Model." In *Comparative Education: The Dialectic of the Global and the Local*, 3rd ed., ed. Robert F. Arnove and Carlos A. Torres (pp. 257–276). Boulder, CO: Rowman & Littlefield Publishers.
Shavit, Yossi, Richard Arum, and Adam Gamoran, with Gila Menahem, eds. 2007. *Stratification in Higher Education: A Comparative Study.* Palo Alto, CA: Stanford University Press.
2tor. 2008. "Online Learning Upscale (And Scaled Up)." *2tor News*, September 12. http://2tor.com.
2tor. 2010. "2tor Raises $20 million Series B to Go after the High School End Online Education." *2tor News*, February 5. http://2tor.com.
Twigg, Carol. 2002. "The Impact of the Changing Economy on Four-Year Institutions of Higher Education: The Importance of the Internet." In *The Knowledge Economy and Postsecondary Education. Report of a Workshop* (pp. 77–103). Washington, DC: National Research Council.
Walford, Geoffrey. 1987. *Restructuring Universities: Politics and Power in the Management of Change.* London: Croom Helm.
Weick, Karl. 1976. "Educational Organizations as Loosely Coupled Systems." *Administrative Science Quarterly* 21 (1): 1–19.
Wolhuter, C. C., P. Higgs, L. G. Higgs, and I. Ntshoe. 2010. "How Affluent is the South African Higher Education Sector and How Strong is the South African Academic Profession in the Changing International Academic Landscape?" *South African Journal of Higher Education* 24 (1): 196–214.
World Bank. 2000. *Higher Education in Developing Countries: Peril and Promise.* Washington, DC: World Bank.
World Bank. 2002. *Constructing Knowledge Societies: New Challenges for Higher Education.* Washington, DC: World Bank.
World Bank. 2010. *Concept Note for the World Bank Education Strategy 2020.* Washington, DC: World Bank.

Chapter 4

Professors in Their Places: Governance in Canadian Higher Education
William Bruneau

Since 1960, Canadian university governance has been the subject of two waves of discussion and debate. The first ended about 1973, marked at its midpoint by publication of the Duff-Berdahl Report (Duff and Berdahl 1966). On the recommendation of that report, the upshot of a yearlong inquiry conducted by authors who represented both administrative and professorial interests, nearly all Canadian universities came to accept that their boards of governors should include professorial, staff, and student representation. In short, university governance became more "participatory" from the early 1970s.

The second wave began in the mid-1970s and continues to the present. The debate now is about politics and ideology as much as about structure (Axelrod 2002). Should universities accept practices of governance drawn from the corporate world and "the market"? How shall professors retain participatory rights acquired in the 1960s and early 1970s—and how might they move ahead to new practices of university government?

In the first wave of debate and action, the professoriate was able to rely on collective bargaining and political action to increase professorial participation (Savage 1994). Bargaining led to modest changes in administrative practice, new definitions of academic freedom, clearer descriptions of due process, and increased wages and improved working conditions. But in the opening decades of the twenty-first century, it is at least questionable whether bargaining and politics will continue to produce the desired result: a clear and effective role for the professoriate in governance.

The two waves were and are rooted in a peculiar history. The historical background helps to explain how and why the demand for governance reform came as late as it did, and to see why reform has come under threat in the past 30 years.

Ecclesiastes claimed, "There is nothing new under the sun," (Ecclesiastes 1:9 [New Revised Standard Version]), but this may not be true of university governance in the latter decades of the twentieth century. Toward the end of this chapter, three examples from recent Canadian history help to show why even the writers of Ecclesiastes might have been surprised by the evolution of university governance.

Canadian universities have been under pressure for decades, and not just three or four. Government and business have long expected universities to educate (and to train) more and more students at all levels, undergraduate and graduate (Woodhouse 2009). In 1800, the British North America colonies were home to nearly 200,000 people of European origin—and two PSE institutions, le Séminaire Laval in Quebec City (Hamelin 1995) and the University of King's College in Halifax (Harris 1976, 27–28). Laval, founded in 1663, trained religious scholars for the New World (Magnuson 2005). King's, organized in 1789, served a small Anglophone community of United Empire Loyalists recently emigrated from the United States of America. Higher education was a marginal activity in a difficult environment.

The rapid growth of the colonies that constituted the new Dominion of Canada brought with it new colleges and universities. As the Dominion came into existence in 1867, the population had grown to just over 3 million people of European origin, and all five Canadian provinces had one or more universities. As Canadians moved west between 1850 and 1914, universities and colleges appeared even in small, rural communities in newly created prairie and coastal provinces (Macleod 2008). Increasingly often, the new institutions were publicly funded and controlled. They were built not only because settler-immigrants wanted them, but also because provincial and national policy, social and economic, called for higher education (Prentice 1977; see also Chapter 6 by Paul Axelrod et al.).

Most Canadians were stubbornly determined to support and maintain "the higher learning." Yet before 1945, participation rates rarely exceeded 3 percent of 18–24 year-olds, and at least half of all universities depended on the goodwill and the financial might of sponsoring Christian churches (Johnston 1976; Burke 1996; Gidney 2004). Student intakes were uncertain, the hiring of able university teachers was a constant anxiety for rectors and presidents, and money was often scarce in Canada's boom-and-bust economy. It is a matter of continuing debate among historians of Canadian higher education, as it is in Britain, the United States, France, and Germany, whether the provision of higher education was a truly "popular" undertaking until after World War II (Müller et al. 1986; Axelrod and Reid 1989).

To put the matter plainly, Canadian higher education was the preserve of social and cultural élites. Universities were entrusted with the job of preparing the men and women who would run the state and the church. Universities and colleges would embody persuasively the dominant public values of Canada's founding "nations," French and English. And from the early twentieth century, Canadian universities would enable the making of a middle class (Axelrod 1990). Oxford, Cambridge, and London's Inns of Court accepted that the university should prepare men for public service (Zeeveld 1948). Canada's idea of the university until the 1950s was essentially practical.

The point of having universities and colleges in Canada was not necessarily to democratize the country, but to make the nation a place of peace, order, and good government, for those were (and are) the watchwords of Canadian political culture (Curtis 1988). From Confederation in 1867, provincial governments had the right, through legislation and charter, to decide if universities could give degrees: their inclination was to use that power to attain limited and highly practical objectives.

From the 1860s, despite encompassing limits on the "idea of the university" in Canada, university governance mattered to provincial governments, to individuals (and sometimes churches) who funded and sustained colleges and universities, and to administrators, professors, and students. To say that governance was a matter of concern to the general public would be an exaggeration, since people outside the academy typically wanted children educated at a reasonable cost; it was beyond their ken to worry about the structure of university administration and government. Thus, if governments cared about the governance of higher education, it was not because of popular sentiment. By the same token, professors could only rarely appeal to public sentiment in their campaigns for a greater role in the higher learning.

For nearly one hundred years, Canadian debates about governance revolved around public higher education as a contributor to national well-being. The idealist philosophers of the 1880s, 1890s, and early 1900s did their best to attract public attention to loftier conceptions of the whole educational "enterprise" (Armour and Trott 1981; Shortt 1976). There was a slow-growing appreciation of those conceptions among the Canadian elites. But, none of this gave university teachers a basis in popular politics on which to rest their case.

Even with the huge expansion of the system after 1950, and the rise of mass PSE, the picture did not change. By 2000, there were over 90 degree-granting public universities, more than half of them created in the previous half-century. They had grown up to answer public demand and to realize official policy. Thus university presidents and professors proclaimed the social and economic value of the higher learning, not just its intrinsic merit as the home of free inquiry and teaching (see Ross Paul's Chapter 5).

Overall, the combined effect of Canada's peculiar economic development (broadly dependent on primary resource extraction), its demography and settlement patterns, and its political history, was to put higher education in a utilitarian light. Artistic creation and scientific research were secondary goals, even for the largest and oldest universities in the nation (Greenlee 1988; Friedland 2002). As Michiel Horn has persuasively argued, demands for transparency in finance and hiring, and on participation in administrative decisions, were muted and intermittent until the mid-twentieth century. On the great questions of academic freedom and tenure, the Canadian university was a late-blooming flower (Horn 1999).

This historical background suggests why Canadian professors' demands for participation have taken the forms they have done, *when* they have done. From 1800 to 2011, the professoriate has had to work hard to make its voice heard above the din (Corbo 2001). But there is no denying of the historic tension in the system, and the remoteness (to most Canadians) of the issue of governance (Axelrod 2002).

Since the mid-1970s, declining public funding, micromanagement by the state, the rise of a large management class (where once administrators stood), the appearance of the idea that students are really customers rather than scholars-in-awaiting, and the appearance of a variety of devices meant to connect the university to the marketplace—all have led to a condition where the *formal* autonomy of universities is nearly all that remains of the substantial independence they enjoyed, however briefly, a half-century ago.

At a distance, the governance arrangements of the university look unchanged from a century ago. The academic senate looks after curriculum, the evaluation of teaching, and student discipline. The board of governors has fiduciary responsibility for the buildings, the funds, and the administrative and management systems of the university (Jones and Skolnik 1997). As before, the president or rector is at the administrative apex of the academic and the "business" sides of the university.

But as case studies of three recent governance crises show (see below), appearances are deceiving. It looks as though the professoriate is still in the saddle. In the sight of the professors, it is not so. To them, the past 30 years have seen growing marginalization.

Perhaps we should not be surprised. After all, when *did* senates and the professoriate truly control university life? At the University of Toronto (U of T), through the nineteenth and twentieth centuries, the authority of the president and of certain college principals was decisive in curricular battles, not the senate (McKillop 1994). At McMaster as late as 1950, the Baptist Church shaped curriculum quite as much as academics did (Johnston 1976). After the great expansion of the 1960s, governments decided much of the content of higher education through their funding decisions. So when university teachers have complained about their relative unimportance in university governance, government and the press have been indifferent or hostile.

Oddly, considering their powers, Canadian provincial and federal governments hesitate to modify the legislative framework of universities and colleges, or to intervene overtly in their governance. If provincial governments intervene, it is usually at the system-wide level (as for instance, limits on the powers of universities to set tuition fees), or to create *new* universities and colleges, or to legislate new powers for the ministries that fund those institutions (Jones et al. 2001; Shanahan and Jones 2009).

On one hand, it is widely agreed among the professoriate that government hesitancy is just what they want. The record of government intervention is not entrancing. On the other hand, the profs frequently call on government to increase its commitment to the finance of public higher education, to fund it, and even to "steer" it.

Yet this paradox is not the salient historic fact of the past 30 years. The main point is that premiers and ministers *have* been only too willing since the late 1970s to interfere. They pay close attention, for example, to university and college rankings, including the *Maclean's* ranking of Canadian universities. They welcome performance indicators in government funding decisions (Bruneau and Savage 2002, 175–196). Alberta threatened at one point to base all university funding on "throughput indicators," the speed at which universities graduate students, and the percentage who find jobs in fields for which they were trained. The federal granting councils likewise have been anxious to find statistical evidence of the industrial and social utility of research. In sum, government intervention has been extensive, but typically indirect.

But why have Canadian universities and their professoriate responded so slowly and ineffectively to this "second wave" of intervention?

One reason is the sheer breadth and depth of the ideological or cultural changes commonly summarized as "managerial," or "market-oriented." Institutional responses to political-cultural events of this magnitude must take many forms and a long time. Robert Birnbaum's important discussion of management fads in higher education (2001), mainly in the United States, makes this point at length. His claim is that these fads have friends, not just in government, but also in the universities themselves. This begs a deeper question: why, one wonders, have university professors, students, nonteaching staff, boards, senates, and even managers countenanced management fads? Why has the professoriate been unable to slow the growth of management practices drawn from the nonuniversity sectors?

Main Actors in Canadian Universities

Come to think of it, one would have expected that at least three constituencies in the postsecondary sector might have stood against the wave.

Students

Canadian students were better organized by the late twentieth century than ever. Their unions and federations, in French and in English Canada—provincial, regional, and national—organized campaigns to discourage increases in tuition fees, to encourage direct grants (not loans) for university studies in Canada, and to make universities fairer and more equitable places (Jones 1995).

But although they mobilize student opinion and maintain energetic lobbies at provincial and national levels, Canadian student unions are internally divided. Left-wing students endlessly face off against right-wingers, divided by social, economic, and professional interests. Their differences are severe enough that these organizations have difficulty changing their own constitutions, let alone revising the structure of university governance. The history of the student movement in Canada is as much about the making of a middle class, as it is about the reform of the university (Axelrod 1990; Clift 2002).

University and college boards of governors have at least two student representatives, and senates have significant student membership. Students pressed successfully in the late 1980s for policies requiring faculty-wide teaching evaluations in the majority of Canadian universities, as they did in the United States and other OECD countries. Graduate and undergraduate students have compelled reluctant administrations and boards to publicize deals that they made with private corporations—Coca-Cola, large mining and timber companies, oil refineries, multinational pharmaceutical companies, and so on.

However, students have been unable to keep the tuition fees as low as they (and their parents) would like, to resist effectively the "corporatization" of higher education, or to make a dent on the entrenched powers of other "actors" in higher education.

Overall, their contributions to debate and action in the field of university governance have been only occasionally effective in encouraging (and sometimes compelling) "transparency" on administrations and boards.

Academic Staff and Faculty Associations

The Duff-Berdahl Report concluded that faculty associations embody a happy balance between academic and economic interests. Duff-Berdahl thus allowed faculty a political space where their associations might eventually assert more than mere "influence," but rather authority and even (dare one say it) power.

After Duff-Berdahl, Canadian faculty members began a campaign to negotiate collective agreements with university administrations. In universities and colleges, collective bargaining acquired real importance, not just as a means of improving professorial compensation, but also giving the professoriate a way to "push back" against the tide of managerialism (Anderson and Jones 1998). It was obvious to many in the Canadian professoriate that Duff-Berdahl style participation and the older governance arrangements it recommended were no longer up to the challenges presented by management fads. Senates and boards were not disposed, not well armed, and possibly unsuited for the fight again management fads.

At a national level, the Canadian Association of University Teachers (CAUT) has responded to longstanding problems in university governance with two major reports, the *Governance and Accountability* (1993) and, in 2004, an important report called *Policy on Governance: Where We Have Been and Where We Should Go*. Work commissioned by the CAUT's Academic Freedom and Tenure Committee, by the CAUT's executive, by regional federations, and by local faculty unions and associations has over the past 20 years helped to constrain management excess.

Even so, there remains a chasm between academics' claims and desires on one hand, and political "reality" on the other. Although academic staff have "influence" on courses and degrees, they have less control than they might or should over pedagogy, fields and disciplines, student discipline, research funding and organization, the physical campus, administrative hierarchy, and of course, the university's operating budget. Faculty associations and unions have, it would seem, decided that their primary worries have to do with compensation and with encouraging university administrations and boards to remember the public interest when they act. The problem of governance is not as high a priority in faculty union work as it might and should be.

The unionization of the professoriate has typically followed chronologically the unionization of technical, maintenance, and secretarial staff, of mid-level administrative employees, and of sessional appointees and teaching assistants (Rogow and Birch 1984). These latter associations and unions may place emphasis on governance matters from time to time, as they did during the great Solidarity Uprising of 1983 (Palmer 1987). On some Canadian campuses all but managerial employees are unionized; this has not necessarily meant that university governance has been modified so as to meet demands for greater transparency, greater consistency with public policy objectives, or new methods for assigning budget priorities.

Boards and Senates

Boards of governors have come to be seen as appurtenances of the university president's office. On occasion a board fires a president ("Did Judith Woodsworth resign...?" 2011), but this exception merely proves a larger rule. Boards in practice act as "rubber stamps" for administrative policy and decision (Jones and Skolnik, 1997). Senates meanwhile have been sidelined again and again (Jones et al. 2004).

As with boards, some senates have found the means to turn back, however briefly, the managerial tide. At the turn of the twenty-first century, Carleton's senate helped ensure the swift departure of an excessively managerialist university president, and later to resist the enticements of globalist corporatization. York, through its 50-year-long history, and Trent, for nearly as long, have shown that a senate can still have a salutary effect on the governance practice and outlook of its institution. But academic senates have not been able to stem the tide. Performance indicators and budget cuts have continued unabated.

Three Studies in Governance: Lakehead, Toronto, and UQAM

Three examples illustrate the shifting balance of academic forces in Canada, and make the more general point that university governance has changed only slightly, despite the historical and ideological pressures that (it is widely agreed) threaten university autonomy and professorial rights.

At the Lakehead

Consider first the recent and intriguing history of Lakehead University (LU) in Thunder Bay, Ontario. Located in the northwestern extremity of Ontario, in a region supported by the transportation, logging, and mining industries, LU relies closely on public funding for its continued survival. From a governance standpoint, Lakehead is little different from any public university in the country, for good and for ill. As of 2011, LU has just over 8,000 students on its main and branch campuses.

In May 2009, LU's President Fred Gilbert, told a news conference that LU was doing well financially, but was about to experience annual deficits of C$35–C$50 million. His language was reminiscent of Aristotle's excluded middle, as President Gilbert asserted *P* and *not-P* at the same time—yes, we're fine, but really, we're not fine at all (Kelley 2009). However that may be, Gilbert said that "reducing costs could mean lay-offs." He would like to be "strategic" about this, saving "quality programmes." According to Gilbert, *popular* programs of study would be kept alive.

The Lakehead senate rejected his "restructuring" scheme, refusing to close programs that would not or could not "increase their attractiveness...to students." LU's vice president (Finance), Michael Pawlowski, said LU was beginning to look like General Motors before the crash, "unable to change quickly enough."

In the end, management plans went ahead, as announced. Management announced (Clutchey 2009a) a four-day shutdown in December 2009 during which no salaries would be paid—a violation of the collective agreement between the faculty association and the LU administration. The management then completed purchase of Port Arthur Collegiate, a stone edifice from the grand days of early twentieth-century educational expansionism, to house a law school unlikely ever to open. The management then created in Orillia (1,261 km to the east of Thunder Bay, 100 km north of Toronto) a C$45 million satellite campus (Clutchey 2009b). Finally, it borrowed C$103.4 million between 2000 and 2009, increasing its accumulated deficit to a sum equal to 78 percent of a single year's budget. All these facts became available *after* the crucial decisions had been made, and were available on public websites from the university, the faculty association, or the government.

There is nothing unusual in LU's actions. All these decisions were taken in the name of "growth" and "flexibility," notions that have wide currency among university managers in the early twenty-first century. Guelph University, a central Ontario institution, has a downtown Toronto campus, not far from York University (in northwestern Toronto). Guelph's campus in Toronto makes no more or less sense than LU's in Orillia. Furthermore these extravagances pale by comparison to the Université du Québec à Montréal's (UQAM) investment in an extended downtown Montreal campus, to be combined with a real estate scheme—a P3 "that landed the university in an almost $400-million hole" (Mandel 2009). LU could and did make the case that its expansion made at least as much sense as the capital growth of other Ontario and Canadian universities.

President Gilbert may have found the Quebec example especially encouraging, since UQAM was saved from bankruptcy at the last moment by provincial government intervention. And indeed, on September 4, 2009, Industry Minister Tony Clement announced that the federal government would provide C$13 million of infrastructure funding for Lakehead's Orillia project.

In short, Lakehead was and is representative of governance practice in Canadian higher education. Management at LU has sought to compete not only with other universities in Ontario, but also everywhere else in the world. At Lakehead the management has answers to decades of underfunding and "formula financing" (where student body-counts decide public funding). The answers typically involve increased tuition, management appeals to donors with deep pockets, and continued dependence on the provincial government to get LU out of messes.

At LU the board of governors acted as a rubber stamp for management policy, providing no reliable check on the fiscal excesses of management. The president has consistently said that a criterion for deciding on courses and pedagogy is their market value and/or their appeal to students. "Marketability" is not the *only* test, of course; senate still has its say on the overall shape of the curriculum.

Yet LU's management persistently asks the university's professors to be flexible, nimble, accountable, and quick to change. Speed is a criterion of "quality" at LU. The phraseology has a familiar ring, drawn as it is from managerial talk at universities across North America and Europe (Burgan 2006). At Lakehead, the faculty union, the provincial federation of faculty associations, and the national association, the CAUT, have sometimes restrained management. The LU senate has played an important public role, but not a decisive one. But nothing has yet led to outright reversal of LU management policy, nor of Ontario government policy.

The University of Toronto

The U of T has played a notable part in the social and economic development of Canada. Its governance has thus been a preoccupation for all Ontario premiers, and even for Canadian prime ministers. The U of T, like all Canadian universities, exists in virtue of legislation creating its senate, board, faculties, and system of accountability. All have deep roots in Canadian intellectual history.

Despite this history, Nancy Olivieri, U of T professor and physician in the U of T hospital system, found that she had no adequate institutional protection at the U of T when she chose to publicize her research findings on *deferiprone*. She had discovered that *deferiprone* made seriously ill many of the children for whom it was prescribed. Apotex, the manufacturer of *deferiprone*, and various colleagues at Sick Kids, opposed Olivieri and her work from 1995 onward (Thompson 2001). Her survival as a researcher and a physician at the U of T was often in doubt from the moment she chose, at personal risk, to go public with her findings.

To the dismay of the international and national academic communities, the governance structure of the U of T—with the exception of the University of Toronto Faculty Association (UTFA)—provided little support, and might be said finally to have sided with the drug company. It took an energetic and costly campaign, shared between UTFA and the CAUT, to save Nancy Olivieri's bacon, and to protect her academic freedom.

Another U of T case saw the cancellation (autumn 2000) of an offer to David Healy of a professorial appointment, just after Healy spoke at an international conference about the inappropriate influence of the pharmaceutical industry in academic research on psychoactive compounds known as SSRIs [Selective Serotonin Reuptake Inhibitors]. Research strongly suggested these compounds might dispose clinically depressed individuals to suicidal behavior (Healy 2003). But it turned out that the U of T was receiving substantial research funding from the manufacturer of a popular SSRI.

The U of T withdrew its offer, and Healy eventually reached a settlement involving his appointment as a visiting professor at the U of T for a specified period. Healy never joined the U of T professoriate. The U of T administration left the impression in some minds that it was concerned, in the Oliveri and Healy cases, to retain links with the pharmacological industry.

The U of T has for almost 40 years functioned under a unicameral system combining the board of governors and the senate (Mcdonald 2000). Under that system, one imagines that financial decisions would not be taken without considering academic consequences, and vice versa. Board and senate would be sitting across from one another, and would eventually have to vote together to decide matters put before them. Things have not worked out in that way. In practice, none of the U of T structure has protected academics from managerialist and outside interference in research and teaching.

UQAM

The UQAM was founded in 1969 as the largest component of the Université du Québec, a provincial university system modeled on the University of California and its many campuses. Scandal erupted at the end of the twentieth century over large cost overruns in the construction of new buildings in central Montreal, and in particular a new science centre, which went over budget by C$100 million. A decision to build a 13-storey student residence in connection with business offices and an intercity bus terminal (Ilot Voyageur), was ultimately abandoned, and the building was eventually purchased by the Quebec government. The Rector, Roch Denis, resigned in late 2006 (Chouinard 2006).

The Quebec auditor-general concluded that untrained academics could not run a university, that too many real estate dealers had been involved, and that the board of governors had failed to exercise proper oversight. The government decided that the whole system of university governance in Quebec was in need of reform. The government proposed in Bill 107 (lost in committee during the 2008 election, but revived as Bill 38 [Québec 2009] thereafter) that 60 percent of board members should have qualifications as "independent administrators," drawn from outside the university system. And, powerful new audit and personnel service committees should be created to advise the board (not necessarily connected to the senate or to the professoriate) (Dorais 2009).

From a governance standpoint, two arguments have been widely discussed vis-à-vis UQAM. The first is Cécile Sabourin's argument that UQAM is the tip of an iceberg, that UQAM got into difficulty in the first place because it (and the entire Université du Québec system) is underfunded. UQAM would not have tried a real estate scheme like the Ilot Voyageur were it not in longstanding financial difficulty. New investment in higher education has begun in Quebec, she writes, but is far from sufficient. Eventually, adequate investment will make it possible to decide responsibly how to apportion funds across the entire public higher education system.

The UQAM "question" shows the absence of cooperation among and between universities, the provincial government, and the growing federal subvention of university research. (Sabourin 2010, author's translation)

In all respects, the provincial commitment is insufficient and erratic, Sabourin writes, and suggests that the government does not understand the connection between university teaching and university research.

On August 27, 2008, yet another student, a graduate student in political science, resigned from the UQAM board. Simon Tremblay-Pépin wrote a lengthy essay to explain his decision, noting that the UQAM administration made a bad situation worse in its public communications during the crisis. The administration sounded as if it were working from a position of weakness against overwhelming forces (the private sector, the government) (Tremblay-Pépin 2008).

But, in fact, the original weakness at UQAM was the board's incapacity to restrain its own managers, along with the absence of an entity to investigate the business dealings of the whole institution, at arm's-length.

All three cases—the Lakehead, the U of T, and UQAM—suggest the pressing necessity of change in Canadian university governance.

Renovation in Canadian University Governance

Arrangements of university governance in Canada owe a great deal to history. Until the 1960s, and the modest reform that followed publication of the Duff-Berdahl Report, those arrangements have held up relatively well. As the three cases above show, the system has, since about 1970, become inadequate. Changes in the dominant political ideology of the age, along with changes in administrative practice, suggest that a further round of renovation is needed.

There is no reason to think that adoption of a new structure—as for e.g., the unicameral experiment at the U of T—would liberate the Canadian university from its own history, or give it magical powers to resist the new managerialism. Rather it makes sense to remember what the professoriate, the public, students, and many critics have always said they hoped for the university: that academic and educational priorities would take precedence in decision making.

If this is the purpose of the university, then new legislation may not be required or helpful. Rather, one way forward is to arrange matters so that two main "actors" take a greater part in academic and institutional leadership—the senate and the faculty association. Their purpose should be to help the Canadian university take into account its own rather complicated past, and understand the traditions that guide it, enable it, and limit it. In a sense, the objective of reform in university governance must be partly *negative*: to remedy the worst effects of the new managerialism.

The history and politics of Canadian higher education invite reform with characteristics that might well include the following:

1) an end to overreliance on metrics—whether from government, from university administrations, or from the private sector.
2) a revival of vigorous senates, with new and substantial influence over the budget and the physical plant of the university.
3) senate-led reviews of university bureaucracies, especially where bureaucrats have enabled irrational budget cuts, or where they encourage misleading rankings.

Much of this could be accomplished through expansion of the scope of collective bargaining, and through new institutional policy argued and agreed at the academic senate.

Bargaining at Canadian universities is limited to faculty compensation, procedures for academic appointments, tenure, and promotion, the definition and protection of academic freedom, professorial discipline, and grievance and arbitration. It should be broadened to include university-wide policies on faculty work and rights, including workload; faculty complement; intellectual property; generalized unfairness and matters of equity; and procedures and conditions of administrative appointments—including the appointment of president or rector. Bargaining would help to limit the damage that ill-conceived managerial schemes have done and might yet do.

Second, it would be helpful to find a new balance between the prerogatives of faculty associations and the rights of senates. At Wilfrid Laurier University, in Waterloo, Ontario, any university policy with academic implications for university teachers and staff, must pass through consultation with the faculty association, whether that policy comes from the administration or from the senate.

Third, there must be an energetic and strong senate finance committee. That committee should meet in public, and often. Its detailed opinion on budget priorities should be given to the Board Finance Committee (meeting in public, of course). Where the final university budget diverges from the compromise version developed by senate, the board must give a detailed rationale to explain that divergence.

Fourth, a senate committee on administrative appointments should meet at least twice a year in public (1) to consider the size and appropriateness of the administrative apparatus of the university, (2) to recommend (or simply to choose) procedures for candidate searches, and (3) to nominate persons who will serve on search committees.

Considering the history and politics of Canadian PSE, these must be considered long-term objectives. When and if those objectives were reached, the system would doubtless have blemishes, but its capacity to resist silly fads and ideological fancies would be greater than it now is.

REFERENCES

Anderson, Barb, and Glen A. Jones. 1998. "Organizational Capacity and Political Activities of Canadian University Faculty Associations." *Interchange* 29 (4): 439–461.
Armour, Leslie, and Elizabeth Trott. 1981. *The Faces of Reason: An Essay on Philosophy and Culture in English Canada, 1850–1950*. Waterloo, ON: Wilfrid Laurier University Press.
Axelrod, Paul. 1990. *Making a Middle Class: Student Life in English Canada in the Thirties*. Montreal, QC and Kingston, ON: McGill-Queen's University Press.
Axelrod, Paul. 2002. *Values in Conflict*. Montreal, QC and Kingston, ON: McGill-Queen's University Press.
Axelrod, Paul, and John Reid. 1989. *Youth, University and Canadian Society: Essays in the Social History of Higher Education*. Montreal, QC and Kingston, ON: McGill-Queen's University Press.
Birnbaum, Robert. 2001. *Management Fads in Higher Education: Where They Come From, What They Do, Why They Fail*. San Francisco, CA: Jossey-Bass.
Bruneau, William, and Donald Savage. 2002. *Counting out the Scholars: How Performance Indicators Undermine Universities and Colleges*. Toronto, ON: Lorimer.
Burgan, Mary. 2006. *What Ever Happened to the Faculty? Drift and Decision in Higher Education*. Baltimore, MD: Johns Hopkins University Press.
Burke, Sara Z. 1996. *Seeking the Highest Good: Social Service and Gender at the University of Toronto, 1888–1937*. Toronto, ON: U of T Press.
Canadian Association of University Teachers. 2004. *Policy on Governance: Where We Have Been and Where We Should Go*. Ottawa, ON: CAUT.
Chouinard, Marie-Andrée. 2006. "UQAM—Roch Denis démissionné." *Le Devoir*, novembre 24.
Clift, Robert F. 2002. "The Fullest Development of Human Potential: The Canadian Union of Students, 1963–1969." MA thesis, University of British Columbia, Canada.
Clutchey, Carl. 2009a. "Faculty to fight university shutdown." *Thunder Bay Chronicle Journal*, April 25.
Clutchey, Carl. 2009b. "New LU campus won't be a drain: president." *Thunder Bay Chronicle Journal*, April 25.
Corbo, Claude. 2001. *L'idée d'université. Une anthologie des débats sur l'ensiengement supérieur au Québec de 1770 à 1970*. Montréal, QC: Les Presses de l'Université de Montréal.
Curtis, Bruce. 1988. *Building the Educational State: Canada West, 1836–1871*. London: Falmer Press.
"Did Judith Woodsworth Resign or Was She Effectively Fired?" 2011. *Globe and Mail*, January 8.

Dorais, François-Olivier. 2009. "La gouvernance en voie de changer au Québec." *Affaires universitaires/University Affairs*, September 8.

Duff, James, and Robert O. Berdahl. 1966. *University Government in Canada: Report of a Commission sponsored by the Canadian Association of University Teachers and the Association of Universities and Colleges of Canada.* Toronto: U of T Press.

Friedland, Martin L. 2002. *The University of Toronto: A History.* Toronto: U of T Press.

Gidney, Catherine. 2004. *A Long Eclipse: The Liberal Protestant Establishment and the Canadian University, 1920–1970.* Montreal, QC and Kingston, ON: McGill-Queen's University Press.

Greenlee, James G. 1988. *Robert Falconer: A Biography.* Toronto: U of T Press.

Hamelin, Jean. 1995. *Histoire de l'Université Laval: Les péripéties d'une idée.* Ste Foy, Québec: Les Presses de l'Université Laval.

Harris, Robin S. 1976. *A History of Higher Education in Canada.* Toronto: U of T Press.

Healy, David. 2003. *Let Them Eat Prozac.* Toronto: Lorimer.

Horn, Michiel. 1999. *Academic Freedom in Canada: A History.* Toronto: U of T Press.

Independent Study Group on University and Governance, CAUT. 1993. *Governance and Accountability.* Ottawa: CAUT.

Johnston, Charles M. 1976. *McMaster University.* Toronto: U of T Press.

Jones, Glen A. 1995. "Student Pressure: A National Survey of Canadian Student Organizations." *Ontario Journal of Higher Education—1995*: 93–106.

Jones, Glen A., Theresa Shanahan, and Paul Goyan. 2001. "University Governance in Canadian Higher Education." *Tertiary Education and Management* 7 (2): 135–148.

Jones, Glen A., Theresa Shanahan, and Paul Goyan. 2004. "The Academic Senate and University Governance in Canada." *Canadian Journal of Higher Education* 34 (2): 35–68.

Jones, Glen A., and Michael L. Skolnik. 1997. "Governing Boards in Canadian Universities." *Review of Higher Education* 20 (3): 277–295.

Kelley, Jim. 2009. "Change Key to Solid Future: LU President." *Thunder Bay Chronicle Herald*, May 20.

Macleod, Rod. 2008. *All True Things: A History of the University of Alberta, 1908–2008.* Edmonton, AB: University of Alberta Press.

Magnuson, Roger P. 2005. *The Two Worlds of Quebec Education during the Traditional Era, 1760–1940.* London: Althouse Press.

Mandel, David. 2009. "The Struggle Has Its Own Dynamic: The Professors' Strike at the Université du Québec à Montréal." *The Bullet*, June 4, 223.

McDonald, John D. 2000. *A Brief History and Description of the Governing Council of the University of Toronto.* 4th ed. Toronto: U of T Press.

McKillop, Anthony B. 1994. *Matters of Mind: The University in Ontario, 1791–1951.* Toronto: U of T Press.

Müller, Detlef K., Fritz Ringer, and Brian Simon. 1987. *The Rise of the Modern Educational System: Structural Change and Social Reproduction 1870–1920.* Cambridge: Cambridge University Press and Maison des Sciences de l'Homme.

Palmer, Bryan D. 1987. *Solidarity: The Rise and Fall of an Opposition in British Columbia*. Vancouver, BC: New Star Books.

Prentice, Alison. 1977. *The School Promoters: Education and Social Class in Mid-Nineteenth Century Upper Canada*. Toronto, ON: McClelland and Stewart.

Québec. 2009. Assemblée nationale, 39e législature, 1è^{re} session, Projet de loi no. 38, "Loi modifiant la loi sur les établissements d'enseignement de niveau universitaire et la Loi sur l'université du Québec en matière de gouvernance." Québec: Editeur officiel du Québec.

Rogow, Robert, and Daniel Birch. 1984. "Teaching Assistant Unionization: Origins and Implications." *Canadian Journal of Higher Education* 14 (1): 11–30.

Sabourin, Cécile. 2010. "Sous-financement des universités—l'UQAM, la pointe de l'iceberg." *Le Devoir,* avril 7.

Savage, Donald C. 1994. "How and Why the CAUT Became Involved in Collective Bargaining." *Interchange* 25 (1): 55–63.

Shanahan, Theresa, and Glen A. Jones. 2009. "Shifting Roles and Approaches: Government Coordination of Post-Secondary Education in Canada, 1995–2006." In *The Routledge International Handbook of Higher Education*, ed. Malcolm Tight (pp. 315–325). New York: Routledge.

Shortt, Samuel Edward Dole. 1976. *The Search for an Ideal: Six Canadian Intellectuals and Their Convictions in an Age of Transition, 1890–1930*. Toronto: U of T Press.

Thompson, Jon, ed. 2001. *The Olivieri Report*. Toronto: Lorimer.

Tremblay–Pépin, Simon. 2008. "Les trois faillites de l'UQAM." *Le Devoir,* août 27.

Woodhouse, Howard. 2009. *Selling Out: Academic Freedom and the Corporate Market*. Montreal, QC and Kingston, ON: McGill-Queen's University Press.

Zeeveld, W. Gordon. 1948. *Foundations of Tudor Policy*. Cambridge, MA: Harvard University Press.

Chapter 5

University Governance and Institutional Culture: A Canadian President's Perspective

Ross Paul

> It does not know what it is doing. Its goals are either vague or in dispute. Its technology is familiar but not understood. Its major participants wander in and out of the organization. These factors do not make a university a bad organization or a disorganized one; but they do make it a problem to describe, understand and lead.
>
> Cohen and March 1986, 3

In 1960s North America, challenges to the dominant forms and practices of university governance came from inside, as students and faculty members took action for civil rights and sought to limit American involvement in Southeast Asia. Although widespread public demonstrations and sit-ins spurred changes on university campuses, broadening representation on boards and senates, introducing human rights and equity policies, and opening up some processes, there was eventual disillusionment with the slow pace of change and campuses gradually quieted. Even where change was substantial, it concerned internal campus communities. The outside world stopped paying attention for several decades.

Today, as universities grow rapidly larger, they attract increasing public interest and scrutiny. No longer content to broaden participation, critics challenge the whole system of governance in academia. Students feel threatened by the double-edged sword of rising tuition fees and declining student support. Governments and taxpayers want assurance of quality and seek to reduce the burden on the public purse. Employers demand better job preparation, practical experience, and skill development.

These developments conspire to make the Canadian university a more complex, publicly visible, and vulnerable institution. Interest groups have proliferated and are well organized. There is much more public interest in the way that institutions are organized, managed, and governed.

What are the implications of these changes for the respective roles of the board and senate? What has been the impact of collective bargaining on Canadian university campuses? Are traditional academic governance models obsolete?

In any given institution, faculty opinion may be divided between those advocating more power for the faculty association and those upholding the traditional authority of the senate. Many will worry about the corporatization of the university just as governments and boards demand more accountability.

Caught in the middle is the university president. Pulled in many directions, the president must be keenly aware of governance, the sources of academic policy, fiscal responsibility, and public accountability. The president and his/her fit to the institutional culture are crucial components of effective governance in Canadian universities.

The World is Changing Faster than the Governance Structure

Writing about the United States, Kenneth P. Mortimer and Colleen O'Brien Sathre (2007, 1) say that the world is changing faster than the governance structures of most universities. This may apply even more to Canada, given the relative autonomy of its universities in a decentralized system of higher education.

In the Canadian university of 1960 only 3–5 percent of the age cohort was enrolled. Students were full time and most lived in residence; few students worked outside the university during the school year. Many faculty members and their families grew up on campus and focused on teaching more than research. Most institutions were small, and the president presided over rather than managed the institution. He (and it was almost always a "he") was accountable to a narrowly constituted board of governors. The university was an ivory tower, usually out of the public eye.

Contrast that arrangement with today's visible universities, where participation rates are over 25 percent of the age cohort and growing annually. Institutions are far larger but with decreasing per capita income, resulting in far less favorable faculty/student ratios, huge first-year classes, and a less personal experience for most undergraduates. Students arrive with a more instrumental view of the university and a consumer's sense of entitlement.

Research has taken priority over teaching in the reward systems and in the socialization of academics. Most Canadian universities are unionized and wrestling with overlapping jurisdiction and authority among boards, senates, and faculty associations. Their local, provincial, and national communities increasingly see universities as instruments of economic and social development, meaning that more players have a vested interest in them. Meanwhile, worldwide interest in academic standards and competitive positioning has lead governments and boards to demand more accountability through performance indicators and quality-assurance schemes.

University leadership and governance is thus more difficult and demanding. In comparison, many institutions in our society (corporations, sports teams, and small businesses) are relatively easy to understand and lead. Their goals are clear (make a profit and keep shareholders happy; win a championship; and provide cost-effective, first-rate customer service), and the chief executive officer (CEO) and employees benefit directly when the objectives are reached.

By comparison, the diffuse goals, multistakeholder groups, externally oriented faculty, diffuse reporting lines, and ambiguous presidential authority render university governance both fuzzier and more complex. The president must play a part not only in forging a common mandate and mission for the institution, but also in making its structures and processes work.

The Major Instruments of Canadian University Governance

Observers see university governance procedures as cumbersome and slow, thus frustrating change. Many were surprised over 20 years ago when Charles Handy (1989, 113) predicted that private sector institutions would look more and more like universities as corporate leaders increasingly supervised highly specialized expert staff. In fact, Handy was right. Like the universities, business is giving employees more freedom to pursue their own interests within a general mandate. Handy thought universities would have to act more like private businesses and this has also ensued, if only as evidenced by the frequency of complaints about the "corporatization" of higher education.

There are four principal instruments of academic governance on most Canadian university campuses—the board of governors; the senate; faculty and departmental councils; and faculty associations and collective bargaining.

The Board of Governors and the Difference between Management and Governance

Although there are differences across Canada's decentralized system of higher education, almost every Canadian university[1] is governed by an act of the provincial legislature assigning full operating authority to a board of governors and senate. Most boards consist of lay members appointed by the provincial government and/or the board itself, the president, and representatives of faculty, staff, students, and alumni.

Boards are primarily responsible for selecting, supporting, and evaluating the president; approving and ensuring pursuit of the institutional mission and mandate; establishing strategic directions and priorities; and assuring fiscal responsibility and accountability. They should also care for the university's intangible assets, "especially academic freedom, the commitment to excellence and impartiality; and its ethical standards" (Freedman 2004, 15–16).

Although the board hires and oversees the president, he/she must take responsibility for board development. An effective president works hard to ensure a board is neither a rubber stamp nor overly interventionist. It is crucial that, led by its chair, the members of the board understand the difference between governance (developing and approving mission, mandate, strategic directions, and institutional policies) and management (ensuring their successful implementation). When the board starts trying to manage, the whole institution and certainly the president are in serious trouble! (Freedman 2004, 16).

The relationship between board chair and president directly effects governance and management. Excellent communications and mutual trust and respect between them are essential. Because universities may be turbulent societies, board members must be active, well informed and supportive of the overall direction of the university, and must back the president. Of course, it is also important for a board, usually through its chair, to take appropriate action if its incumbent president is not performing at the expected level (Freedman 2004, 18–21).

Ironically, despite their responsibility to uphold academic freedom, board members themselves may be the most challenging on this matter. They may object to controversial pronouncements of a professor or visiting speaker, the awarding of a particular honorary degree, or otherwise want to intervene in matters clearly delegated to the senate and faculty of the university.[2] In such circumstances, it is incumbent upon the president to ensure that the board is well informed on the matter at hand and, where necessary, to champion academic freedom in the face of controversy and opposition from board members.

The Senate[3]

Almost all Canadian universities function in a bicameral system with the senate responsible for academic matters and the board for overall direction and fiscal responsibility. This relationship has evolved considerably over the past few decades, given that a complete bifurcation of academic and fiscal matters is artificial and even unworkable. For example, a senate will quickly lose credibility if it advocates a tightening of admissions criteria that threatens the institution's enrollment base or proposes a new program without having considered its financial implications.

In many ways, the senate is at the heart of the current debate on university governance in Canada. Although its importance was underlined as far back as 1966 in the landmark Duff-Berdahl Commission on university governance in Canada, and reaffirmed in different ways by the CAUT commissioned report of the Independent Study Group on University Governance (ISGUG) in 1993, there is still significant disagreement about the role and effectiveness of senates on most university campuses (Benjamin, McGovern, and Bourgeault 1995).

In preparation for a book on university leadership in Canada (Paul 2011), I interviewed 11 of the country's most successful university presidents. I found strong consensus on a wide range of issues, but the role and importance of senate was not one of them. Some presidents saw the senate as central to their ability to work with faculty, staff, and students to ensure academic quality, whereas others were less convinced of its value, experiencing it too frequently as a forum for blather, blarney, and resistance to change.

Robert Birnbaum (1991) has provided perhaps the most comprehensive analysis of the role and effectiveness of university senates. Characterizing their manifest functions as rational decision making, formulating and clarifying goals or policies, and serving as a political agency to help develop shared values leading to a consensus, he concludes that they seldom succeed at any of these. He then asks why senates persist in most universities. His answer is that, even where they have fallen short of their manifest roles, they continue to play important latent functions on campus. He identifies eight of these, ranging from the senate as a symbol of administrative acceptance of faculty participation in governance to senate as scapegoat for the institution's problems and shortcomings.

Birnbaum's recognition of the latent roles of senates is extremely useful in helping to explain the durability of long-standing academic governance models in universities. Academia's vaunted resistance to change can be frustrating to reformers but it does ensure that proposals are vetted thoroughly so that, once approved, they will be easier to implement because of widespread participation in their consideration. The most effective academic leaders are those who are thoroughly socialized into the system of governance and the cut and thrust of university politics.

As a senior academic administrator in four institutions in three provinces over 35 years, I always enjoyed senate and found it to be an important instrument of my own academic leadership. It helped me to stay abreast of institutional politics, to identify potential campus leaders, to encourage student participation and development,[4] and to keep the campus informed on major challenges and achievements. I put myself on the side of those who value the role of the senate, but recognize, as Mortimer and Sathre (2007, 30) have found, that administrators routinely attribute more influence to senates than do members of faculty. Indeed, one of the best litmus tests of the status and effectiveness of a senate in a given university is the quality and reputation of faculty members who participate in its deliberations.

In all but a handful of cases across Canada, the president chairs the university senate. I have experienced both approaches, chairing the Windsor Senate while Laurentian's was chaired by an elected faculty member. Although the latter arrangement theoretically allows the president more freedom to speak and to vote (not only to break a tie[5]), this advantage is outweighed by his/her presence in the chair. Chairing not only reinforces the president's symbolic status as academic leader, but ensures that it is demonstrated in practice, with the incumbent directly accountable for the effectiveness of senate. It also provides an opportunity for the president to demonstrate openness in management, an issue discussed further at the end of this chapter.[6]

Faculty and Departmental Councils

Faculty and departmental councils deal with the daily academic business of the institution and are the source of many ideas and proposals that gravitate to senate. They also provide an excellent "early warning system" for complaints and problems that swirl around the corridors of academia before they get to higher levels. Depending on institutional practice, departmental chairs may be influential leaders or rotating caretakers, but the dean is almost always the most important player in faculty governance. The effectiveness of these councils of local governance will be directly correlated with the performance of senate (and vice versa). Although most of the interface between the administration and these councils will be via the vice president, academic, and his/her academic management team, an effective president will develop good relationships with deans, chairs, and faculty members and monitor their issues and concerns closely.

Faculty Associations and Collective Bargaining

The role of senate and its relationship to the board has been further complicated by the rise of unions and collective bargaining since the mid-1970s. Although collective agreements have sometimes strengthened faculty roles in areas such as protection of academic freedom and formalizing standards and procedures for promotion and tenure, there are also significant differences between the traditional collegial culture of the senate and the negotiating culture of collective bargaining that have confused and complicated the board/senate relationship.[7]

The 1993 report of the CAUT-commissioned ISGUG dealt with this very matter, noting that the earlier Duff-Berdahl Report did not anticipate the rise of faculty associations and suggesting that the latter have actually helped strengthen senates. At the same time, the ISGUG reaffirmed the role of senate as distinct from collective bargaining in a number of ways, including representing a broader range of interests and stakeholders than faculty associations do and separating university policy interests and collegial governance from vested interest deliberations at the bargaining table.

The latter point underlines a critical aspect of being a representative on either a board or senate. Although individuals are often chosen or elected to the role by a particular constituency, they should act for what they believe to be the best interests of the institution, not necessarily the individual group they represent. They will, of course, be expected to consult their own constituency regularly on the issues of the day and are on the board or senate to represent those viewpoints. As with the Canadian parliamentary system, however, they should be free to make their own judgments and to vote according to their conscience on a given issue. Their accountability to the constituency comes primarily at election time.

The Critical Issue of Institutional Culture

The first task of a new president is to learn and understand the local institutional culture. At first glance, that might seem an easy task. Canadian universities are unusually homogeneous, not only in their make-up as public comprehensive research intensive institutions with a narrow band of academic standards across the country, but also in the ways in which they are governed (as outlined above). The overwhelming majority of those appointed as presidents have significant prior academic management experience in one or more Canadian universities. Notwithstanding the similarities across institutions, each one has its own distinct local culture. For the 90 percent of Canadian presidents appointed from outside their institution, learning and appreciating that culture is critical to their success.

According to Edgar H. Schein (1999, 19), an organization's culture is deeply embedded and an incoming change agent must delve beyond its artifacts and espoused values to discover the assumptions that influence its members' behavior. Building on the earlier work of William H. Bergquist, Bergquist and Kenneth Pawlak (2008) have provided a useful examination of what they term the six cultures of the academy—collegial, managerial, developmental, negotiating, virtual, and tangible. Knowledge of these dimensions and their variable representations can help a new president in understanding how to achieve change.

Institutional fit may be the single biggest determinant of a president's success. The variance of governance outcomes from campus to campus cannot be explained only by differences in structures and procedures. An institution used to personalized, informal leadership may react badly to a formal president; meanwhile a president who spends almost all the time off campus may be underappreciated by faculty, staff, and students that are used to highly accessible leaders. The vital importance of institutional culture helps explain why several recent presidents who were successful in their first institution did not last long in their second.

The point is reinforced by Cynthia Hardy's (1996) findings that six Canadian universities facing similar financial challenges during retrenchment experienced very different outcomes, the major factor being each institution's local culture and styles of management and governance.

Some Key Issues of Institutional Governance

In judging the effectiveness of governance in a given institution, it is useful to consider some issues of concern on any university campus, with particular attention to the role of the president.

Academic Freedom

As already noted, a university president must be a champion of academic freedom. This means more than the defense of controversial faculty opinions or protection from inappropriate external interventions. Ironically, academic freedom is too often abused when it is taken for granted.

For example, academics too readily support and promote those with whom we agree and ostracize those whose opinions are outside the prevailing politic. Too often, departments hire and promote like-minded colleagues rather than seeking out the best qualified individuals for an academic post. Would Galileo be tenured in today's university? Given the radical nature and unpopularity of his beliefs, he probably would not even be hired! Thus, it is incumbent upon the president and other academic leaders to ensure that hiring, promotion, and tenure decisions are based entirely on qualifications and quality of performance, and not skewed by personality or a tendency to hire and promote "people like us." Diversity is usually used today to refer to representational mixes of people by ethnic background, gender, or sexual orientation, but its most important outcome for a university is diversity of viewpoint and perspective.

Institutional Academic Standards

As set out in a number of books, such as *Ivory Tower Blues* (Côté and Allahar 2007), there are legitimate concerns about what is happening to academic standards. Grade inflation, an increasing sense of entitlement, consumerism, and a more instrumental approach to higher education among students have conspired to threaten the academic integrity of our institutions. These have greatly complicated the faculty role, at the same time the pressures for productivity in research and scholarship have escalated. Too many students blame faculty for their own shortcomings and professors lack the time or personal contact to help students develop the requisite skills, attitudes, and work habits to succeed at traditional university work. There is also evidence that faculty evaluation systems are skewed in favor of the easier markers, reinforcing the notion of student as customer with less and less responsibility for his/her own learning and academic performance.

This presents a wonderful opportunity for a president and the senior academic administrative team to lead university governance. Nothing could be more central to the role of the senate than a frank, open, and well-documented discussion about issues like grade inflation, academic integrity, and the relationship between teaching and research. There are no simple answers, but concerted and sincere efforts to come to grips with these questions will help establish the credibility of the senate in overseeing academic management. To the extent that the president's approach is collaborative, there may be spin-off benefits in improved communications and better relations among the various groups that help the institution.

Institutional Quality and Government Relations

Across Canada for several decades, government funding formulae and, therefore, internal budget allocations, have overwhelmingly rewarded increased enrollments. Although universities are consequently accessible to a broader cross-section of society, rapid expansion has meant a steady annual decline in per capita revenues and thus in institutional quality, especially for undergraduate students.

It is easy to blame governments for the decline in institutional funding, yet university presidents have not helped by failing to limit enrollment growth without full funding. The lack of a united university front often undermines the effectiveness of government lobbying. Presidents argue for more money, students want lower tuition fees and smaller classes, and faculty want competitive salaries and better working conditions. Meanwhile universities rely on managers and tough-minded decision making that tends to undermine collegial relations.

An effective president will work to find common ground with student and faculty leaders in representations to the various levels of government while ensuring an open budget process so that when the inevitably difficult decisions are made, at least the rationale for them is clearly understood.

Assuring the Quality of the Undergraduate Student Experience

Reversing the trend to less personalized undergraduate education requires more than money. It may be unrealistic to expect a return to small classes, close faculty-student interaction, and a strong residential and extra curricular experience for students, but universities can still do much to enrich the undergraduate experience.

First, there is an encouraging trend to more differentiated systems of higher education, notably in Alberta and British Columbia, where former colleges recently converted to universities are striving to be first-class teaching institutions, joining a few others across the country (notably in Atlantic Canada) in emphasizing the undergraduate learning experience. They are also avoiding the trap of second-class status by continuing to support and promote faculty research.

Larger institutions are paying close attention to the undergraduate student. Large classes are not necessarily a disadvantage, if led by superb communicators giving stimulating presentations supplemented by small-group seminars. Lectures and supporting seminars may be presented online, increasing their availability to students. Many social networking technologies can be used to enhance a student's learning.

There is increasing recognition of the importance of the first-year experience and concern about the impact of the budget squeeze. As Ian Clark and his colleagues (2009, 11) have shown, the proportion of first-year classes taught by sessional instructors or teaching assistants has grown steadily in recent years, even exceeding 50 percent in a couple of universities. In response, some institutions are trying to ensure that first-year students are taught as much as possible by tenured faculty members. Encouragingly, the Association of Universities and Colleges of Canada (AUCC) hosted a workshop on undergraduate education in the spring of 2011 where participants, exclusively presidents, and vice presidents academic, were to bring a student as a third member of their institution's team (Zundel and Dean 2010).

Conclusions: The Case for Open Governance and Management

One of the biggest enemies of effective governance at all levels of any institution is cynicism. University faculty are trained to be skeptics, to question, and to demand proof of any assertions. They work in a rarefied atmosphere of freedom to pursue their own interests in their own way. A corporate culture where everyone shares the same goals and benefits from the same outcomes is not only much more difficult to achieve in a university, but it is also often antithetical to its values of open dialogue and dissent in the search for truth. At its best, university governance will recognize the legitimacy of and find ways to accommodate competing aspirations and concerns. Faculty need freedom to do what they do best. Students deserve to know where their tuition dollars go. Governments and taxpayers have a right to demand fiscal accountability and the highest performance standards. Presidents must ensure effective and efficient management within the parameters of academia. A healthy skepticism is at the heart of what a university is, but it can easily degenerate into cynicism and distrust when differences of opinion are personalized and the politics become petty. The president, especially, has a responsibility to ensure that this does not happen.

This is easier said than done. Many believe that procedures and practices in university governance are hopelessly outdated and that presidents are powerless to do much about them. Still, I argue that our systems of governance can work effectively when several key ingredients are in place.

It starts with open management, the concept that an institution should be managed according to the values that define it.[8] In the case of the university, this means the supremacy of academic freedom, the encouragement of debate and dissent, the love of curiosity and the thirst for knowledge, the development of independent and interdependent learners, and a collegial form of governance that fosters the institution as a "learning organization."[9]

Among the elements that best ensure open and effective governance are the following:

1) A president who understands the institutional culture and knows how to work effectively within it.
2) A strong and trusting relationship between the president and the board, notably through its chair.
3) A president who believes in the role of senate and attracts the best people to it by taking it seriously.
4) An institution with a very clear mission, mandate, and strategic plan that has been developed through broad consultation and consensus among the key stakeholder groups and which clearly differentiates the university from its competitors.
5) An institution where the administration, faculty, staff, and students work together.
6) A president who works tirelessly to ensure that governance embodies the best values of academia and ensures others get credit for successes.

The key to any system of effective governance, whatever its details, is trust among the key players, a direct product of the extent to which the system of governance is an open one (Mortimer and Sathre 2007). This is to agree with Mortimer and Sathre that academic governance is an art form, one requiring significant political savvy. The challenge is to ensure a campus climate that encourages debate and dissent but puts institutional interests first.

In defining an appropriate role for university presidents in governance, we turn again to Birnbaum (1992, 178) and his emphasis on finding an appropriate balance between tradition and change. An effective leader recognizes how governance systems differ from campus to campus, shaped by local history and culture. Birnbaum cites four key principles to effective university governance—faculty must believe they have influence in decision making; that influence can come through participation and/or accountability; to be accepted, good governance must conform to the expectations of participants; and the leader must be particularly sensitive to the interpretative importance of governance structures and processes in the institution.

Borrowing from Darwinian medicine, Susanne Lohmann (2004, 72) makes a useful distinction between *defects* and *defenses* in her analysis of university governance. Defects must be eliminated but defenses, even when they look bad, are necessary to protect the integrity of the institution in striving to achieve its goals and purposes. The challenge is to distinguish between them in determining what changes to traditional governance models are needed in the twenty-first century.

> The university's built-in tendency to ossify and the commingling of defects and defences explain why the structures of the university are so resistant to change and improvement—why they are hard to change in the first place, and hard to change for the better. (Lohmann 2004, 72)

So, the incoming president has to recognize that, in endeavoring to improve the organization, he/she must first take the time and trouble to understand it, to appreciate its history and culture, and then to build change. The best way **not** to change a university is to trumpet from the outset that one is going to transform it. Even if a president manages to ram innovations through, if they are not accompanied by concomitant cultural changes, they will probably be reversed by the next president if their impact even lasts that long.

No participant in governance (faculty, administration, and board) should forget that the university is, above all else, an educational institution. Some of the elements seen as problems (endless process, vocal dissent, frequent conflict, slow decision making, and student participation) may be strengths. If the overriding goal is to make the university truly a learning organization for everyone involved, then worries about governance will disappear.

Notes

1. The discussion refers to public universities that cover the overwhelming majority of Canadian postsecondary institutions. There are relatively few private universities, most of them confessional in nature and none very large.

2. Recent examples of how a Canadian university board has been tested include Concordia University's cancellation of a 2002 speech on campus by Israeli premier Benjamin Netanyahu because of fears of violence, the University of Western Ontario's awarding of an honorary degree to the noted Canadian abortionist and women's rights advocate, Henry Morgentaler in 2005, and the University of Ottawa's cancellation of a visit by controversial right-wing pundit, Ann Coulter, in 2010. These are discussed further in Paul (2011).
3. The term "senate" is used to describe the major academic policy body in the university that, in Alberta and Saskatchewan, is called "general faculties council" and, in some other institutions, "academic council."
4. It is hard to be a student senator or board member. Student representatives are usually on such bodies only for one or two years and thus at a disadvantage in learning the governance procedures and figuring out the impact of various campus personalities and hidden agendas. Effective student governments provide orientation programs for student representatives at all levels.
5. In my first meeting as the chair of the Windsor Senate, I had to break a tie on a controversial organizational issue, supporting those who opposed a significant structural change. Although stressful, it gave me an early opportunity to show that changes in academic structures would work only with faculty support and that I was prepared to take the additional time necessary to find consensus.
6. Of course, a president can also demonstrate controlling tendencies in the way he/she chairs the senate but, in such cases, they can be challenged by concerned senate members.
7. The terms "collegial" and "negotiating" are used as defined by Bergquist and Pawlak (2008).
8. This concept is developed further in Paul (1990) and is based in part on the work of Badarraco and Ellsworth (1989) and their concept of "value-driven management."
9. This term was coined by Peter Senge (2006) and applied in the university context by Chris Duke (2002, 55).

References

Badaracco, Joseph L., Jr., and Richard R. Ellsworth. 1989. *Leadership and the Quest for Integrity.* Boston, MA: Harvard Business School Press.

Benjamin, Ernst, Ken McGovern, and Guy Bougeault. 1993. *Governance and Accountability: The Report of the Independent Study Group on University Governance.* Toronto: CAUT.

Bergquist, William H., and Kenneth Pawlak. 2008. *Engaging the Six Cultures of the Academy.* Revised and Expanded Edition of *The Four Cultures of the Academy.* San Francisco, CA: Jossey-Bass, John Wiley and Sons.

Birnbaum, Robert, ed. 1991. *Faculty in Governance: The Role of Senates and Joint Committees in Academic Decision Making.* San Francisco, CA: Jossey-Bass.

Birnbaum, Robert. 1992. *How Academic Leadership Works: Understanding Success and Failure in the College Presidency.* San Francisco, CA: Jossey-Bass.

Clark, Ian D., Greg Moran, Michael L. Skolnik, and David Trick. 2009. *Academic Transformation: The Forces Reshaping Higher Education in Ontario.* Queen's Policy Studies Series. Montreal, QC and Kingston, ON: McGill-Queen's University Press.

Cohen, Michael D., and James G. March. 1986. *Leadership and Ambiguity: The American College President.* 2nd ed. Boston, MA: Harvard Business School Press.

Côté, James E., and Anton L. Allahar. 2007. *Ivory Tower Blues: A University System in Crisis.* Toronto: U of T Press.

Duff, Sir James, and Robert O. Berdahl, 1966. *University Government in Canada.* Toronto: U of T Press.

Duke, Chris. 2002. *Managing the Learning University.* Buckingham, Uk: Society for Research into Higher Education, Open University.

Freedman, James O. 2004. "Presidents and Trustees." In Ronald G. Ehrenberg, ed. *Governing Academia.* Ithaca, NY and London: Cornell University Press, 9–27.

Handy, Charles. 1989. *The Age of Unreason.* London: Arrow.

Hardy, Cynthia. 1996. *The Politics of Collegiality: Retrenchment Strategies in Canadian Universities.* Montreal, QC and Kingston, ON: McGill-Queen's University Press.

Lohmann, Susanne. 2004. "Darwinian Medicine for the University." In *Governing Academia*, ed. Ronald G. Ehrenberg (pp. 71–90). Ithaca, NY and London: Cornell University Press.

Mortimer, Kenneth P., and Colleen O'Brien Sathre. 2007. *The Art and Politics of Academic Governance: Relations among Boards, Presidents and Faculty.* Westport, CN: Praeger.

Paul, Ross H. 1990. *Open Learning and Open Management: Leadership and Integrity in Distance Education.* London: Kogan Page.

Paul, Ross H. 2011. *Leadership under Fire: The Challenging Role of Canadian University President.* Montreal, QC and Kingston, ON: McGill-Queen's University Press.

Schein, Edgar H. 1999. *The Corporate Culture Survival Guide.* San Francisco, CA: Jossey-Bass.

Senge, Peter. 2006. *The Fifth Discipline: The Art and Practice of the Learning Organization.* Rev. ed. New York: Crown Business.

Zundel, Pierre, and Patrick Deane. 2010. "It's Time to Transform Undergraduate Education." *University Affairs Newsletter.* http://www.universityaffairs.ca/its-time-to-transform-undergraduate-education.aspx.

Chapter 6

The Politics of Policy Making in Postsecondary Education in Canada and in the Province of Ontario: Implications for Governance*

Paul Axelrod, Theresa Shanahan,
Richard Wellen, and Roopa Desai-Trilokekar

Introduction

Governance in higher education is, in some crucial senses, about the management of universities. This chapter probes not the management of universities so much as decision making in government and its impact on university governance. Drawing on a larger study of postsecondary policy making in the federal and Ontario provincial jurisdictions, and relying on primary documents and interviews with individuals directly involved in policy making, this chapter illustrates how certain Canadian PSE policies were made and executed.

Using historical evidence and argument, we consider external factors and internal dynamics that shaped decision making, and interpret federal Liberal Party policy making in PSE in light of Conservative Party politics in Ontario between 1990 and 2000. As in Western European OECD countries, federal and national educational policies in Canada do not run in parallel with regional and provincial decisions. In Germany's federal system, for example, the federal role in higher education is negotiated through a higher education framework act with which the *Länder* (states) must comply. A ruling of the German federal constitutional court in 2005 stated that although the *Länder* could not be restricted by federal law from charging tuition fees. They were responsible for following a national standard of equal opportunity to education. Thus Germany represents an interlocking relationship of the federal and the state governments in what has come to be characterized as "cooperative federalism." By contrast, Canada's decentralized federalism means that the management of federal-provincial tensions and boundaries depends to a greater extent on informal factors such as negotiations and the agility and political organization of elites and policy networks inside and outside of government. The effects of these distinctive features of Canadian federal and provincial structures appear in the course of our discussion.

Federal Liberal Policy Making 1990–2000: The Liberal Party "Vision"

We begin with a story of defeat—the electoral defeat of the Liberal government in 1984 and subsequently in 1988, followed by the ascension to the leadership of the Liberal Party by Jean Chrétien, who defeated Paul Martin in 1990. The growing unpopularity of the Conservative government led Liberals to think the party was in a strong position to win the next election, but that it had entered the 1990s bereft of direction. Jean Chrétien appointed two individuals to help solve this problem, Eddie Goldenberg and Chaviva Hosek.[1] When the Chrétien government was elected in 1993, both these individuals assumed senior appointments in the Prime Minister's Office: Hosek became policy director and Goldenberg was appointed senior policy adviser.

Following an important policy conference in Alymer, Quebec, in 1991, Martin and Hosek embarked on a cross-country policy consultation tour, visiting communities and speaking with experts who provided them with "off the record" advice (Hosek interview 2009; Chrétien 1992; Chrétien 2008a). They then prepared *Creating Opportunity: The Liberal Plan for Canada*, subsequently dubbed *The Red Book* that was employed effectively in the 1993 election campaign (Liberal Party of Canada 1993). The *Red Book* made a general case for the importance of research and innovation and thus for potential investment in universities. The absence of detail in the *Red Book* disappointed the AUCC, a national advocacy group representing most degree-granting colleges and universities in Canada, which had been lobbying for a stronger statement.[2] The AUCC remained uncertain as to what priority investment in universities might have in a Liberal government (Best Interview 2009).[3]

The Liberals won the 1993 election. The Department of Finance produced a "Purple Book," containing specific references to the value of investment in research and postsecondary education, something the AUCC did find promising[4] (Best Interview 2009; Greenspon and Wilson-Smith 1996, 199). Lloyd

Axworthy, the new minister of human resources development (HRD), was then allowed to impose some of his own policy priorities, including a reform of Canada's patchwork of social security programs. A leading reform advocate in the Liberal Cabinet, Axworthy was determined to make major changes in unemployment insurance, social assistance, and postsecondary education funding (Greenspon and Wilson-Smith 1996, 148–149; Chrétien 2008b, 72).

Income Contingent Repayment Scheme (ICR)

Following considerable discussion, public hearings, and occasionally querulous internal debate, Axworthy produced a "Green Paper" listing his policy goals, with a proposal for a contingent loan repayment (ICR) scheme for Canadian postsecondary students. The ICR approach was designed to link the overall funding of postsecondary education with the funding of student assistance. Students would be given large loans to be repaid according to the level of their future incomes.

The proposal was dramatic, vaguely articulated, and aroused skepticism in the university community and particularly from student groups who thought that it would mean higher fees and more debt, notwithstanding the "contingent" aspect of the repayment program. Students argued that those receiving loans would have to repay them too quickly, and that those with low incomes would have long-term debt. They mounted an intensive campaign against Axworthy, at one point pelting him with macaroni on Parliament Hill, and calling a national day of protest (Greenspon and Wilson-Smith 1996, 192).

The AUCC criticized the ICR even though it had earlier publicly called for its consideration. It believed there had been too little consultation with the postsecondary subsector (Best Interview 2009) and feared a total federal withdrawal of transfer payments to the provinces for postsecondary education (an unfounded rumor, according to a Department of Finance official). University presidents, including Robert Prichard of the U of T, had been looking for an alternative to the transfer payment approach for the funding of universities. They now opposed the proposal because of its vagueness and because it mentioned tuition fees, a matter of provincial, not federal constitutional jurisdiction. From the postsecondary education subsector's perspective, the document went too far. The Finance Department concluded that the battle was no longer worth fighting, and the government withdrew the proposal. Axworthy had lost control politically of the debate and was unable to build a constituency in the postsecondary educational community. As David Dodge, the deputy minister of finance indelicately noted, his "friends" in the universities were "kicking the shit out of him" (Greenspon and Wilson-Smith 1996, 229). His plans were in any event overtaken by the deficit war, which interrupted the reform of social security and other grand policy plans (O'Leary Interview 2009).

The Deficit

In the wake of the wounding recession of the 1990s, the continuous federal deficit became a priority for the Liberals following their election in 1993. Officials in the Department of Finance convinced the Prime Minister's Office that the country's future required the nation's accounts to be balanced (Gray 2003). All of this was discussed at a dinner attended by David Dodge, deputy minister of finance, and senior officials in the Prime Minister's Office who came away persuaded that the deficit must go (Goldenberg 2006, 114; Hosek Interview 2009). Peter Nicholson, special advisor in the Department of Finance,[5] was similarly influential. Martin agreed that "this fiscal problem isn't a matter of ideology; it isn't something that should separate left from right. It is the arithmetic of compound interest. And if we don't deal with this, no government is going to be able to achieve the social objectives the public wants it to" (Martin 2008, 133). The 1995 Budget and the imposition of Program Review—C$20 billion in expenditure cuts—followed, with substantial reductions in transfer payments to the provinces and cuts in the budget of every federal government department excepting Indian Affairs.

The failure of Axworthy's social security review, combined with Program Review, led to a significant policy departure in the transfer payment system and thus the funding of PSE. With the ICR put on the back shelf, a new Canadian Health and Social Transfer (CHST) enabled Ottawa to reduce transfers to the provinces from C$17 billion to C$11 billion annually and to combine health, education, and social assistance funding into a single package. The provinces responded to the CHST by cutting budgets for public health and education. For PSE in Ontario, reductions in provincial funding totaled 15 percent in 1996–1997 (Trick 2005, 156). University presidents disapproved of this scheme because it did nothing to reform the transfer payment system, reduced funding dramatically, and allowed provinces to spend money (supposedly) intended for postsecondary education on other things. But the purpose of the new federal policy was not to reform the transfer system or to increase funding of public postsecondary education. It was meant to kill the deficit demon. And it did.

Spending the Surplus: The Birth of the Canada Foundation for Innovation (CFI)

The speed with which Program Review succeeded in eliminating the deficit surprised even the Department of Finance, which held back this news from Cabinet as it did not want to generate competition for the spoils around the Cabinet table. Nor did Finance want to encourage departments to replenish their budgets and accumulate long-term, and possibly unsustainable, commitments, all of which they had been used to doing before 1995. After discussions with Finance, Chrétien resolved that half the surplus should go to deficit reduction and half to new programs (Chrétien 2008b, 260; O'Leary Interview 2009). These new projects would build a knowledge economy. But if government wished to alter normal allocation practices, how *would* the government spend its windfall?

The year 1991 had witnessed formation of the "Group of 10" (G-10), a self-declared alliance of research-intensive universities in Canada (later the G-13). In the view of Robert Prichard (president of the U of T), the collective advocacy of a group of 60 institutions, members of the Association of American Universities (AAU), had driven Washington policy on higher education on the funding of research. There was nothing like this in Canada. A meeting of the AAU in Toronto enabled some of its delegates to meet with an "embryonic" group of 10 Canadian university presidents of "research intensive universities" at Prichard's home, where they discussed how the US research model might work for Canada. That night the G-10 was created. Prichard, among others, believed the AUCC was moribund and ought to be more assertive. He thought that Canada could not sustain several dozen major research universities. Thus the G-10 would encourage differentiation of university mandates (Confidential Interview 2009[6]). It began to promote research and infrastructure investment directly with the government and the Liberal Party officials and through the AUCC.

The 1995 budget cuts interrupted the G-10's advocacy campaign, beginning what Prichard described as the worst period in half a century for university funding in Canada (Prichard 2000, 17–18). Following a "depressing" meeting of the G-10, he proposed that the group secure a conference with the finance minister. With assistance from Peter Nicholson, the meeting occurred in Montreal on August 18, 1995. In attendance were representatives from the G-10, including Prichard and Paul Davenport, president of the University of Western Ontario, AUCC Board Chair Howard Tennant, and president of the University of Lethbridge, and Arthur May, president of Memorial University—not a G-10 member, but present because of his role as chair of the AUCC standing advisory committee on university research. Peter Nicholson accompanied the finance minister (O'Leary Interview 2009). AUCC had the delicate task of managing and reconciling G-10 demands with those of the organization's much larger non G-10 membership.

Finance Minister Martin was skeptical at the outset but by the end of the three-hour meeting, he was persuaded of the need for infrastructure support, and for research funding, as such initiatives fit the federal government's knowledge economy plans. Visibly engaged in the conversation, he made this commitment to the group: "I'll be there for you *not* in the upcoming budget but in the next year (1997)" (Confidential Interviews 2009). The whole

AUCC had, it seemed, agreed to the G-10's schemes (Confidential Interviews 2009, Martin 2008, 185). Martin now created an advisory group of university academics, who were "sworn in" to government service and required to keep discussions with Finance Department officials confidential. On the advice of Peter Nicholson, Martin appointed Robert Giroux, who had become president of AUCC in December 1995, Martha Piper, who assumed the presidency of the University of British Columbia in 1997, and Robert LaCroix, who was appointed rector of Université de Montréal in the same year, as members of the advisory group (O'Leary Interview 2009). His office drew counsel from this group in advance of the 1997 budget in formulating its approach to the funding of research, student assistance, and a reinvigorated Registered Educational Savings Plan (RESP) to give tax incentives to Canadians to save money for their children's postsecondary education.

Meanwhile Eddie Goldenberg, from the Prime Minister's Office, spoke frequently with Martha Piper and Robert LaCroix, members of the advisory group and fervent proponents of the importance of research, and particularly of the need for new infrastructure. Chrétien's brother, Michel, a research scientist at Université de Montréal, also encouraged the prime minister to support the research agenda. (Chrétien 2008b, 264; Confidential Interviews 2009). With the Prime Minister's Office and the Finance Department seeing eye-to-eye, and the universities pressing collectively through AUCC and through the advisory council, Scott Clark, associate deputy minister, prepared a plan that led to the creation of the Canada Foundation for Innovation (CFI) to support research infrastructure. The "Foundation" model permitted the government to assign a financial endowment to the CFI and thus spend some of the federal surplus and avoid allocating it to debt reduction. Neither Martin nor Chrétien thought that was necessary or politically desirable (Confidential Interviews 2009; Lopreit and Murphy 2009, 126). As an arm's length agency the CFI would use the endowment to fund its operations over many years. Research grants would be allocated to universities by CFI through competitive peer review, freeing academics from "political interference" by government, and thereby respecting the principle of academic freedom (Goldenberg 2006, 343; Confidential Interview 2009). David Strangway, former president of the University of British Columbia, was appointed the first president of the CFI.

Federal-provincial tension over this new initiative had to be contained. Although Quebec officials raised initial complaints about federal intrusion into provincial constitutional jurisdiction, the province yielded when it became apparent that rejecting CFI funding would prove costly to Quebec's academic community (Thompson 1977a; Thompson 1977b; Willis 1997). As one federal official recalled, having new money to spend "buys goodwill with the provinces" (Confidential Interview 2009). This new venture also had an important impact on institutional research culture in Canada. For the first time, to qualify for federal funds, universities had to present strategic institutional plans—an important change from the traditional Tri-Council approach to allocating grants that were and remain directed exclusively to individual researchers. Many universities struggled at first to generate these strategic plans.

In cultivating support for these new postsecondary initiatives, one other group played an indirect but key role, the Liberal Government Caucus on Post Secondary Education and Research. Two Members of Parliament first elected in 1993 started the group, Peter Adams, a Trent University geography professor, and John English, a history professor at the University of Waterloo. The caucus consisted of some 20 members, mostly backbenchers, who met regularly with postsecondary education lobby groups, promoted the importance of government investment in research, and lobbied for it in weekly Liberal caucus meetings attended by the prime minister and his Cabinet. The "quiet encouragement" the caucus received from Chrétien and Martin helped sustain its advocacy (Adams 2001, 2007; Adams Interview 2009). In addition, monthly "Bacon and Egghead Breakfasts" sponsored by the Natural Sciences and Engineering Research Council (NSERC) and the Partnership Group for Science and Engineering (PAGSE), along with "Breakfasts on the Hill" organized by the Canadian Federation for the Humanities and Social Sciences (CFHSS), supported by the Social Sciences and Humanities Research Council of Canada (SSHRCC), became regular entries on the schedules of MPs and senators (Adams 2007, 7).

Ontario Policy Making, 1995–2000: Conservative Party Vision

Federal Liberals were well into their first mandate when the Progressive Conservatives were elected in Ontario in 1995.[7] The 1990 recession and the federal government's transfer payments reorganization and cuts to the provinces had hit Ontario particularly hard (Courchene and Telmer 1998). The debt, deficit, and taxes had set the stage for the provincial Conservatives' campaign platform of fiscal restraint and dramatic retrenchment—*The Common Sense Revolution (CSR)*. Once elected, the Conservatives proceeded aggressively to implement their CSR platform, including reorganization of municipal and public institutional governance and implementation of sharp fiscal cutbacks (Courchene and Telmer 1998; Shanahan et al. 2005). The CSR was controversial, especially in the education sector where massive cuts were planned and where the Conservatives moved quickly, with little consultation, to implement the plan, diminishing the opportunity for organized opposition. Within 18 months of the election, all CSR policies had been introduced (Royce 1997; Courchene and Telmer 1998; Shanahan et al. 2005).

Three separate but related policy documents affected Ontario's postsecondary subsector. *New Directions-II: Blueprint for Learning in Ontario, 1992* outlined Conservative plans for education and foreshadowed the extension of postsecondary degree-granting privileges, the lifting of restrictions on private degree granting, increases in student tuition fees, and the expansion of student loans, bursaries, and scholarships, including a possible income contingent loan scheme.[8] In November 1995, the same month Conservatives took power, the minister of education and training, John Snobelen announced a plan to review postsecondary education. The review commenced in July 1996 with the release of a government-prepared discussion paper, *Future Goals for Ontario Colleges and Universities*, which specifically solicited recommendations on the most appropriate cost sharing between student, private sector, and the provincial government for PSE funding; accessibility; program rationalization; and cooperation between public education institutions. The government then established the Advisory Panel on Future Directions for Postsecondary Education, chaired by David Smith (and subsequently known as the Smith Commission), to conduct the review of PSE in Ontario.

The commission issued a report affirming the binary structure of public education in Ontario and calling for restoration of public funding to the postsecondary subsector. In key areas its recommendations nonetheless mirrored the Conservative education platform. It proposed greater private sector support, institutional program differentiation, an income contingent loan plan, and tuition deregulation, the latter conditional upon enhanced government and institutional assistance for students in need. Affirming the principle of institutional autonomy it called for strengthened institutional accountability to be exercised by governing bodies of universities and colleges but within an overall less-regulated PSE environment (Ontario Ministry of Education and Training 1996a, 1996b).

Partial Deregulation of Tuition Fees

The questions of tuition fees and cost sharing between government, students, and the private sector were hardly new in Ontario. Still, the Harris Conservative government was the first to tackle the tuition dilemma by partially deregulating fees. Although it was foreshadowed in their platform, and recommended by the Smith Commission, the decision to deregulate, according to one government policy advisor, was driven more by the constrained economic circumstances in the province than by the market ideology that infused the Conservatives' political approach. Nor, according to one official, did the policy flow from research on appropriate tuition levels and student assistance (Scott Interview 2010).

In November 1995, shortly after being elected to power, Finance Minister Ernie Eves announced a C$400 million reduction in postsecondary operating grants. Universities and colleges would be allowed immediately to increase tuition fees by 10 percent and 15 percent respectively. Higher tuition would bring students' contributions to 26 percent of the total cost of their postsecondary education in 1995–1996 (Snobelen 1996). A senior government policy advisor suggested that the ultimate aim was to increase student tuition contributions to 35 percent PSE operating costs (Confidential Interview 2010).

Anticipating the cuts, university presidents had asked for an increase in tuition. Most presidents favored tuition deregulation and used cuts in operating grants to argue their case. They had a receptive government and a freshly penned government report advocating tuition deregulation.[9] The Conservatives deregulated fees in graduate programs and certain professional programs (business/commerce, dentistry, law, optometry, pharmacy, and veterinary medicine). Under Ministry approval, a number of undergraduate program fees were also deregulated, among them engineering and computer science, whereas undergraduate arts and science programs and selected professional programs such as education continued to be regulated (Shanahan et al. 2005.) Deregulation was allowed in fields where graduates could obtain high-earning jobs and could better afford increased tuition.

A five-year cap at 2 percent on tuition fees was introduced for most programs. Institutions were required to set aside 30 percent of the tuition increases for needs-based aid to ensure accessibility for lower-income students. Student assistance funding increased and a variety of scholarships were created. In consequence average overall student university fees between 1995 and 2001 increased by 60 percent. By 1997/1998 university income from tuition represented 37.8 percent of university revenue, whereas 57 percent came from government operating grants and 5.1 percent from other sources, including the federal government. The cost of PSE had significantly shifted to students, and the reforms extended the role of the market in specific program areas, particularly in engineering and information technology, business, law, medicine, and dentistry (Shanahan et al. 2005, 23).

Expansion of Degree-Granting Rights

The Conservatives did not expand degree-granting rights until their second mandate. The final report of the Smith Commission had called for the limited establishment of privately financed, not-for-profit universities under strict conditions developed by an advisory body on postsecondary education. The panel had recommended that the awarding of secular degrees should continue to be a responsibility of universities, but called for a mechanism allowing colleges to acquire polytechnic degree-granting power and eventual university status. The commission had stopped short of recommending degree-granting rights to private, for-profit institutions for fear of opening Ontario to degree mills and inferior-quality institutions (Smith et al. 1996).

The government acted on the report and went further. Insiders suggest that behind the legislation was a desire to end the universities' monopoly on degree-granting. The government intended to unleash the private sector on the university degree-granting world and to support colleges whose programs were explicitly oriented to the job market (Confidential Interview 2010). It passed new legislation entitled the *Post-Secondary Education Choice and Excellence Act*, 2000 (Ontario Ministry of Training, Colleges and Universities 2000) that permitted organizations to offer programs leading to a degree, or to operate a university, either with the consent of the minister of training, colleges and universities or by an Act of the Legislative Assembly of Ontario. The act also permitted the Ontario colleges to offer applied degrees in certain areas subject to the approval of government and upon the recommendation of a new advisory body established under the act called, the Postsecondary Education Quality Assessment Board (PQAB) (Shanahan et al. 2005).

The number of institutions offering degrees in Ontario slowly expanded. Yet the legislation imposed onerous standards of financial reporting that deterred private institutions from applying for degree-granting status. One senior policy advisor suggested that civil servants opposed the policy and drafted legislation so as to minimize its impact (Confidential Interview 2010). There was little consultation with the university subsector, and many were caught off guard.[10] The government saw the changes as controversial and anticipated the historical resistance that always came from the universities in discussions of system integration and degree-granting. It therefore proceeded largely without them (Scott Interview 2010; Confidential Interview 2010).

The Creation of the University of Ontario Institute of Technology

After the *Post-Secondary Education Choice and Excellence Act*, 2000, the Conservative government's 2001 budget included plans to build a new (technical) university, the University of Ontario Institute of Technology (UOIT), in partnership with Durham College. A persistent campaign led by Gary Polonsky, president of Durham College, and the political interests of Jim Flaherty, minister of finance and MPP in the Durham area (Confidential Interviews 2009, 2010, 2011) combined to make UOIT possible. Polonsky involved the local mayor, community, and industry and acquired the support of Flaherty, who pitched the proposal to Premier Harris during a speaking engagement in Durham

(Confidential Interviews 2009, 2010, 2011). Once the Premier approved, the creation of UOIT was assured. Flaherty was receptive to Polonsky's appeals for a university, since it would encourage the region's automotive and power industries and provide the government with political capital in nearby communities (Scott Interview 2010; Shanahan et al. 2005). According to one senior official, the budget announcement "came out of the blue... This was not something that had been negotiated around Cabinet table. This was Flaherty exercising his power with budget to spend funds to create a new university" (Confidential Interview 2010). In less than six months, on October 4, 2002, the minister of finance and the minister of training, colleges and universities announced the opening of the first entirely new university in Ontario in almost 40 years.[11]

The original vision for UOIT was a university-college, a hybrid institution. It was to be called simply the "Ontario Institute of Technology" but in the end, to enhance its status, "University" was added. It was integrated with the Durham College campus, Gary Polonsky was named the new president (but remaining president of Durham College), and after considerable controversy, obtained a seat on the Council of Ontario Universities, an association comprised of the presidents of all provincially assisted universities. The provincial government invested C$60 million in the new university, which was to offer market-driven programs ranging from auto manufacturing to nuclear technology and safety (Shanahan et al. 2005). The university's "bizarre" overlapping of college/university governance structure and its integrated financial and administrative mechanisms made accountability difficult and created a conflict of interest (Confidential Interviews 2010, 2011). In the postsecondary subsector the new university was nicknamed, "Flaherty's Folly." Many viewed it as "completely driven by political needs. There was no (overall) policy around it" (Scott Interview 2010), and no real policy discussion regarding its creation (Confidential Interview 2010).

Interpreting Policy Making

Federal and provincial PSE policy making exhibits many similarities. In the cases profiled in this chapter, both jurisdictions initiated policies in response to turbulent economic circumstances. The fiscal circumstances that governments faced when they came to power cast a shadow over policy discussions. Both governments grappled with recession. Following their election in 1993 the federal Liberal government had to confront the ballooning and potentially structural deficit. The 1995 federal budget called for cuts and reorganization of transfer payments and granting councils, all of which affected postsecondary education across the country. Similarly, in 1995 the provincial Conservatives inherited record high debt, deficit, and tax policies from the previous New Democratic Party administration. Consequently, deep cuts were featured in mid-decade federal and provincial government budgets. Policy making in this fiscal context necessarily shaped and was shaped by the economy. PSE policy was driven by economic imperatives during this time but it was also expected to contribute to the government's economic objectives. For example, the dramatic fiscal situation in Ontario in 1995 created conditions conducive to the implementation of partial tuition deregulation, allowing the government to cut PSE operating grants and providing another source of revenue for PSE institutions. Five years later, albeit in brighter fiscal circumstances, the same government invested C$60 million in the UOIT, justifying it, in part, as an economic stimulus since the institution's mandate was to provide the region's growing nuclear and auto industry with trained workers. In both cases the economy played a role in the policy decision to cut or invest in PSE.

The federal Liberal case for research and innovation as part of a broader global economic forecast was outlined in the *Red Book*. As part of their fiscal strategy to reduce the provincial deficit, the provincial Conservatives detailed their platform in the Common Sense Revolution document. The differing party ideologies of the Liberal federal government and Conservative provincial governments led to divergent economic policy, the one more investment-driven, and the other more market-driven. Party platforms provided a road map for government policy direction. They embodied the visions, philosophy, objectives, or promises of each government which, in turn, steered policy initiatives.

One cannot underestimate the influence of internal policy systems through which initiatives were channeled. Minimalistic structures and streamlined processes could be found in both the federal Liberal and provincial Conservative governments. Chrétien's Liberal Cabinet was divided into three committees for social, economic, and foreign policy. Policy proposals coming to Cabinet were to be vetted in advance by Cabinet colleagues and the Prime Minister's Office (Chrétien 2008b, 34–35). Similarly, to achieve efficiency, the provincial Conservatives integrated elementary, secondary, and postsecondary education into a single ministry. Minimalistic structures enabled key people within government to influence policy directives. For example, senior government officials interviewed for this study described inner sanctums of provincial cabinet ministers who, through several provincial administrations, dominated policy making. For PSE policy this included the finance minister, the minister responsible for postsecondary education, and the Premier. One senior official described them as "the Blessed Trinity for getting approvals for new initiatives" (Confidential Interview 2010). This was illustrated poignantly in the creation of UOIT. Similarly, at the federal level, the policy alignment between Prime Minister Chrétien and Finance Minister Martin contributed more than any other factor to the realization of new initiatives. The role of Finance was critical in both jurisdictions, with the budget being "the government's major policy statement" that can drive any other policy areas that the finance minister and his department "deem necessary" (Savoie 1999, 189). While enabling key individuals to direct policy decisions, minimalistic structures also allow for minimal consultation around policy. For example, ideas for spending the federal surplus were conceived and developed outside of the Cabinet committee structure through the collaboration of officials in the Prime Minister's Office and the Finance Department. Likewise, the establishment of UOIT was decided away from Cabinet and caucus by the Premier and finance minister. Little consultation preceded the passage of the provincial *Post-Secondary Choice and Excellence Act*. At both the federal and provincial levels, swift implementation of policies truncated policy discussion both inside and outside government, and reduced the prospects of opposition.

Policy networks, lobbyists, and constituents also contributed to policy making. However, each administration has its own approach to including individuals and groups outside government. Some governments are inclusive while others limit the channels for outside influence (Shanahan et al. 2005; Cooke Interview 2009). In either case when they do consult, government decision makers will recruit and seek out organizational members or other individuals whose values they share and whose opinions they trust. These may include relationships among colleagues within government, Cabinet or caucus, informal associations, policy development networks, leaders in postsecondary education, or other relevant sectors (Cooke Interview 2009; Confidential Interview 2010). With respect to the issues discussed in this chapter, the AUCC—especially Robert Giroux—played a significant role in Ottawa, as did individual sectoral leaders in federal and provincial venues.

Effective lobbying depends on understanding government decision-making powers and processes, especially in the postsecondary subsector. Constitutional jurisdiction over education lies with the provinces in Canada. There is no federal department of postsecondary education. Yet the federal government has a long history of engagement with the postsecondary field especially in the areas of research, student assistance, and labor-market training through numerous departments (in the case of the latter two issues, usually in collaboration with provincial governments). The scope of federal postsecondary initiatives is limited by this constitutional arrangement as the provinces may object to "intrusions" into provincial jurisdiction. Lobbyists and network groups must understand which federal government department has responsibility for specific postsecondary files and identify the leverage points within this jurisdictional framework.

Individuals who can formulate their message in the language and priorities of the government are effective in their advocacy (Chambers 2010, Scott 2010, and Levin 2009 Interviews). At the provincial level, university presidents who advocated increased tuition fees could make arguments consistent with the

Smith Commission recommendations for reduced government expenditures and tuition deregulation. Similarly, the federal government's initiatives for reinvestment in university research and student assistance were both influenced and supported by the successful lobbying of university leaders such as Martha Piper and Robert LaCroix

Faculty and student associations or university administrators can influence government policy if they are prepared to discuss and negotiate as they advance policy positions. Oppositional politics and approaches have some, but limited, effect. For example, the Canadian Federation of Students' opposition to the federal income contingent loan scheme factored into the demise of the proposal, but new funds flowed into student assistance through measures such as the Millennium Foundation Scholarship Program only when the organization was prepared to collaborate with other postsecondary stakeholders (Axelrod et al. 2011). Conversely, at the provincial level the federal and Ontario student associations were unsuccessful in stopping partial tuition deregulation because they were unable to make their case in terms that were congruent with the Conservatives' determination to reduce government expenditures on PSE (Junor and Usher 2004). As one of our interviewees suggested, it is as important to show appreciation of government initiatives as it is to promote new policies or criticize those in place (Usher 2009).

Canadian federal "innovation" initiatives and provincial government deficit reform were peculiar to the 1990s, and may or may not be replicated. Still, the decision making that led to these policies has wide implications with respect to policy analysis. The cases examined in this chapter demonstrate the importance of a number of factors in postsecondary policy making: the impact of external forces, including the fiscal environment and economic imperatives; the goals and values embedded in party platforms and ideologies; the political consequences of Canada's constitutional idiosyncrasies; the nature of internal policy systems and structures; the ability of networks, lobbyists, and constituents to align their interests with those of governments; and the role of old-fashioned, political pragmatism. This analysis increases our understanding of policy making in postsecondary education and potentially other policy fields, including, potentially, those in international jurisdictions. Those of us in universities affected by such policies, or who seek to change them, have much to gain from a deeper understanding of the complexity and peculiarities of post-secondary education policy development.

Notes

* Portions of this chapter appeared in Paul Axelrod, Roopa Desai-Trilokekar, Theresa Shanahan, and Richard Wellen. 2011, "People, Processes, and

Policy-Making in Canadian Post-secondary Education, 1990–2000." *Higher Education Policy* 24 (2): 143–166, and are included here with the permission of the publisher.

1. Eddie Goldenberg was a long-time associate of, and advisor to, Chrétien, and Chaviva Hosek was a well-known feminist and recently defeated cabinet minister in the Liberal government of the Province of Ontario.
2. AUCC has functions similar to those of the American and European associations of university rectors and presidents.
3. Robert Best was AUCC's director of government relations from 1991 to 2001.
4. See Government of Canada (1994), published by the Department of Finance under Paul Martin's signature in 1994, and released initially as the *Purple Book* in 1993. See also AUCC's response in AUCC (1995).
5. Nicholson was a scientist, self-taught economist, and a long-time associate of Finance Minister Martin with a "formidable intellect" who had spoken at the Aylmer Conference.
6. Interviews were conducted with several dozen individuals responsible for developing and implementing policy decisions in Ottawa and Ontario. These included elected officials, appointed public servants, and other members of policy networks. Those cited directly provided their permission to be named; anonymous interviewees are designated "Confidential Interview(s)." Each interview was conducted by one or more of the authors. Most were face-to-face, and some were by telephone, and took place between 2008 and 2011.
7. Ontario, Canada's most populous province (13.2 million), comprises some 1 million square kms, and is bordered by the provinces of Manitoba on the west and Quebec on the east. Ottawa, Canada's capital city, is located in Ontario. More than one-third of Canada's 1.7 million college and university students (full time and part time) attend Ontario institutions. See Statistics Canada (2011a, 2011b).
8. New directions also called for a smaller role of government in PSE, more partnership funding, greater private sector support for higher education research and development, institutional competition within PSE, and new public accountability value-for-money audits (Michael D. Harris and Ontario Progressive Conservative Caucus 1992).
9. Robert Prichard (U of T) and Paul Davenport (University of Western Ontario) were important advocates of deregulation. A noted exception was Lorna Marsden from York University who was concerned about the impact of the policy on student accessibility (Marsden Interview, 2009).
10. Mike Harris's remarks in November 1999, which were widely reported, revealed the government's intention: "We would welcome advice on whether we ought to allow those who seek to create private universities, fully funded by private money, with no taxpayer dollars, in the province of Ontario. That is an option we are looking at" (Ibbitson 1999).
11. See Ontario Ministry of Finance (2002). Prior to the creation of the UOIT, the last entirely new publicly funded university in Ontario was Brock University, which opened in St. Catharines in 1964. Other new universities, such as Ryerson, Nippissing, and Algoma, involved a change in status of existing institutions.

References

Adams, Peter. 2001. "Research in Parliament." Paper presented to a joint meeting of the Geophysical Union (CGU) and the Eastern Snow Conference (ESC), Ottawa, ON, May 2001.

Adams, Peter. 2007. "The Importance of University-Community Interaction: Community Involvement and Political Sustainability in Canada's Publicly Funded Research and Teaching System." Prince George, BC: University of Northern British Columbia.

Adams, Peter. 2009. Interview with the authors, Peterborough, ON, October 9, 2009.

AUCC. 1995. "Notes for a Presentation to the House of Commons Standing Committee on Finance Regarding Bill C-76, The Budget Implementation Act." Ottawa, ON: AUCC.

Axelrod, Paul, Roopa Desai-Trilokekar, Theresa Shanahan, and Richard Wellen. 2011. "People, Processes and Policy-Making in Canadian Post-secondary Education," *Higher Education Policy* 24 (2): 143–166.

Best, Robert. 2009. Interview with the authors, Ottawa, ON, August 20, 2009.

Chambers, Mary Anne. 2010. Interview with authors, Toronto, ON, May 21, 2010.

Chrétien, Jean, ed. 1992. *Finding Common Ground: The Proceedings of the Aylmer Conference*. Hull, QC: Voyageur Publishing.

Chrétien, Jean. 2008a. "Comments on the Receipt of the David C. Smith Award." Toronto, ON: Council of Ontario Universities. http://www.cou.on.ca.

Chrétien, Jean. 2008b. *My Years as Prime Minister*. Toronto, ON: Vintage Canada.

Cooke, David. 2009. Interview with the authors, Windsor, ON, November 30, 2009.

Courchene, Thomas, and Colin Telmer. 1998. *From Heartland to North American Region State: The Social, Fiscal and Federal Evolution of Ontario*. Monograph Series on Public Policy. Toronto, ON: Centre for Public Management, Faculty of Management, U of T.

Goldenberg, Eddie. 2006. *The Way it Works: Inside Ottawa*. Toronto, ON: McClelland and Stewart.

Government of Canada. 1994. *Agenda: Jobs and Growth. A Framework for Economic Policy*. Ottawa, ON: Department of Finance.

Gray, John. 2003. *Paul Martin: The Power of Ambition*. Toronto, ON. Key Porter Books.

Greenspon, Edward, and Anthony Wilson-Smith. 1996. *Double Vision: The Inside Story of the Liberals in Power*. Toronto, ON: Double Day Canada Limited.

Harris, Michael D., and Progressive Conservative Caucus of Ontario. 1992. *A Blueprint for Learning in Ontario*: Toronto, ON: Progressive Conservative Caucus of Ontario.

Hosek, Chaviva. 2009. Interview with the authors, Toronto, ON, April 23, 2009.

Ibbitson, John. 1999. "Harris Weighing Whether to Open the Door to Private, Non-Profit Universities." *Globe and Mail*, November 18, 4.

Junor, Sean, and Alex Usher. 2004. *The Price of Knowledge 2004: Access and Student Finance in Canada*. Ottawa, ON: Canadian Millennium Scholarship Foundation.

Levin, Ben. 2009. Interview with the authors, Toronto, ON, November 18, 2009.
Liberal Party of Canada. 1993. *Creating Opportunity: The Liberal Plan for Canada.* Ottawa, ON: Liberal Party of Canada.
Lopreit, Débora, and Joan Murphy. 2009. "The Canada Foundation for Innovation as Patron and Regulator." In *Research and Innovation Policy: Changing Federal Government-University Relations*, ed. Bruce Doern and Christopher Stoney (pp. 123–147). Toronto, ON: U of T Press.
Marsden, Lorna. 2009. Interview with the authors, Toronto, ON, May 12, 2009.
Martin, Paul 2008. *Hell or High Water: My Life in and out of Politics.* Toronto, ON: McClelland and Stewart.
Ontario Ministry of Finance. 2002. News Release: "Canada's Newest University to Meet the Demand for Market-Driven Degree Programs—Province to Invest $60 million in Ontario Institute of Technology," October 4, 2002. Toronto, ON: Ontario Ministry of Finance.
Ontario Ministry of Training, Colleges and Universities. 2000. *Directives and Guidelines for Applying for Ministerial Consent under the Post-Secondary Education Choice and Excellence Act, 2000.* Toronto, ON: Ministry of Training, Colleges and Universities.
O'Leary, Terrie. 2009. Interview with the authors, Toronto, ON, October 29, 2009.
Ontario Ministry of Education and Training. 1996a. *Excellence, Accessibility and Responsibility.* Toronto, ON: Ontario Ministry of Education and Training.
Ontario Ministry of Education and Training. 1996b. *Future Goals for Ontario Colleges and Universities.Discussion Paper.* Toronto, ON: Ontario Ministry of Education and Training.
Prichard, J. Robert S. 2000. "Federal Support for Higher Education and Research in Canada: The New Paradigm." *The 2000 Killam Annual Lecture.* Halifax, NS: Killam Trusts.
Royce, Dianne. 1997. "University System Co-ordination and Planning in Ontario: 1945–1996." Unpublished PhD thesis, U of T, Canada.
Savoie, Donald. 1999. *Governing from the Centre: The Concentration of Power in Canadian Politics.* Toronto, ON: U of T Press.
Scott, David. 2010. Interview with the authors, Toronto, ON, June 6, 2010.
Shanahan, Theresa, Donald Fisher, Glen A. Jones, and Kjell Rubenson. 2005. *The Case of Ontario: The Impact of Post-Secondary Policy on Ontario's Higher Education System.* New York: Alliance for International Higher Education Policy Studies (AIHEPS).
Smith, David C., David M. Cameron, Fred Gorbet, Catherine Henderson, and Bette M. Stephenson. 1996. *Excellence, Accessibility, Responsibility.* Toronto: Ministry of Training, Colleges, and Universities.
Snobelen. John. 1996. "Letter" to Ontario University Newspapers, University of Waterloo. *Gazette*, March 13, n.p.
Statistics Canada. 2011a. *College Enrolments by Registration Status by Sex, by Province.* Ottawa, ON: Statistics Canada. http://www.statcan.gc.ca.
Statistics Canada. 2011b. *University Enrolments by Registration Status by Sex, by Province.* Ottawa,ON: Statistics Canada. http://www.statcan.gc.ca.
Thompson, Elizabeth. 1997a. "Don't take Federal Funds, Quebec Warns Universities," *Gazette*, December 9, A1, A8.

Thompson, Elizabeth. 1997b. "Quebec Relents on Federal Fund," *Gazette*, December 17, A12.
Trick, David. 2005. "Continuity, Retrenchment and Renewal: The Politics of Government-University Relations in Ontario 1985–2002." Unpublished PhD thesis, U of T Canada.
Usher, Alex. 2009. Interview with the authors, Toronto, ON, September 8, 2009.
Willis, Terrance. 1997. "Blocking Federal Money is Stupid," *Gazette*, December 10, A1.

Chapter 7

Liberality and Collaborative Governance in a New Private University: The Experience of Quest University Canada

James Cohn

Introduction

Discussions of reform in higher education often look away from the elephants in the room. The sheer size of most Canadian postsecondary institutions, the complexity of their administrative structures, the stasis of their traditions, and the bulk of their contractual obligations and labor agreements—all these tend to weigh reform down. Changing the course of such a juggernaut is more than a challenge. Even with a clear sighting of the reefs ahead, it takes extraordinary leadership and unusual unanimity of buy-in from all the stakeholders to turn such a ship around. We all must admit that, even with genuine goodwill and genuine spending, genuine reform seldom happens. What to do?

Sometimes you jump ship and hop into a canoe.

The Need for Innovation

When David Strangway left the presidency of the University of British Columbia in 1997 after 12 years in that office, he had come to believe that PSE in Canada need not continue in the direction it was headed. Although he himself helped transform University of British Columbia (UBC) into a globally recognized research institution, he saw that financial pressures were squeezing the blood out of undergraduate education. To compete against each other, and to answer their governments' clamorous demands to become "economic development engines," provincial universities felt compelled to pour money into research, laboratory equipment, costly buildings, and flashy programs. They were under formidable pressure to do whatever it took to make names for themselves.

Meanwhile provincial governments and taxpayers had (and still have) limited resources with which to fund them. More and more students want an education. Whether one is an administrator, a professor, or a student in higher education, one has doubtless done the math: larger classes, especially introductory and service classes, cost far less to run. The quality of teaching—and of education—naturally suffers.

Leaving UBC, Strangway was particularly concerned about three problems. First, even though there were many excellent teachers among the professoriate, large institutions offer nearly irresistible incentives that short-change undergraduate teaching in favor of faculty research and graduate programs. Undergraduates are all too often left to fend for themselves. Second, increasing academic specialization leads to narrowly educated undergraduates, ill prepared to grasp or to solve the real problems of our century. Since his essay appeared in 1959, the gap between C. P. Snow's famous "two cultures"—the sciences and the humanities—has, if anything, widened into an unbridgeable abyss for the average undergraduate—if undergraduates have even heard of the problem.

Finally, students are insufficiently aware of, and ill prepared for, the so-called flattening of the world: while global interdependence and competition increases, students' comprehension of other peoples, cultures, and languages decreases.

To respond to this educational distress, it was deemed insufficient—and perhaps impossible—simply to reform an existing institution. Strangway's idea was to start from scratch, bringing the most suitable innovations to light, and incorporating the best practices into a new university. Strangway and his advisors traveled around North America and the world looking for ideas. The mission of the Sea to Sky University—later renamed Quest University Canada—would offer an "intimate, integrated, and international" undergraduate education. Ever since, the school has aimed to support that mission by creating a facility, inventing an administrative structure, developing a faculty and staff, designing a curriculum, and fostering a rewarding student experience.

The Practical Difficulty of Founding a New University

Compared to the size today of the UBC or Michigan State University at about 50,000 students each, or the University of Ottawa at about 38,000, Quest with its 291 students looks like a canoe in a harbor of a super tankers. If anything, the metaphor understates the difficulty of floating a new institution. The task is harder than anyone might think, even for big minds and a small boat. The material obstacles alone might have put off any reasonable person. First, in British Columbia, the founders required legislation passed by the provincial legislature to create a new degree-granting university. The *Sea to Sky University Act* of 2002, introduced as a private member bill by Ralph Sultan of West Vancouver-Capilano, set up the skeleton in law—and thus one towering hurdle passed. To put flesh on the skeleton, they had to build a campus, and to do that, they needed financial support. Strangway persuaded a fellow geologist who was keenly interested in education, the codiscoverer of the Ekati diamond mine in the Northwest Territories, to provide the bulk of the funding for the campus—another towering hurdle passed. Building a campus entailed intricate problems of siting, design, permitting, and construction: each of these formidable barriers was successfully vaulted in turn. The campus in Squamish, British Columbia, opened in the fall of 2007, ten years after Strangway had left UBC.

Numerous intellectual and bureaucratic barriers also had to be cleared. The founding administrators and faculty had to design a curriculum from scratch that not only would meet the objectives of the mission, but would also satisfy the Degree Quality Assessment Board (DQAB) of the British Columbia Ministry of Advanced Education and Labour Development. Although Quest receives no direct financial support from the Ministry, by law it is nonetheless answerable to its standards. Without the imprimatur of the DQAB, no university in the province can operate or grant degrees.

Education consultants began the job of rough-hewing the program of study, and they hired the founding faculty in 2006. The seven members of the founding faculty had the job of shaping the program of study into an actual set of courses that they would teach. They also advised on the myriad decisions, big and little, that go into establishing an institution of higher learning—everything from the kind of chairs and tables that would furnish the classrooms, to setting down the requirements for graduation. Except for reminders to pay due attention to its mission, Quest's consultants and founding faculty were never told what the content of the curriculum had to be. All of them understood that they were designing the best liberal education for undergraduates that they could come up with.

Quest aims solely at excellence in undergraduate education, and consequently offers only one program and one degree: a four-year liberal arts and sciences curriculum leading to a Bachelor of Arts and Sciences degree. The DQAB gave Quest its formal approval for the prospective program of study in the fall of 2006, and has, upon review of Quest's progress, and several subsequent site visits, renewed its approval every year.

Although the authority of the DQAB alone carries legal weight in British Columbia, Quest also sought accreditation from the American Academy of

Liberal Education (AALE) in the United States. The AALE follows a strict set of standards and criteria grounded in the ideals of the American liberal arts tradition. Before Quest opened, in March 2006, the AALE allowed Quest affiliate status on the strength of its curricular design. After four years, the AALE brought in a team to conduct a rigorous review—including a four-day site visit by leading Canadian and American academics. The AALE granted Quest full international program accreditation in June 2010. Quest became one of only a handful of Canadian institutions to be fully accredited in both Canada and the United States.

Due to the less-than-edifying example of some for-profit and fly-by-night institutions, the foundation of Quest as a private (albeit not-for-profit) university was met with skepticism in Canada. The imprimatur of the DQAB and the AALE therefore helps to show that Quest's academic program meets the standards and criteria of serious reviewers, and deserves recognition on a par with the notable Canadian public universities. The founding faculty of seven put together the first syllabi and taught the initial classes at Quest with the freedom to design them as they saw fit, and with no programmatic interference from the president or board. (The greatest curriculum challenge had less to do with the content of classes, with which the founding faculty already had ample teaching experience at other institutions, and more to do with the adjustments required for teaching on the "block plan" of one course at a time.) The DQAB was interested in matters of curricular integrity and quality, in the organizational and administrative capacity, and in the financial and physical basis for higher education at Quest—but it did not base its approval on the presence or absence of any particular model of academic governance. Academic governance has evolved considerably in its first five years, as Quest has progressed from a start-up to an established institution. Everyone at Quest—students, staff, and faculty—knows that they are constantly under scrutiny from the established universities. Such is the lot of the outlier and innovator, and it works as a magnifying lens for everything that Quest does. That enhanced scrutiny helps explain how a pebble like Quest, which is tiny by any university standard, could make a splash in the pond at all.

Inadmissibility for membership in the AUCC remains a barrier to Quest's recognition in Canada. The AUCC is not, technically speaking, a federal or national accrediting agency; it understands itself, rather, to be a voluntary professional association representing the aims of its members. In the absence of federally supervised accrediting in Canada, however, membership in the AUCC looks like de facto accreditation—and generally functions as such. Although Quest has every reason to seek membership in such a powerful organization, at its present size it is ineligible to apply. The AUCC requires an enrollment of five-hundred Full-Time Equivalent (FTE) students for two years prior to, and in the year of, application. Although enrollment at Quest is increasing rapidly, it will not meet this criterion for a number of years to come. Since so many other organizations in Canada and worldwide rely on the AUCC to validate the bona fides of its members, this impediment disadvantages the new institution significantly—a conservative force that works against reform and innovation. Needless to say, the AUCC is not intending to create an obstacle, but does so unwittingly by its prominent position and well-established rules.

Current Operation

Quest's doors opened in the fall of 2007 to welcome 73 students, and its first class graduates in April 2011. As of this writing in summer 2011, 291 students are taking classes from 21 faculty members, and Quest is offering a total of 139 class sections in 2010–2011. Approximately 60 percent of its students come from Canada (from nine different provinces and territories), 25 percent from the US (from 19 states), and 15 percent from 22 other countries around the world. The five-year business plan calls for steady increases in enrollment until it reaches something more than six hundred students on campus at any one time. Running a summer term would allow Quest to reach an enrollment of up to eight hundred students—beyond which it would need to begin a second phase of building. In other words, the founders adhered to the idea of intimacy as a priority in education, and built it into the architecture and the long-term plan. No one at Quest thinks that bigger is necessarily better.

True to the spirit of its mission to offer an "intimate" education, both the curricular design and the course delivery at Quest center on the student—as opposed to, say, on the research interests of the faculty, or the development of economic spin-offs, or training for specific labor needs in business and industry. To this end, Quest reformed course delivery. All Quest classes are seminars, without exception. Faculty must go outside of their disciplinary silos and be willing to guide a seminar class of eager students rather than to profess their discipline by lecturing to a passive audience. All Quest faculty are officially called "tutors" rather than "professors" so as to emphasize their primary role: to guide the conversation of engaged students rather than to perform as "the sage on the stage."

Moreover, Quest teaches on the "block plan," a course delivery innovation by which students take, and teachers teach, only one course at a time. Colorado College developed it 40 years ago, and members of that institution helped implement it at Quest. Instead of taking four courses (or more) simultaneously per semester, students take just one at a time, very intensively, three hours per day for 18 days—for a total of 54 contact hours; each semester, they take four classes in a row. (Funnily enough, most faculty from other institutions think that the block plan would be a great idea for everyone *else*, but that it would never work in *their* department.) Any discussion of higher education reform must address the method of course delivery. Like it or not, taking that question off the table amounts to refusing reform right from the start.

The aim of "integration" in undergraduate education involves a further reform of curriculum design, course delivery, and administrative structure. Quest eschews "majors," thus preventing students from slotting themselves into programs before they have had a chance to explore the life of the mind. To the end of integration, the program of study at Quest is organized into two tiers of two years each. To deliver *breadth*, the curriculum design mandates the first two years (that is, 16 courses) of study for all students—the "Foundation Program." To provide *depth*, students organize their third and fourth years of study around a question of their choosing—the "Individual Concentration Program." No academic firewalls isolate students into departments; on the contrary, Quest insists that all its students gain at least a basic comprehension of scientific and humanistic endeavors, and emphasizes competence in rhetoric as well as quantitative reasoning.

Superior undergraduate education is expensive because it relies on small classes and intensive advising. Although a bargain by the standards of American liberal arts colleges, Quest has the unhappy distinction of being the most expensive university in Canada, with tuition of CAN$27,000 this year, and room and board charges of CAN$8,660. The price notwithstanding, Quest distributed several million dollars in bursaries and scholarships for 2010–2011, making it possible for students from all economic classes and countries of the world to attend. David Strangway speculates that what Quest collects per student might not be very different from the amount per student collected by large research institutions. They receive a combination of tuition and government subsidies on a headcount basis, but must often divert money from undergraduate education to fund research and graduate programs (D. Strangway, personal communication).

Quest receives no direct support from the provincial or federal government. The school depends on the generosity of its donors until it reaches sustainable numbers. Its independent, not-for-profit status does not free it from Ministerial oversight (for we answer to the DQAB), but it does give Quest extraordinary freedom to innovate—an enviable position when it comes time to talk about reform. Indeed, one government official commented during a visit to the campus, "If the government gave you money, we would ruin you."

New Structures

The five-page *Sea to Sky University Act* of 2002 establishes the legal framework for the institution. According to the act, the university is a not-for-profit corporation governed by its board, and administered by its president and vice chancellor, who is also the CEO. Most of the powers involved in running the university are invested in the president, who may delegate them to an academic council. The academic council as foreseen would be chaired by the president, and its members appointed by the board—giving disproportionate weight to the administration, and saying nothing about the role of the faculty.

It must be remembered that the act created an institution *ex nihilo* that had no staff, faculty, or students. There was no tradition from which the power-sharing structures typical of most Canadian universities could derive or evolve, and by which a faculty senate usually has the preponderance of authority. Strangway stated that "as a very small institution—at least in the early days—it seemed wise to build a strong collegial atmosphere with administration and faculty and for that matter staff all on the same page" (D. Strangway, personal communication). He recognized that, as the institution grew larger, Quest might need an academic council or senate. He was nonetheless wary of a governance structure that would set the faculty against the administration, instead of fostering a common aim. Such an internal division might have crippled a fledgling university.

In any event, the academic council permitted (but not required) by the *Sea to Sky University Act* has not materialized because Quest is still so small that there has been no need. The whole faculty can—and do—meet together in a seminar room to discuss policy questions with the president. The challenges of getting a new institution up and running are formidable enough that everyone has been kept sufficiently busy with the day-to-day tasks at hand, and everyone has to row the same boat. In time, I believe that the faculty will want to implement an academic council of some kind, in which case it might prefer a structure other than that specified in the act. Amending the provincial legislation is a matter of considerable political complication and delicacy, and not to be undertaken lightly, but perhaps it will be the preferred route.

To date, Quest has striven to foster a collegial atmosphere between the faculty and administrators, with some success. It is a very small institution, and its administration remains flat. Four areas—which means only four individuals—report directly to the president: the chief financial officer, the dean of student affairs, the vice president for operations and development, and the chief academic officer (CAO). The entire administration can fit around a café table, and often does. Large institutions educating tens of thousands of students simply cannot do the same thing, for very good reasons, but those good reasons raise good questions about the relationship between size and aims.

Academic Governance

The greatest administrative challenge in academics at Quest has been to transform an ad hoc start-up into an enduring institution. Since nothing existed, all of the policies and structures of academic governance have had to be created from scratch—the job is hardly finished, but the board has passed the rough outlines of the necessary policies. The process has involved an iterative consultation between the faculty, the board, and Quest's legal counsel. Quest has tried to find institutional structures that will put the collegial nature of its governance on a firm foundation for the long term. Needless to say, this is an ongoing experiment, and only time will tell whether the foundation will last. The main structures follow.

Academic Freedom, Rank, Tenure, and Performance Review

First shocker: from the outset, Strangway and the consultants who worked with him began by hiring faculty without tenure, without ranks, and without departments. They wanted to do things differently in an effort to promote collegiality.

Strangway nonetheless understood academic freedom as intrinsic to the work of a university, and the Quest board passed a comprehensive statement guaranteeing academic freedom well before hiring began. There is room for disagreement about whether academic freedom depends on the institution of tenure, or whether Canada's Charter protections and academic labor unions would suffice against employment discrimination. But the establishment of a clear and wide-ranging policy at Quest makes the argument moot.

As for tenure, its steady decline is one of the bigger elephants in the room at reform conferences. Proportionally fewer and fewer academic employees in the United States are on a tenure track, while proportionally more and more are contingent (Curtis and Jacobe 2006). No one—neither the overwhelming majority of hardworking professors, nor university administrators responsible for budgets—likes the fact that tenure and its concomitant job security has the potential for abuse by professors who do less teaching and research than their colleagues. The contracts of the reserve army of adjuncts and sessionals typically provide low pay, few benefits, and no job security at all. Sessionals are cheaper and less risky to employ than full professors. Academic employers are tempted to hire sessionals instead of full-time, tenure-track professors, especially when it is a buyers' market, despite the implicit unfairness of hiring two tiers of workers. Given these two trends—the drop in tenure-track positions and the increase in sessional positions, obverse sides of the same coin—it is hard to argue that the system is not broken. In Canada, neither Statistics Canada nor the Association of Universities and Colleges of Canada collects information about the percentage of contingent academic employees, but it is often acknowledged that they number at least half of the postsecondary teaching staff.

As one instance of reform of the tenure structure, appropriate for a very small institution, Quest has established a faculty employment policy by which faculty members are hired on a series of term-limited contracts. The renewal of contracts is subject to a successful performance review. The contracts run for one, two, three, and six years; after one reaches the six-year level, the contracts continue to be renewable for periods of six years.

An essential element of the policy is that an elected committee of the faculty undertakes the performance review, seeking outside expertise as needed. That committee ultimately makes its recommendation to the president, who makes a recommendation to the board, following the established lines of legal authority common to many universities. The committee must make an effort to reach consensus, but if it cannot do so, it must give reasons to the president for the disagreement. At Quest, as elsewhere, it is conceivable that the president could gainsay the recommendation of the Faculty Performance Review Committee (FPRC), but only at the risk of the type of confrontations that presidents tend to avoid. Moreover, Quest's policy requires the president to give reasons for his/her disagreement with the FPRC in an effort to reach a consensus with the committee if at all possible; if impossible, the board must ultimately weigh the reasons and make a determination about the renewal of a faculty contract.

Since there are no departments at Quest, the faculty as a whole nominates and elects members to the FPRC. There is likewise no rank among the faculty. Therefore, the FPRC might count relatively new faculty among its numbers, as indeed is the case at Quest. The policy implicitly trusts the faculty to nominate and elect their best representatives. Successful self-governance relies on democratic and friendly trust, a risk more easily taken in a small institution where everyone knows everyone else personally, but a risk nonetheless. Although the committee could make its own job easy by simply recommending that all their colleagues continue on to their next contract after a merely perfunctory review, the university is small enough, and has staked its reputation on successful teaching to such an extent, that it would be imprudent and counterproductive for it to do so. Every system of review relies ultimately on the goodwill of its members. The design at Quest emphasizes democratically elected peers charged with an important task that they agree to take seriously.

As another innovation, the standards of performance review are included in each tutor's employment contract, but they are flexible, allowing the individual tutor to grow and develop in unique and self-determined ways. All tutors submit a work plan to the CAO outlining what they expect to achieve during the contract period. Teaching six blocks per year is standard, as is some sort of university service. Faculty members are expected to stay intellectually alive and up-to-date in their fields with their research, and to share their inquiries in the field publicly. Quest is not a publish-or-perish environment, but rather allows faculty members to decide where they will invest their intellectual energies. It might well happen that tutors want to pursue pedagogical questions or develop their teaching skills or new courses; they might seek to broaden their knowledge of other fields and explore interdisciplinary connections without knowing ahead of time what those connections will be. The work plan system lets individuals make those decisions themselves so that they can strive to do their best work, while allowing the university to offer appropriate classes and take care of its service needs. The policy aims at allowing tutors the maximum freedom to innovate and explore, on the theory they will become better teachers by doing so, while ensuring that such freedom is exercised responsibly.

A faculty-nominated and elected Dispute Resolution Committee has the authority to review grievances pertaining to academic freedom and unsatisfactory performance reviews. The grounds for a dispute must involve either a violation of the Academic Freedom Policy, harassment, intimidation, or bias on the part of the FPRC, or the presentation of new evidence that was unavailable to the committee. The design emphasizes peer review by elected representatives of the faculty, always in an attempt to make the faculty self-governing and to accept the responsibility that self-governance implies.

Administration of Faculty

The CAO has the explicit task of leading and directing the faculty, and the office is considered equivalent to that of the provost at other institutions. The president nominates the CAO, and the CAO serves at the pleasure of, and reports to, the president. For the well-being of a small school, the CAO and the president must get along, and these rules about the appointment of the CAO will help to ensure that they do.

A couple of checks, however, limit the dependence of the CAO on the president. First, the president may only appoint a CAO who is currently a faculty tutor, or is qualified to be one, as determined by the FPRC. This provision ensures that the faculty will have an immediate supervisor who understands what they do—first and foremost, the trials, demands, and joys of teaching. As a tutor himself or herself, the CAO ought to give due weight to issues that matter to his/her peers, such as the scheduling of courses, assigning committee work, setting academic standards, and finalizing the curriculum. Moreover, the CAO is likely to be someone who shares their concern for undergraduate education as a priority, since he/she will either come from the ranks, or will have passed the same sort of test for hiring that a faculty candidate would undergo.

As a second check, any nominee for CAO must also receive the approval of two-thirds of the continuing tutors in a secret ballot. Thus, while the office is not directly elected, the president and the faculty must come to a virtual agreement about candidates for the job. Neither the president nor the faculty can simply force a candidate into position against the will of the other. Once again, while conceding that different interests may well coexist in a university, the guiding principle has been to find institutional means to promote collaboration and collegiality, rather than adversarial positioning. Although a president could in principle dismiss any CAO at any time, to restore him/her to the tutors' ranks, these two checks are likely to prevent rash action. The president would merely have to start over again, facing the difficulty of finding another candidate who was—or could qualify to be—a tutor, and who had in addition the approval of two-thirds of his/her colleagues.

The four area coordinators make up the next level of faculty supervision. Although Quest recognizes no ranks and no departments—institutionalized by the contractual provision that all faculty are equally tutors and all report directly to the CAO—Quest does recognize the obvious difference between the kinds of specialized training that PhDs must have. (All continuing faculty at Quest have a PhD.) We have divided academics into the Life Sciences, Physical Sciences and Mathematics, Social Sciences, and Arts and Humanities, each with its own coordinator. Coordinators advise on the curriculum and scheduling of courses within their areas; they are ex officio members of the FPRC for tutors in their area; and they take the lead for hiring new faculty and sessionals, as needed. In day-to-day practice, most of a coordinator's tasks, like those of the CAO, involve quotidian decisions: Can we run a new, proposed course? What is the student demand? Who should teach it? When should it be scheduled? Do we need to hire a sessional to fill the slot? The CAO chairs the coordinators' meetings, at which various problems, policies, and decisions can first come up for discussion.

Here too the structure promotes democratic collaboration rather than adversarial confrontation. Although only faculty members of a given area may nominate candidates for the coordinator of their area, the faculty as a whole elects the coordinator from among the nominees. This provision aims to ensure that no faction of tutors in any area can push through a candidate against the wishes of the majority of their colleagues. Insofar as the coordinators work together as a sort of elected cabinet, the faculty as a whole has a strong interest in making sure that all coordinators represent the tutors' shared goals for the university. The structure makes it virtually impossible for a rogue area of study to obstruct the work of the whole. There are no departments to fight over slices of the budget and to seek advantage against each other in a zero-sum game. Moreover, the areas do not need to fight over students, and the height of their silo walls can come down to promote integrated teaching and learning.

Reference

Curtis, John W., and Monica F. Jacobe. 2006. "Consequences: An Increasingly Contingent Faculty." In *AAUP Contingent Faculty Index 2006*. Washington, DC: AAUP. http://www.aaup.org.

Part III

Latin America

Chapter 8

International Forces Shaping Latin American Higher Education Governance*

Alma Maldonado-Maldonado

It is difficult to find a resolution for current global problems without the participation of an international organization. Three recent examples are the organized responses to the economic crisis by agencies such as the International Monetary Fund (IMF) in close alliance with the G-8 or G-20 in 2008; the international actions coordinated by the World Health Organization (WHO) to combat the influenza A (H1N1) virus pandemic crisis in 2009; and the 2010 United Nations Climate Change Conference—the COP16 Conference—organized in Cancun, Mexico. These three cases show the punctual intervention of international organizations in the discussion and resolution of global problems. These organizations "make authoritative decisions that reach every corner of the globe and affect areas as public as governmental spending and as private as reproductive rights" (Barnett and Finnemore 1999, 3).

Globalization has caused several transformations and set many challenges to current societies. In particular, it "has affected and changed the way power is realized in the nation state" (Rutkowski 2007, 243). There is an extensive literature on globalization and the influence of international organizations in education and higher education in terms of financial support or document production, since these are two very concrete ways to materialize their impact in national states and their policies. However, the study of the more sophisticated influence of international organizations in education has been a more difficult challenge. The aim of this chapter is to provide a conceptual framework to understand the more indirect ways of affecting higher education institutions from the context of global governance.

The Tool Box: Global Governance, Soft Laws, International Regimes, and...

Michel Foucault thought of his books as tool boxes from which people could use a phrase or idea to disqualify the power systems, just as if they were a screwdriver or an adjustable spanner interrupting the circuit (Eribon 1992, 291–292). This chapter aims to provide a tool box with the concepts that will be used in the understanding of the international pressures on higher education institutions in Latin America.

The first concept, "global governance," is understood as an intellectual effort to describe changes that are produced at the technological, economic, social, and political levels identified with globalization. One of the first definitions of global governance was produced by an international commission in 1995. According to this commission global governance is

> the sum of many ways individuals and institutions, public and private, manage their common affairs. It is a continuing process through which conflicting or diverse interests may be accommodated and cooperative action may be taken. It includes formal... as well as informal arrangements that people and institutions have agreed to or perceive to be in their interest. (Commission on Global Governance 1995, 2 cited in Karns and Mingst 2004, 4)

It is a challenge to discuss the idea of global governance regarding the field of educational public policies and reforms, considering that literature about global governance and education (and higher education) is basically nonexistent. For instance, an examination of the journal *Global Governance* contains little material on educational policies and reforms. A Review of Multilateralism and International Organizations shows that there are practically no articles that refer to education between 2001 and 2007. The main issues included are security, economy, environment, health, human rights, diplomacy, and other topics.

In this sense, global governance is a concept embedded in the field of international relations. Margaret Karns and Karen Mingst (2004, 4) state that "global governance is not global government," but the key question is what are the implications of having one without the other. As Joseph Stiglitz (2002, 22) points out, the problem of having "a global governance without global government," is that "many of those affected" by the decisions of international organizations "are left almost voiceless." Thomas Nagel cited by Sen (2009, 25) says that "if Hobbes is right, the idea of global justice without a world government is a chimera." There are four elements identified as integral parts of global governance: "international rules of laws; norms or soft law; structures, formal and informal; and international regimes" (Karns and Mingst 2004, 5). A characteristic of globalization is the participation of several actors—national governments, civil society, private entities or corporations, and/or groups or networks of experts—and the role of international organizations in the production of such soft laws and regimes is crucial.

International organizations are the "formal embodiment of institutions and regimes." (Martin and Simmons 2011, 2). For Friedrich Kratochwil and John Ruggie (2001, 347), regimes are "broadly defined as governing arrangements constructed by states to coordinate their expectations and organize aspects of international behavior in various issue-areas." These issues include the trade, monetary, and oceans regime or "nuclear weapons proliferation, whaling, European trans-boundary air pollution, food aid, trade, telecommunications, and transportation" (Karns and Mingst 2004, 12). The same authors mention that "where an international regime exists, participating states and other international actors recognize the existence of certain obligations and feel compelled to honor them" (Karns and Mingst 2004, 12). This is perhaps the most important difference when using the concept of "regime" in education. In this area, regimes exist in the sense of establishing "governing arrangements" and affecting the national and international (and in this case regional) behavior of their higher education institutions. The application of the concept of "international regimes" in education remains less strict than what the technical definition sets, perhaps with the unique exception of the educational regimes that the World Trade Organization (WTO) establishes; and even at the WTO there are no disputes until today related to education or higher education, the only related disputes have to do with intellectual propriety.

In the field of education, international regimes lack "settlement procedures to resolve conflicts" (Karns and Mingst 2004, 12). Nevertheless, the means to apply pressure and impact do exist. This is perhaps the most important paradox when attempting to use regimes as defined in international relations to discuss reforms and changes in higher education.

A more helpful definition of regimes to understand some current reforms in higher education is offered by Stephen Krasner (1983). He defines a regime as implicit or explicit principles, norms, rules, and decision-making procedures around which actors' expectations converge in a given area of international relations.

Norms and soft laws should be considered as part of the international regimes. Soft laws are even less common in the field of education and higher education, because very few elements from the field of international law are considered in the discussion of education. According to David J. Rutkowski (2007) and Hwa-Jin Kim (2001), "soft laws" are powerful tools of modern international law that have become a significant instrument in influencing global, national, and local agendas.

"Soft" law is a general term, and has been used to refer to a variety of processes. David M. Trubek and his colleagues, as cited by Rutkowski (2007, 233), suggest "that the only common thread among the vast definitions of 'soft' law is that they are not formally binding." Rutkowski further argues: "Where 'hard' law encompasses strong obligation, precision, and delegation, 'soft' law allows for one or two of these three criteria to be relaxed or absent" (233).

An important part of the discussion is whether international law may or may not have the aim of "imposing constraints on domestic political behavior" (Raustiala 2006, 9). International law can be used as a tool "by which strong states couch their demands to weak states," suggesting that the scope of these reforms may affect developing countries more directly than developed countries. Clear examples of this are some WTO norms or requirements to create "extensive judicial remedies and sweeping changes to local intellectual property laws" (Raustiala 2006, 11). In fact, some of the rules that are part of international law might be considered as "effective enforcement" (Kim 2001, 49).

In education, there is a debate on what constitutes international law. The most widely defined as laws or hard laws are the three treaties that make up the International Bill of Human Rights adopted by the UN General Assembly on December 16, 1966: the Universal Declaration of Human Rights; the International Covenant on Civil and Political Rights (ICCPR); and the International Covenant on Economic, Social and Cultural Rights (ICESCR). Nevertheless, there is no agreement on whether they can be considered hard or soft laws. For instance, the ICESCR that went into force in 1976 states: "Higher education shall be made equally accessible to all, on the basis of capacity, by every appropriate means, and in particular by the progressive introduction of free education" (United Nations, Office of Public Information 1978, cited in Rutkowski 2007, 234). This article was used in both senses in part given the reservations that each country established before signing.

However, the 26 article of the Human Rights Declaration says: "Technical and professional education shall be made generally available and higher education shall be equally accessible to all on the basis of merit." In comparison with the ICESCR, the Human Rights Declaration has a more limited scope.

In 1998 and 2009 UNESCO organized the First and Second World Conferences on Higher Education and each of them produced a declaration signed by all the participants (members of the organization). These are a clearer example of soft law, yet one of the main problems in defining them as soft laws is understanding their limitations and importance.

Finally, formal and informal structures of international organizations will not be discussed in this chapter, but it does not mean that some additional concepts may be included in this tool box later.

Two Concrete Ways International Organizations Influence Higher Education

As mentioned before, the two more widely studied and quoted examples of the concrete work and influence of international organizations are in terms of direct financing and the knowledge production and information that these agencies produce.

Economic

According to Alma Maldonado-Maldonado and Brendan Cantwell (2009, 284), from 2002 to 2006 about US$61.2 billion were assigned to education. This represents approximately 12 percent of the total spent on international aid. In 2002, the financial commitment was approximately the same between multilateral and bilateral organizations. However, this distribution changed in 2006 when an important growth on bilateral aid was reported, while the multilateral kept stable. The World Bank is the main international organization providing financial funds, so these data have to be considered carefully because the allocation of resources has to do with the size of the country and its particular needs.

The sheer number of publications that are produced by these organizations is immense (Robertson 2009). The World Bank for instance has at least 80,000 documents, books, reports, studies, and papers with free access. The OECD is in a similar situation, although a lot of its production is not free to access.

Another aspect of this knowledge and information production has to do with the role of experts and personnel. In most cases, there is a small network of experts that are working from one international organization to another and keep moving between organizations.

The study by Joel Samoff and Carrol Bidemi (2003) is interesting in terms of how the international organizations have been able to put together some of the top experts in every field. Among other things, in the case of Africa but perhaps as well in Latin America, a job in one international organization solves for these experts many financial problems and works inevitably as a mechanism to co-opt them. A discussion on experts, epistemic communities, and interest groups would be very difficult to do in this chapter.

Four Cases from the Global Context That Impact Higher Education Institutions

Millennium Development Goals

Eight Millennium Development Goals (MDGs) were coordinated by the UN and approved by 189 countries in 2000. Goal number two looks to achieve universal primary education: "Ensure that, by 2015, children everywhere, boys and girls alike, will be able to complete a full course of primary schooling" (UNDP 2011). Because this goal had been a long-term ambition; support for the MDGs was very clear on behalf of most international organizations and groups, such as UNESCO, the World Bank, IMF, and the EU. It has had important consequences in previous debates about the ongoing tension between primary versus higher education.

When the conference "Education For All" took place in Thailand in 1990, the emphasis that most international organizations put on supporting primary education became clear. This changed somewhat in 2000, when UNESCO and the World Bank published the report *Higher Education in Developing Countries: Peril and Promise,* written by the task Force on Higher Education and Society. Their two main conclusions discussed the importance of higher education for all developing countries, independent of their size and region; as well as a critique of the rate of return approach that favors the social impact of primary education over the tertiary sector.

The MDGs are a good example of what can be defined as a soft law in education, because they establish a frame of action about a very specific topic and one of the effects created is a change in international behavior regarding primary education and its support. One of the clear effects that these goals produced is that it became difficult for foundations, countries, or stakeholders to go against the prioritization of this educational level over any other.

The review of data, with its limitations, supports this idea. Available data on the public expenditure per pupil in primary and tertiary education as percentage of the Gross Domestic Product (GDP) in Latin America, from 1998 to 2007 and 2008, provide some interesting tendencies. In the cases of Argentina, Bolivia, Brazil, Chile, Colombia, and Mexico, there is a clear tendency where the public expenditure per pupil as percentage of GDP per capita in primary education has increased in a period of ten years. In some cases that increase was very limited; Bolivia went from 13 to 14 percent; Mexico from 12 to 13 percent. Other increases were more significant, such as the Brazilian case from 11 to 17 percent or Argentina from 11 to 15 percent. However, the increase was still very restrained.

These same countries share the tendency of decrease in the public expenditure per pupil in tertiary education as a percentage of GDP per capita in the same period. In some cases, there is an important reduction. Brazil went from 80 to 30 percent, a 50 percent decrease; Bolivia went from 52 percent to 36 percent, with 16 percent less; Chile, decreased from 21 to 12 percent, a 9 percent reduction; Colombia first spent 34 percent and later 27 percent, decreasing by 7 percent; and Mexico went from 48 to 42 percent, a decrease of 6 percent. Among these countries, Argentina lost fewer points from 20 to 16 percent (World Bank 2011).

It is important to mention that there is no constant increase or decrease in the percentages because in every case the percentages vary considerably. Another issue to consider is the differences in percentages between primary and tertiary education. In most countries, the largest expenditure per pupil is in higher education because it is more expensive and there are fewer students enrolled.

There is not enough evidence to affirm that this tendency to prioritize primary education in the region is the result of the Education for All Conference and the MDGs. However, it may have affected the increase of tertiary enrollment in the region within the last ten years, perhaps a steady enrollment in primary education as an effect of the demographical changes in these countries. The sum of these factors reflects that states spent less money per students in tertiary education and more in the primary level than ten years ago.

The Education for All Conference and the MDGs have become a figure very close to a soft law that has caused several international organizations, groups of countries, networks, and coalitions to join together with the aim of achieving a specific goal: to make basic education universal and spend accordingly the first priority in developing countries.

Accreditation and MERCOSUR

MERCOSUR (Customs union of four Southern-cone countries [Argentina, Brazil, Paraguay, and Uruguay] established under the 1991 Treaty of Asunción) is a trade regime like the North American Free Trade Agreement (NAFTA). MERCOSUR was created in 1991 as a response to several challenges, especially the economic integration of other regions and the need to construct something similar in Latin America. For Michael Mecham (2003, 377), "One early success was in driving an expansion of trade among members." Also, MERCOSUR "provided a basis for cooperation in foreign economic policy."

As with NAFTA, Mexico was forced to reform its accreditation system (Aboites 2010); Mexican higher education institutions were pressured into establishing evaluation mechanisms more similar to those existing in the United States.

Perhaps because of NAFTA or MERCOSUR, in the nineties the whole region of Latin America had to create several accreditation agencies (Fernández Lamarra 2003). The most prominent feature of the higher education convergence policies in MERCOSUR has been the development of a common accreditation system for degrees that, in turn, has given rise to related policies and spurred major projects in the higher education sector (Verger and Hermo 2010, 113).

Norberto Fernández Lamarra (2003, 266) presents advances made in 2003 regarding the constitution of the accreditation efforts: "first, the Ibero-American Network for Higher Education Accreditation (RIACES); and second, the work carried out by the ALFA-ACRO Project (Accreditation for Official Recognition) constitute important advances in this direction." Despite the fact that the establishment of accreditation systems is still not similar everywhere, there have been some considerable advances since Lamarra's article. This is reported by RIACES (2011), who by 2011 included 35 evaluation and accreditation agencies of higher education quality, as well as organizations involved in the development of instruments and policies related to its improvement.

Another related initiative is ALFA-Tuning, a project that attempts to establish "30 generic competencies in Europe and 27 in Latin America. Of those, 22 are 'convergent' or identical with the European ones" (Aboites 2010, 448). Indeed, Tuning is the methodology developed in Europe to create the higher education European space (Beneitone et al. 2007). The Bologna Process has become more "successful" than MERCOSUR-Educativo (Verger and Hermo 2010, 117). The explanations have to do with the existence of governance structures and resources along with stronger regional policy coordination than those in South America.

Finally, it is important to consider that the implementation of accreditation and evaluation systems has become a very powerful mechanism to reform higher education institutions and is shaping systems worldwide, as Guy Neave (1998) has previously discussed.

World-Class Universities and Rankings

In 2003, the first worldwide ranking of universities was created by the Institute of Higher Education at the University of Shanghai Jiao Tong. The following year, the *Times Higher Education* produced another important ranking. More recently, the *U.S. News and World Report's* ranking has greatly increased its influence (Maldonado 2010). The effects of rankings have to do with the role of prestige, the stratification effect, the methodological problems, the disadvantages for non-English speaking countries, and the ways in which they have been used by policy makers (i.e., some national agencies have started using them to provide scholarships to foreign students).

Another concept that has acquired a lot of relevance is that of world-class universities. According to Jamil Salmi (2009) the World Bank started the discussion and exploration of the issue of world-class universities after two ministers from two different countries asked for help to define a world-class university. In fact, the top ranked universities are those considered within a world-class rank. There are two complementary perspectives in examining how to establish new world-class universities.

The first dimension, of an external nature, concerns the role of government at the national, state, and provincial levels and the resources that can be made available to enhance the stature of institutions. The second dimension is internal. It has to do with the individual institutions themselves and the necessary evolution and steps that they need to take to transforms themselves into world-class institutions (Salmi 2009, 7).

The final issue mentioned by Jamil Salmi refers to the internal challenges that many universities face—whether they have real possibilities or not—to aspire to become a world-class institution.

An examination of the 2010 Shanghai Jiao Tong ranking shows that nine Latin American universities are among the top two hundred. The top ranked is the University of Sao Paulo, located between spots 101–105; there are six other Brazilian ones, followed by an Argentinean, Chilean, and Mexican university respectively. However, in the *Times Higher Education* ranking the National Autonomous University of Mexico (UNAM) is the only Latin American university to rank in place 190. Finally in the third ranking, the *U.S. News and World Report*, there are three universities from Brazil, two from Mexico, and two from Argentina and Chile. The Latin American region only ranks better than Africa.

It is important to question the extent to which we should consider the ideas of rankings and world-class universities as a new type of regime that forces universities to reform themselves to become better established and to acquire the prestige that is implied by being better ranked. Some of these institutions already know what the ranking criteria are and are acting in consequence, for example, by increasing the number of international students or hiring more international faculty. It seems a new "nonformal" regime was born in 2003 for higher education institutions internationally.

AHELO

The OECD has established several large-scale international assessments, such as the Program for International Student Assessment (PISA) focusing on 15-year-olds at compulsory school level, and the Program for the International Assessment of Adult Competencies (PIAAC). PISA began in 1997, and by 2006 it already had the participation of the 30 OECD members and another

57 nonmember countries (OECD 2010–2011). Interestingly, many of these nonmembers still participate despite the fact that their PISA results have not been very satisfactory (Rutkowski 2007, 241). This clearly is the case of Latin American countries.

In the context of these programs, the OECD is currently developing a new initiative: the Assessment of Higher Education Learning Outcomes (AHELO) that will test students in higher education. It will evaluate student performance across countries. The test will look at common generic skills (critical thinking, analytical reasoning, and problem-solving and written communication), discipline-specific skills (economics and engineering), and contextual information.

According to the official information, AHELO will be a tool for universities "to assess and improve their teaching," for students "to make better choices in selecting institutions," for policy makers "to make sure that the considerable amounts spent on higher education are spent well," and for employers "to know if the skills of the graduates entering the job market match their needs" (OECD 2010–2011). The standing of the project reported in 2010 is as follows:

> The OECD will be working with a consortium of world experts and teams in 15 participating countries to develop and administer the tests. By the end of the feasibility study in 2012, we will determine if such tests can indeed be developed and successfully administered to students. (OECD 2010–2011, 5)

It is interesting to notice the influence that the United States exerts in the project. They acknowledge that many of their questions "will be based on an international adaptation of the US Collegiate Learning Assessment (developed by the Council for Aid to Education)" (OECD 2010–2011). Further, two of the project's sponsors are from the United States—the Lumina Foundation for Education and the Spencer Foundation—while the rest are from Portugal, Sweden, England, and Ireland (OECD 2010–2011, 8). Also there are 16 countries that are currently participating in the project.[1]

Tom Schuller and Stéphan Vincent-Lancrin (2009, 66) argue,

> The OECD differs from many other international organizations in that it is not a regulatory, still less legislative, body (though with some "soft law" exceptions). It does not distribute financial support, either. Its legitimacy and influence depend to a high degree on the perceived quality of its information and analysis, not on its power as a rule-making body (as with the EU) or as a provider of funds (as with the World Bank).

In this sense, what would happen with AHELO if this initiative works? Neither AHELO nor PISA is any type of governance instrument or initiative that governments must follow, but there are some practices that affect most educational systems in a nonnormative way, that is, "non-binding and intended to serve as a reference point" (Kim 2001, 34). Besides, these practices are "grounded in what is desirable and appropriate for liberal, market-friendly, economic policies" (Amaral and Neave 2009, 85). To some extent the popularization of a standardized test like PISA has become a new type of "non formal" regime that countries need to follow. If AHELO works, it could be constituted as something similar in higher education. Colombia and Mexico are the only Latin American countries participating in AHELO testing their generic skills; Mexico is also participating in the Economics test. All of the participating countries take part in the analysis of their contextual dimension.

Discussion

The four cases presented above provide important information about global governance, regimes, and reforms in Latin American higher education. They help in the understanding of how universities are changing and what strategies global actors have created to bring about these changes.

They are all international in scope. The MDGs could be considered a soft law, the accreditation mechanisms are an established regime, the rankings a regime in progress, and AHELO could eventually become a regime. However, as was mentioned before, this idea of "regime" must be considered carefully because it does not fully comply with the technical definition that has been used in other fields, especially international relations.

The MDGs are an example of an international initiative that was not directly addressed to higher education but has nevertheless affected it. Their influence has been more circuitous. The case of accreditation refers to a set of policies that have produced a regime. The policies have been implemented for some time and have resulted in the establishment of institutions, norms, standards, and networks. Their focus is specific and relates directly to higher education institutions. The expansion and acceptance of these policies throughout the region is evident.

The popularity of rankings and the concept of "world-class universities" seem to have increased in strength since the publication of the first worldwide ranking. It is still difficult to evaluate the extent that these worldwide rankings have impacted institutions, but looking at the way higher education institutions and educational systems are using and quoting their yearly results shows a growing relevance. Even though two of the worldwide rankings are produced by independent agencies—the *Times Higher Education* and *U.S. News and World Report*—it is not possible to affirm that the rankings' initiative comes solely from university outsiders; the Chinese ranking was a university initiative. Alternatively, the discourse around the idea of "world-class universities" does come from outsiders and represents a broader frame of action.

Finally, AHELO is a project that may end up establishing a focused frame: its target and objectives are very specifically directed to higher education. It is an initiative that comes from outside higher education institutions. It is an OECD initiative and its stakeholders are not higher education institutions.

After presenting the four cases, there is a concept that makes a lot of sense to compel their discussion: "techne of government." This concept is used by Dean (1999) (cited in Sidhu 2007, 206), as one of the four dimensions to study government. They are as follows:

> Forms of visibilities. The picturing and constituting of objects that are to be governed, ways of seeing and perceiving "the problem" at hand; Techne of government—The means, tactics technologies, and strategies though which authority is constituted and rule legitimized; Episteme of government. The forms of thought, knowledge, expertise, and calculation that arise from and inform the activity of governing; forms of identification—The actors, subjects, identities, and agents that presuppose the practices of government.

Discussing four specific constructs to analyze the influence of international organizations in national educational policy "in a movement towards global 'soft' convergence," David Rutkowski (2007, 232) offers some ideas for the analysis of these technes of government:

> (1) construction of a multilateral space for "soft" laws to be formed; (2) construction of the means to directly implement policy through loans and grants; (3) construction of a multilateral space to create and exchange policy knowledge; and (4) construction of the concept of being experts in measuring and evaluation educational policy.

This classification helps to better understand how to place the cases presented in this chapter. According to these technes of government, the MDGs are an example of the soft laws; the case of credits and loans directly influenced by international organizations has purposely not been discussed in this chapter; and the other three—accreditation systems, worldwide rankings, and AHELO—correspond to the third and fourth slots of Rutkowski's definition. In a broader sense, this chapter attempts to contribute to answering a question posed by Margaret Karns and Karen Mingst (2004, 24): "the question is not will globalization be governed, but rather, how will globalization be governed?" Here the question is not whether higher education will be governed in this globalization context; but rather, how will higher education be governed? This chapter provides some theoretical points to articulate an answer.

The reality is that higher education institutions have had to change because of these new forms of global governance. Either they receive less money and have to adjust; or they are established and actively participate in the international, regional, and national accreditation processes; or they must find ways to obtain better scores in the worldwide rankings; or they consider participating in a project like AHELO that may exert worldwide pressure in the future.

Final Remarks

Given the novelty of this topic in the field of higher education, there are more pending issues to discuss than conclusions to make. Some of the issues have to do with the way the specific role of agendas are developed within the frame of global governance; the need for a deeper analysis of the role of power, agency, and hegemony; or to continue exploring the possibilities of the concepts of regime and soft law.

The concepts of "international forces" or "international technes of government," "regimes," or "soft laws" are hard to place theoretically in the traditional/classical governance models (New Public Management, Network governance, and Neo-Weberian narrative) or in their main aspects (decision-making processes, power, leadership, and institutional composition). This has posed a challenge in this chapter.

Perhaps global governance and the concepts of soft law and regime help as a scaffolding, or as a tool that belongs in the tool box previously mentioned, that set or hold different elements involved in the topic of development of a global agenda in terms of who participates, how this agenda is established, and the reasons why certain actors (organizations, networks, or group of countries) take part in this, and what the role of national states is. As Susan Robertson (2009, 114) argues:

> The converging agenda of market multilateralism is amongst the powerful international agencies as a mechanism of global governance; together with the strategic use of governmental techniques, such as the construction of indexes and other methodologies, to produce the conditions and social relations for a new long wave of accumulation.

In sum, reforms in higher education public policies in Latin America are moving toward some form of global governance, including soft laws and regimes. But at the same time, the way this is happening, the strategies used, and the implementation processes still require more research and analysis. This is a pending task for people interested in these issues.

Notes

*The author would like to thank Nicte-Ha Dzib Soto for her assistance in reviewing the journal *Global Governance*. A Review of Multilateralism and International Organizations and Scarlett Zamudio for their help in reviewing the data on public expenditure per pupil in primary and tertiary education in Latin America.

1. Australia, Belgium, Colombia, Egypt, Finland, Italy, Japan, Korea, Kuwait, Mexico, the Netherlands, Norway, the Russian Federation, the Slovak Republic, Sweden, and the United States (with particular state institutions)

References

Aboites, Hugo. 2010. "Latin American Universities and the Bologna Process: From Commercialisation to the Tuning Competencies Project." *Globalisation, Societies and Education* 8 (3): 443–455.

Amaral, Alberto, and Neave, Guy. 2009. "The OECD and Its Influence in Higher Education: A Critical Revision." In *International Organizations and Higher Education Policy. Thinking Globally Acting Locally?* ed. Roberta Malee Bassett and Alma Maldonado-Maldonado. New York: Routledge.

Barnett, Michael, and Martha Finnemore. 1999. "The Politics, Power, and Pathologies of International Organizations." *Internacional Organizations* 53 (4): 699–732.

Beneitone, Pablo, Cesar Esquetini, Julia Gonzalez, Marty Malet Aida, Gabriela Siufi, and Robert Wagenaar. 2007. *Reflexiones y perspectivas de la Educación Superior en América Latina. Informe final -Proyecto Tuning- América Latina 2004–2007.* Bilbao, Spain: Universidad de Deusto, Universidad de Groningen.

Eribon, Didier. 1992. *Michel Foucault*. Barcelona, Spain: Anagrama.

Fernández Lamarra, Norberto. 2003. "Higher Education, Quality Evaluation and Accreditation in Latin America and MERCOSUR." *European Journal of Education* 38 (3): 253–269.

Karns, Margaret, and Karen Mingst. 2004. *International Organizations: The Politics and Processes of Global Governance.* Boulder, CO: Lynne Rienner Publishers Inc.

Kim, Hwa-Jin. 2001. "Taking International Soft Law Seriously: Its Implications for Global Convergence in Corporate Governance." *Journal of Korean Law* 1 (1): 1–50.

Krasner, Stephen, ed. 1983. *International Regimes*. Ithaca, NY: Cornell University Press.

Kratochwil, Friedrich, and John Gerard Ruggis. 2001. "International Organization: A State of the Art or an Art of the State." In *International Institutions: An International Organizational Organization Reader*, ed. Lisa L. Martin and Beth A. Simmons. Boston, MA: The MIT Press.

Maldonado-Maldonado, Alma, and Brendan Cantwell. 2009. "International Organizations and Bilateral Aid." National Interests and Transnational Agencies." In *International Organizations and Higher Education Policy. Thinking Globally Acting Locally?* ed. Roberta Malee Bassett and Alma Maldonado-Maldonado. New York: Routledge.
Martin, Lisa L., and Beth A. Simmons. 2001. *International Institutions: An International Organizational Organization Reader.* Boston, MA: The MIT Press.
Mecham, Michael. 2003. "MERCOSUR: A Failing Development Project?" *International Affairs* 79 (2): 369–387.
Neave, Guy. 1998. "The Evaluative State Reconsidered." *European Journal of Education* 33 (3): 265–284.
OECD. 2010–2011. *Assessment of Higher Education Learning Outcomes (AHELO).* Paris: OECD. http://www.oecd.org.
Raustiala, Kal. 2006. "Refining the Limits of International Law." *ILSA Journal of International and Comparative Law* 34 (1): 1–21.
RIACES. 2011. Official website. Buenos Aires: RIACES. http://www.riaces.net.
Robertson, Susan. 2009. "Market Multilateralism, the World Bank Group, and the Asymmetries of Globalizing Higher Education: Toward a Critical Political Analysis." In *International Organizations and Higher Education Policy: Thinking Globally Acting Locally?* ed. Roberta Malee Bassett and Alma Maldonado-Maldonado. New York: Routledge.
Rutkowski, David J. 2007. "Converging Us Softly: How Intergovernmental Organizations Promote Neoliberal Education Policy." *Critical Studies in Education* 48 (2): 229–247.
Salmi, Jamil. 2009. *The Challenge of Establishing World-Class Universities.* Washington, DC: The World Bank.
Samoff, Joel, and Carol Bidemi. 2003. "From Manpower Planning to the Knowledge Era: World Bank Policies on Higher Education in Africa." Paper presented at the UNESCO Forum on Higher Education, Research and Knowledge, Paris, October 2003. Paper commissioned by the UNESXO Forum Secretariat (ED-2004/WS/8).
Schuller, Tom, and Stéphan Vincent-Lancrin. 2009. "OECD Work on the Internationalization of Higher Education: An Insider Perspective." In *International Organizations and Higher Education Policy: Thinking Globally Acting Locally?* ed. Roberta Malee Bassett and Alma Maldonado-Maldonado. New York: Routledge.
Sen, Amartya. 2009. *The Idea of Justice.* London: Allen Lane.
Sidhu, Ravinder. 2007. "GATS and the New Developmentalism: Governing Transnational Education." *Comparative Education Review* 51 (2): 203–227.
Stiglitz, Joseph. 2002. *Globalization and Its Discontents.* New York and London: W.W. Norton & Company.
Verger, Antoni, and Javier Pablo Hermo. 2010. "The Governance of Higher Education Regionalization: Comparative Analysis of the Bologna Process and MERCOSUR-Educativo." *Globalisation, Societies and Education* 8 (1): 105–120.

United Nations Development Programme (UNDP). 2011. *The Millennium Development Goals: Eight Goals for 2015*. New York: UNDP. http://www.beta.undp.org.

World Bank. 2011. *World Development Indicators (WDI) Global Development Finance (GDF)*. http://databank.worldbank.org.

Chapter 9

Reforms of University Governance in Mexico: Inducements for or Impediments to Change?

Wietse de Vries and Germán Álvarez-Mendiola

Señor, Señor,
Can you tell me where we're heading?
Lincoln County Road or Armageddon?

Bob Dylan, Señor

Introduction

University governance in Mexico has gone through many reforms over the last two decades.[1] From a traditional collegial model, it has moved toward a more managerial one. But what has really changed and why?

To evaluate the reforms and their outcomes, we will discuss four aspects of the reform of university reform in Mexico. First, we look at changes in the relationship between the state and higher education. Second, we review changes in governance structures at the universities. Third, we review possible explications for the new structures and processes that emerged as a result of the changes. Fourth, we discuss the implications of these changes for the daily operation of universities and for its central actors and processes.

Our analysis is motivated by several observations that indicate that, after two decades of reforms, system and institutional governance seemingly continues to be hunch-based, making little use of existing information. The goals of efficiency and efficacy do not seem to have been reached. At the same time, research on higher education shows uneasy truths: student retention, learning outcomes, employment, or curricular content do not seem to have improved.

As such, what Eric Ashby (1963, 93) observed nearly five decades ago seems to remain true:

> All over the country these groups of scholars, who would not make a decision about the shape of a leaf or the derivation of a word or the author of a manuscript without painstakingly assembling the evidence, make decisions about admission policy, size of universities, staff-student ratios, content of courses, and similar issues, based on dubious assumptions, scrappy data, and mere hunch.

In Mexico, several governance reforms were introduced to better decide about exactly these issues. Our central question is: why do governance reforms at universities not automatically lead to better, or more efficient, institutional performance?

The Problem of Assessing Change in Governance

How to assess the new forms of governance? Governance is a broad concept that includes leadership, management, and administration. As such, it encompasses aspects like the setting of the institutional mission and goals, decision-making processes, the allocation of resources, and the patterns of authority and power (Marginson and Considine 2000). To analyze changes, we adopt Edwards's definition of governance, in the sense that what matters is not what an organization does, but how it does it. Governance in this sense concerns how an organization manages itself, and the processes and structures it uses to reach its goals (Edwards 2001).

In the Mexican context, the analysis of changes of governance has centered mostly on the legal adjustments of the institutional structures, and on the interaction of these structures with public policies or other external factors (Acosta 2002). This type of analysis tends to review organizational arrangements—both formal and informal—and the decision-making processes that develop within them, to explain how power is exercised. These analyses reveal interesting histories about how different actors, such as rectors, use the rules of the game, or try to bend the rules in their favor, to rise to, and remain, in power (López 2011).

But the analysis of this "game of power and knowledge" (Gradilla 1995), generally remains limited to reviewing the outcomes of the political struggle for power between several actors with winners and losers within an ever-changing legal framework that imposes certain constraints on each actor. Rarely do these analyses review whether or not the logic of regulation has changed, or why and how this change takes place.

We opt here for a slightly different focus. As Adrián Acosta (2002) points out, there are three paradigms that can be used to analyze university governance: The first concerns the symbolic representations about power within the university, complete with its myths and "false currencies," whereas the second analyzes the internal political configuration of power. The third studies the profile of university governance (including management and bureaucracy), and the tools of government used to exercise power within universities.

We focus on the third aspect. Adopting an internal point of view, we review the profile of university bureaucracies, their daily operations, how they justify their work, and the instruments that they use to exercise power. We ask why these particular forms have come to the fore, and what the implications are for several actors and processes.

Changing Relationships between the State and Higher Education

Changes in university governance have largely been attributed to a new relationship between the state and the universities. Even though many public universities were in crisis due to internal political conflicts two decades ago, it is unlikely that governance structures would have changed as rapidly and profoundly as they did without outside pressure.

Since 1990, Mexican federal and state governments have sought to regulate and to modernize the system of higher education through several policies. As in other countries, the declared goals have been to guarantee quality and transparency, as well as to improve efficiency, efficacy, and pertinence. The changes have been defined as part of a new "social contract" (Brunner 2006), between the state and higher education, which implied the introduction of evaluation and new forms of funding. As part of its modernizing strategy, the Mexican federal government introduced special funds, in addition to regular subsidies. At the same time, it introduced several evaluation processes, reviewing everything from the system level, to faculty, students, and curriculum majors. The expressed goals were to improve quality and at the same time to broaden access (de Vries and Álvarez-Mendiola 2005).

To achieve these goals, the reform of governance—both at the national and the institutional level—was declared a linchpin. The emphasis on governance reforms had several motives. First, by 1990 public universities were seen as highly inefficient and ungovernable. The existing forms of governance chronically led to the absence of decision making and innovation (Gago 1989). A second reason, less often mentioned, was that the federal government needed brokers or middlemen for the implementation of public policies. Until the end of the 1980s, policies were practically nonexistent. Universities were either autonomous or private, and each institution was free to decide upon matters such as governance, hiring and promotion of faculty, admission of students, or curricular content. Under these conditions, a first crucial step for federal authorities was to convince institutional authorities of the benefits of their new policies.

These reforms are inscribed in an international context, where many government and university officials stated the need for a type of governance that would be more agile, leading to a more efficient and pertinent management and administration, and better academic results (de Boer and File 2009). Generally considered within a context of New Public Management, the reforms should lead to a better balance between costs and benefits, with more attention devoted to different clients, more accountability and better quality (Casanova 2009).

Mexican federal policies initially seemed to comply with a global logic of the "Evaluative State": based on an evaluation policy that reviewed the compliance with system goals, additional performance-based funding would allow government to steer higher education by "remote control" (Neave 1988). Over time, however, the regulatory relationship between the state and universities in Mexico became more and more complex, leading to a scheme of microscale planning rather than distant steering. The growing complexity of state regulation was due to successive instances of "disenchantment" by different federal officers regarding the effects of the new policies (Kent 2005). The adjustments, however, share a peculiar characteristic: existing policies were never phased out, but rather were complemented by new ones. The result is an increasing complexity, not only because of the growing number of policies, but also for the proliferation of rules and regulations that dictate how and to whom these policies should be applied (de Vries and Álvarez-Mendiola 2005).

And, while modernization started with one special fund (the Fund for the Modernization of Higher Education [FOMES]) in 1989, by 2010 there were 18 similar funds, each one aimed at resolving a particular problem within the system (SEP 2010). Most of these are not performance-based funds, but rather need-based or compensatory. And while in the 1990s these special funds comprised less than 10 percent of the budget for higher education, by 2010 they represented 30 percent (SEP 2010). For each one of these funds, public universities have to submit proposals for improvements.

In the area of evaluation, several additional initiatives appeared, and by 2010, there were three distinct processes to evaluate faculty, and two different organizations to accredit programs.

After two decades of reform, there is a highly complex set of policies that seek to regulate higher education. Several of these policies apply to specific sectors, such as the public state universities, but not to others, such as the federal public universities or the private sector. Over the last few years, however, there have been moves to apply similar policies to regulate the private sector (Álvarez-Mendiola 2011).

Changing Governance Structures within Universities

The emphasis the federal government placed on governance induced many changes in public universities. In discourse and theory, these reforms were promoted under the guise of New Public Management.

In its ideal form, these reforms would lead to management systems that are coherent and integrated, that focus on results in terms of efficiency, quality of service, rational distribution of funding, optimization of labor, and the systematic evaluation of performance (Amaral et al. 2002). Management would be guided by strategic decision making, attending demands from both the market and the state. This requires an optimum use of information about the institution and its environment, to transit from a mere struggle for power to the rational use of resources. Other aspects of this new form of governance include the following:

1) A decentralized environment of management that leads to a better interplay between authority and responsibility, so that decisions about resource allocation and service provision are located closer to the location where services are provided, allowing for better feedback from clients and stakeholders.
2) A strong emphasis on the provision of services to clients, through the creation of competitive environments within public sector organizations and the participation of nongovernmental competitors.
3) The necessary flexibility to explore more cost-effective alternatives in the provision of direct public services and regulations, including (semi) market mechanisms such as costs for clients, vouchers, or the selling of property rights.
4) Accountability based on results or on the introduction of adequate procedures, rather than compliance with particular rules and regulations, additionally a shift from the avoidance of risks to risk management.
5) Transparency, based on the availability of information to the public, and the obligation for authorities to provide information (Keating and Shand 1998; Brunner 2006)

Integral to this model is the evaluation of the performance of several actors and processes, with decision making based on reliable and objective information, hence the need for evaluation. In Mexico, however, this new idea of governance was introduced in institutions that had a very peculiar historical form of organization. This form is generally considered as collegial, but had its particular characteristics in Mexico.

Governance Before 1990

Before 1990, day-to-day governance of institutions was administered by a small body of appointed officials, assisted by administrative personnel. The latter typically consisted of people with, at most, only an upper-secondary education. These administrators tended to be unionized and to have a permanent appointment. Their main task was to register data on students and their qualifications and to administer the payroll. Access to their ranks, however, was largely based on political or patrimonial practices: each head of department had a certain liberty—restrained by the budget—to appoint new members of his administration, who would obtain "tenure" after a few years. But, while these administrators were immovable, they received an inferior salary compared to faculty.

This apparatus was coordinated by a level of higher ranked officials, such as directors, deans, coordinators, and the rector. The typical process was that university rectors were elected by the community (sometimes on a one-man one-vote basis) for a period of three-to-four years. After election, they were free to appoint their closest collaborators. Just like the rector, these officials tended to be "amateurs": they were professors that temporarily left their academic job to dedicate themselves to management. Most lacked any administrative experience. Furthermore, they would receive some additional pay to their academic salary, but most gained just a little bit more than ordinary faculty.

Just like the rector, officials tended to have a short administrative lifespan: they would enter their post with the newly elected rector and leave when he/she did. The common procedure was that every newly elected rector would appoint his loyalists to the several administrative posts, as a way to reward their support during elections. While officials came and went, the underlying bureaucratic structures remained stable, carrying out daily administrative work.

While this apparatus complied in some ways with Max Weber's description of "bureaucracy," it was not particularly efficient. Information systems tended to be rudimentary, based on paper records. No clear information existed as to student or faculty numbers, and analysis of information over time was rare. Administration was seen as an auxiliary function to faculty work, as something tedious but unavoidable.

The higher ranks of administration, however, were not very bureaucratic. They operated within the political arena: officials designated by the rector occupied their post with an eye on the following elections. The executive branch had its counterpart in the legislature. In public universities, the university council formally was the supreme decision-making body. In several cases, the principle of parity or shared governance operated: faculty representatives equaled student representatives, while administrative personnel had a minor share.

This form of governing universities is still considered by some as the ideal model. Universities enjoyed full autonomy, and all decisions regarding faculty appointments, student admissions, or the internal allocation of public funding corresponded to institutional actors, not to outside parties. Faculty and students were represented in several legislative bodies. Authority was not imposed top-down within a hierarchy, but rather negotiated through collective agreement.

As several researchers have pointed out, however, this form of government was not ideal. In many public universities, the charter and rules were not updated for decades, so that government and administration tended to be based on informal customs and practices, defended or contested by several political groups or factions. While rectors would invoke autonomy to shield their university from outside interference, faculty would invoke academic freedom to shield their work from intrusion by the university administration. The practical outcome was that few decisions could be made, or that any attempt at reform could be reversed (Fuentes et al. 1991). As such, the Mexican collegial model led universities to pay little attention to outside demands, to consider no other stakeholders than inside interest groups, and not to care about efficiency and efficacy. By the end of the 1980s, many actors, both inside and outside the universities, considered that this form of governance was one of the reasons for the crisis in which many public universities were submerged.

A Peculiar Mexican Hybrid Model?

By the beginning of the 1990s, there was a consensus that governance had to be reformed. Less clear was how this would be accomplished. New Public Management was in vogue in several countries, but it was diametrically opposed to the existing collegial forms of governance in Mexican public universities.

As a result, while changes since 1990 meant a departure from the old collegial model, universities do not seem to have reached the objectives of New Public Management. In between these two extremes there are other models or hybrids. As Adrián Acosta (2009) points out, the resulting hybrid models require that rectors and their teams must combine conflicting roles: they not only continue to be the traditional Machiavellian prince, but also have to be rule-following bureaucrats and innovative managers.

In fact, there continues to be confusion on how university management should be organized or reformed. There is a continuous stream of "novelties" coming from the private business sector as well as from different federal governments, including fashions such as planning by objectives, strategic planning, benchmarking, reengineering, or Total Quality Management. But at the same time, many traditions are defended by internal actors.

If we consider the collegial and the managerial models as the two extreme ends on a continuum, university governance in Mexico today sits somewhere half between. This, however, raises the question of how to characterize the new model.

In the shift between the two extremes, several changes occurred. Initially, the rules for political participation began to change. In most universities, election procedures were changed, which meant that the influence and participation of students and auxiliary staff declined (López 2003). Shared government (between students and faculty) practically disappeared altogether.

A second change related to the criteria for elections. To qualify for rector, official, or councilor, candidates had to meet new norms: candidates coming from the academic ranks needed to be full professors with tenure and a graduate education. Students needed to have good academic qualifications. Although these moves might seem trivial, they are not, as only about 30 percent of professors in Mexican universities are full-time and only a few students pass all courses. The changes in legislation put an oligarchy of professors in a powerful position, alongside a small segment of students.

A third change concerns university management and administration. At the top layer of administration, rectors maintained their right to appoint collaborators. However, in several university charters there were amendments made requiring officials to possess a university degree, preferably a graduate one.

Perhaps the most important changes occurred at the middle management level. Here, the traditional bureaucrat without a university degree was gradually replaced by middle managers or policy operators, who were appointed on a temporary basis, but must have at least an undergraduate degree.

These changes are best exemplified by the current job descriptions and salary structures in universities. As to faculty, these remain relatively simple: there are full and associate professors; some are full time, others part time. At the beginning of the 1990s, salaries in the public universities were homologized nationally, which means that the maximum salary for a full-time professor is currently around 20,000 pesos (US$1,800) a month, while the junior ranks earn a corresponding fraction of this salary.

By contrast, the administrative labor conditions were left to the discretion of each university. As a result, when it comes to administrative job descriptions, a bewildering variety exists, ranging all the way from rector to janitor. There are directors of departments, vice directors, assistant directors, and assistants to the director. There are executive, bilingual, and personal secretaries. Each has a special position on the payroll.

And, while academic salaries were regulated nationally, administrative salary scales were left unregulated. In practice, this meant that university managers were left the freedom to establish their own salary. As a result, most middle managers currently earn above 50,000 pesos and most rectors well over 100,000 pesos (US$9,000 a month).

Thus, governance reforms produced several consequences: university administration ranks became leaner; employing fewer personnel (most public universities had more administrators than faculty by the end of the 1980s). But, as administrative salaries increased, university spending on administration remained over 50 percent of the total budget. Through this process, a new layer of modern bureaucrats was created, generally earning more than full professors.

A second consequence was that administration changed its role: from an auxiliary apparatus, it transformed into a profession in itself and the central actor in the process of modernization.

However, in general, university governance structures today are hard to characterize. In some aspects, governance has become more bureaucratic: during the last two decades, there has been an effort to introduce specific rules and regulations within the universities, linked on occasions to external quality certifications such as ISO 9000. At the same time, however, it has moved to a more task-based form of organization, to better respond to outside demands from both government and markets. In fact, responding successfully to public policies, with their financial stimuli, has become a crucial task. This model comes closer to Burton Clark's (1998) description of the entrepreneurial university.

Politics, however, have not disappeared. The central aspect of university governance continues to be that it concentrates power and exercises it in an autocratic fashion. Power is put into effect through multiple layers of subalterns, a sort of royal court that has to guarantee the political balance of power. Management now supervises what is left of the traditional bureaucracy, but operates through a new, more dynamic layer of middle managers. This new layer thrives on the successful operation of procedures that derive from public policies, and the additional funds linked to it.

How can we characterize modern-day university governance? In practice, there seems to be an intricate mix of models, where collegial modes continue to exist, but are mixed with practices from the entrepreneurial extreme. In some aspects, bureaucracy seems to have won terrain. In others, university governance still resembles an organized anarchy or a loosely coupled system. Some parts are operating with an entrepreneurial or market-oriented logic, while others are fixed on due bureaucratic process. As Robert Birnbaum' (1988) observes, decision making takes place on the move, always under pressure and with insufficient information. But what nowadays seems to count more is adherence to due process, prescribed by federal policies, not an evaluation by results.

In conclusion, a central tenet of these reforms was that institutions would become better adapted to their environment and would improve their internal processes obtaining higher levels of efficiency and quality. However, doubts remain as to whether these changes have led to a better process of decision making within the universities or to profound changes in day-to-day academic work. As Adrián Acosta (2009, 143) points out: "it is difficult to demonstrate that there exists a direct relationship between the administrative and organizational reforms of university government and the improvement of quality of institutional performance."

Possible Explanations for Hybrid Forms

If governance reforms did not lead to the ideal model posed by New Public Management, but rather to some sort of hybrid intermediate model, what could be the reasons? Research provides several explications, both internal and external.

Internal Factors

One possible explanation, popular with university administrators, is that universities have grown more complex since 1990, making it far more difficult to manage the university because of these changing dimensions. At face value, this seems to be valid: a typical public university in 1990 comprised some 20 academic majors and a few postgraduate studies. Today, most offer over 50 majors and an additional 50 graduate options. Student and faculty numbers have increased. An increase in student and faculty numbers, combined with an increase in programs, placed additional pressure on university administration. However, this explanation does not seem very convincing if one considers that the underlying administrative process has not changed radically: the daily operation continues to consist of linking a teacher with a course, a classroom, and a number of students, and to record the final qualifications. Furthermore, much of this process is now computerized, making it easier to register and consult data.

Another factor to consider is that university bureaucracies appear to have inherited many of the vices, but few of the virtues, of the ideal type described by Max Weber. The ideal type of bureaucracy, according to Weber, is characterized by clear norms and rules that apply to all, guaranteeing as such not only efficiency but also equity and justice, instead of adhocracy and favoritism. Qualifications and performance should be the criteria used for hiring and promotion. The ideal bureaucracy would also entail stability, discipline, and confidence in the organization.

University bureaucracies in Mexico, however, still show various characteristics that separate them from the ideal type: after the election of each rector, the administration is overhauled, and new managers are appointed. Additionally, most bureaucratic structures in Mexican universities have seen a shift from unionized administrative personnel toward temporarily hired executives, introducing more instability.

Both at the federal and institutional level, most executives and middle management personnel are appointed at the discretion of their superiors, and these appointments tend to be based on loyalty to the superior in turn. Furthermore, most of these functions have no clear job description. By the same token, many rules do not seem to operate in practice, or are unknown by most actors. In those cases, adhocracy prevails.

As to rules of the game, important gaps still remain within each university's legislation. For example, there may be extensive legislation concerning merit pay programs, because such legislation is mandated by the federal government, but at the same time there can be an absence of legislation regarding tenure or promotion. Thus, some processes have become very bureaucratic, while others remain highly discretional.

A Culture of Distrust. An additional part of the continuing complexities of university management might be explained by cultural inheritances: policies operate within a bureaucracy with peculiar Mexican traits. In Mexico, bureaucracy has always been surrounded by distrust and a lack of confidence: civil or voting registers have traditionally been considered unreliable. This lack of confidence, however, goes two ways: citizens do not trust the workings of bureaucracy, and bureaucrats do not trust data provided by the citizenry. Additionally, there is a shared belief that these problems will only be resolved through more specific legislation. This leads to processes that are characterized by a lot of red tape, extensive rules, and an enormous amount of formal verification, for example, for the cross-checking of photocopies with originals.

Examples of this tradition of mistrust abound: qualification for the National System of Researchers requires faculty members to submit copies and originals of their work, complete with letters from their universities that certify that they actually work there. Qualification for institutional merit pay programs requires much the same. And even today, when students can register online for their courses, they have to present a printed copy of payment at central offices. And a curious common trait in all Mexico, not only in universities, is that each and every bureaucratic procedure requires that the client presents an original birth certificate.

This cultural inheritance explains why the introduction of modern digital systems of information does not lead to more agile administrative processes. First, the introduction of new procedures does not insure that the older ones will disappear, which, in turn, implies that the number of requisites and steps increases. Second, there is a strong tendency to consider new technologies as basically identical to the old forms: what was once registered on paper is now registered on a spreadsheet and then printed out and stamped.

The Use of Evaluation and Information. A second set of explanations concerns the use of evaluations. The central principle of New Public Management and the Evaluative State is that decision making should be based on information that results from evaluation.

In the Mexican case, many evaluation processes have been introduced since 1990. However, none of the information resulting from these processes seems to be used. Examples abound: the introduction of entrance exams in public and private universities has led to increasing selectivity, but not to studies about who is effectively admitted and how they fare. Even though most universities have reliable databases on students, no university carries out student tracking studies. The few studies that do exist are carried out by small groups of researchers and do not seem to have an impact on policies (Casillas et al. 2008). Alumni tracking studies are scarce and are mainly carried out to comply with accreditation criteria. In other words, students and alumni are still unknown actors, in spite of discourse that stresses curriculum change to better attend to students and their learning.

The same logic applies to faculty. There is much information collected on faculty, as a result of many evaluation processes. But each process was designed to satisfy a specific need, usually defined externally, and not to introduce a systematic follow-up of faculty development. Thus, merit pay schemes require evaluation of performance every two years, leading to additional income, but they are not related to promotions or tenure. Additionally, separate processes are in place to qualify for the National System of Researchers (SNI). For each of these programs, a faculty member must present his/her curriculum vitae in a distinct format, which leads to the development of a different database.

The same logic applies when it comes to the establishment of new academic majors or new institutions. Over the last two decades, the federal government has created several new institutions, without any studies about the adequacy of these new offerings. In practice, most were set up because the institution or a group of faculty deemed they were necessary and responded to needs of the labor market, but surprisingly little information exists as to whether this is the case.

Thus, both at the national and the institutional level, one characteristic stands out: there is no practice of consulting and analyzing information that results from evaluation. The problem has two sides: first, Mexican higher education has no culture of systematic institutional research, and has very few personnel trained in this area. Second, most databases are created for administrative ends, not for comparisons or follow-up studies.

This aspect relates to other factors: most universities collect data with surprisingly few persons capable of managing ever-increasing databases, let alone analyzing and interpreting the data. Furthermore, each database tends to have its own design, making it incompatible with others. Most are set up for impromptu administrative needs, such as when the university needs to report on a specific issue, such as the number of teachers with a particular profile. To aggravate matters, each department tends to consider the resulting database as its sole property and restricts access by others.

The Permanent Reform of Governance Itself. Another possible explanation is that management reform has become a goal in itself. Within each university, there tends to be a competition between several management fads. This implicates that, with each change of rectors and managers, there are not only discontinuities in the daily work of administrative workplaces, but also theoretical ruptures: each new manager picks his/her own favorite from the list of possible management theories. As Robert Birnbaum (2000) observes, university governance seems to be particularly prone to "fashions" in the field of management theories, randomly adopting examples or models from public or private organizations. As a result, over time, administrative departments experience shifts from strategic planning to management by objectives, to quality management, or whatever fad is currently most popular. These rivaling theories (or rather, recipes) tend to be presented to managers at multiple symposia and courses, generally by outside managerial experts. Then, each change in theoretical focus tends to require a reengineering of administrative processes and lower-ranked administrative personnel need to be retrained. But as higher-ranked managers tend to remain in their position for only a few years, reengineering and retraining becomes a continuous process.

As such, a distinguishing aspect of modern university management in Mexico is the continual reform of administrative structures and processes. On the whole, much more reform and change seems to be taking place at the administrative level than within the academic units, where tenured faculty remain in the same position, teaching the same courses using the same didactic methods. Overall, academic practices do not seem to have changed a lot (Grediaga et al. 2004).

External Factors

The new relationship between the state and higher education is an additional explanatory factor. This relationship, in the case of public universities, has historically been dominated by politics.

Political confrontations or arrangements between universities and state governors remain common today. However, this relationship has gradually become dominated by policies, rules, and regulations. At the federal level, public universities have developed two types of action: year after year they lobby intensively in Congress to negotiate increments of their regular subsidies, which are assigned by the federation (Mendoza 2009). Second, they have to elaborate development plans and propose actions that follow the guidelines for the special funds administered by the Undersecretary for Higher Education (SES). Third, at the state level, following the reactivation of the local state planning committees, public universities must participate in decisions about local development. State governments tend to have little leverage over state public universities, as they provide only a fraction of funding, but much of this additional funding is free (not designated to the payroll), and has to be permanently negotiated. To complicate matters more, local government (the state governor and congressmen) must be mobilized to participate in negotiations with the federal Congress. All this not only requires technical know-how, but also political prowess to obtain resources, as many of the rules are obscure.

Apart from the political relations with state and federal governments, there are large amounts of technical or bureaucratic aspects that derive from policies. The new part of the relationship is the introduction of many bureaucratic and administrative dimensions. That is, many policies not only establish goals to reach, but also a myriad of administrative procedures to reach them. As a result, universities today count with new bureaucratic procedures, or even wholly new offices, that are a direct result of public policies introduced during the last two decades.

Some of these offices are a direct result of federal policies. For example, to participate in the national program of student assistance, it is necessary to have an office where students can register for financial help. In the case of other policies, the process can be embedded in existing structures, but even so there tends to be a special group of administrators dedicated to the specific needs of a policy. On many occasions, these new structures adopt or mimic the logic of federal offices, in a process that Paul DiMaggio and Walter Powell (1983) characterized as "isomorphism." Mimicking the logic of outside funders leads to perceived legitimacy, in the eyes of external parties, and to additional funding. The corollary of this process, however, is that institutions do not seek to become more rational or efficient, but rather try to demonstrate that their organization has the offices, and the officeholders, that can effectively implement the policy. In practice, this suggests that participation in federal programs entails important additional costs for a university, as it requires the creation of offices and the hiring of administrators. These reforms also introduced completely new actors, such as outside consultants, advisors, and experts in evaluation and accreditation.

The emblematic example is the federal Integral Program for Institutional Development (PIFI). Since 1990, the federal government grouped together several special funds that address specific needs of higher education, such as infrastructure, faculty development, or the organization of new academic majors. The extraordinary funds grouped together in the PIFI, however, were originally assigned based on annual (currently biannual) development plans. This means that every two years each university must elaborate proposals for improvement, preferably with the broad participation of faculty, according to the guidelines (Díaz-Barriga 2008). These proposals are then sent to the undersecretary for higher education, where they are evaluated by committees of external experts, using another set of guidelines. If proposals are approved, the funds are sent to the university. To disburse these funds, each university must tender each acquisition to at least three possible providers. Once products are bought, reports have to be submitted to the SES. Finally all funds are audited by the federal Congress, not only in financial terms, but also as to the attainment of declared goals.

On the upside, this process introduced a practice of institutional planning and financial control (Díaz-Barriga 2008). However, from a practical point of view, it means that the acquisition of a computer today involves a lengthy process (about one year); complicated by paperwork, in which many actors intervene. No official data exists on the overhead costs of these special funds, but they must be considerable.

What is important to point out is that these new programs or policies have led to the creation of new tasks, carried out by newfangled experts (*pifiologists* is the term coined by a former undersecretary for higher education for these officers), new processes, and new offices. Furthermore, while the 1990s started with one special funding program, by 2006 there were eight, and by 2010, eighteen (SEP 2010). While mainstream funding (subsidies) remains relatively simple and involves little bureaucracy, special funds are allocated through a highly complex process, involving an increasing number of bureaucrats.

A collateral effect of the large number of public policies and funds is that public universities today pay more attention to the activities of the state, rather than the market. The reason is straightforward: more than 90 percent of public university income originates from public sources. As such, it is far more convenient to show that the university complies with federal guidelines than to procure higher efficiency.

In practice, considerations about efficiency are notably absent: there are no incentives to reduce costs or to pursue income from alternative sources. Public universities in Mexico do not compete for students (demand continues to exceed available spaces). Income from tuition has increased in some public universities, but even so, tuition revenues tend to be lower than in the private sector. Furthermore, under current legislation, public universities are not allowed to show surpluses in their budget at the end of the fiscal year.

In any case, showing a surplus at the end of the year would not be wise if the intention is to negotiate a major budget with the state. In a situation where the state is far more important than the market, it is convenient to show deficits and to present new needs. Thus, opening new academic majors is an ideal way of creating new needs, as they require hiring more faculty members and administrators.

The lure of additional or special funds clearly incites universities to do so. Most of these funds are considered as compensatory: they seek to remedy deficiencies within the universities, such as the lack of infrastructure or the absence of pension plans. As such, what would be considered as possible fatal deficiencies in a private enterprise tends to be considered as an opportunity for additional funding by the public universities.

Implications

After decades of reform of Mexican university governance, there is no evidence that these changes have led to organizations that are more efficient, agile, or pertinent. This, however, does not mean that nothing has changed: the culture of reform seems to have produced a series of side effects.

Some of these changes are the result of modifications of formal structures and rules, as in the case of elections. Others are an outcome or a redefinition of the themes of debate, the language used, and the procedures and solutions proposed. This redefinition assumes that management is a science, that leadership is crucial, and that new forms of governance, based on rational decision making, will produce desired outcomes (Pfeffer 1981).

The stress on managerialism resulted in the introduction of several externally defined processes in the university. Today, universities must deal with accountability procedures, with self-evaluation and accreditation agencies, demonstrate that they have updated their mission and vision statements, developed a strategic plan linked to proposals for improvement, and a strategic planning process that will allow it to comply with all the above. They furthermore must prove that these actions will lead to increased results and satisfaction of students, alumni, and employers; better performance of faculty; and a better use of funding. At least, this is what the PIFI proclaims.

An implied benefit of this process is that a good university needs modern governance, able to respond to multiple outside demands. These reforms situate the establishment of university management as a distinctive and significant sector. Central to this reform is a growing professionalization of management: instead of an administration guided by amateurs, today there is a growing number of managers with a background in administration, accountancy, or law that have dedicated themselves exclusively to management. As such, university management appears to have established itself as a profession (de Vries 1996; Marginson and Considine 2000; Meek et al. 2010).

A second outcome concerns a change in the internal balance of power. Over the years, numerous studies in many countries have concentrated attention on the internal changes in governance. They generally conclude that, over time, the executive branch has started to dominate the traditional collegial forms of government (López 2003; OECD 2003). As a result, some levels, such as the president or rector and their collaborators, have increased their power, while others, particularly faculty and students, saw their influence diminish (Ibarra 2001; López 2003; Acosta 2006;).

The changes, however, have not been limited to the introduction of new structures or rules, but also new procedures. A crucial side effect is that the academic profession gradually has lost its self-regulating authority, and has increasingly become subjected to management procedures operated by administrators. This change has been most notable in specific areas. For example, to access merit pay programs, faculty must submit themselves to continuous evaluations, designed and operated by administrators. In other areas, change has been more tacit, but follows the same venue: curricular content is increasingly becoming an institutional issue, instead of being left to professors. Research priorities are increasingly defined by government agencies and institutions. Bureaucracy has become the *owner* of processes that formerly were carried out by faculty. Today, processes that used to be carried out by academic units, such as student admission, faculty hiring and promotion, and the evaluation of performance and curricular organization are carried out by managers, rather than faculty. It should be noted that these processes were not necessarily carried out in an efficient way when they were in the realm of faculties. However, there are no guarantees or evidence that efficiency improves once these processes become the responsibility of bureaucracy. On the contrary, we observe processes of costly microplanning, mimicking federal policies.

The shift in the balance of power suggests that faculty, in the Mexican case, might not be moving toward "academic capitalism" (Rhoades and Slaughter 1997), but rather toward "academic bureaucratism," where academic production is managed and allegedly improved by institutional and national administrators, through an increasing formalization and evaluation of faculty work (Gumport 2000).

A third aspect to consider is the cost of managerialism. Over the last two decades, efficiency, efficacy, and accountability have become dominant goals. To achieve these goals, universities must respond to markets and become more competitive. Governance must be reformed to increase teaching and research productivity. Managerialism is considered as a key to this reform.

A side effect of the rise of managerialism, however, is that Mexican universities today spend more than half of their budget on management. For some reason, faculty productivity seems to be enhanced only when there is a core of highly paid administrators who carefully document the improvements. In terms of corporate management, this would spell disaster, but somehow, within universities, this is called progress. In other words, the adoption of private sector management practices does not necessarily lead to a more efficient university, but rather to more spending on management, without clear improvements in productivity.

Conclusions

How can we judge governance in Mexican higher education today? Certainly, compared to 1990, things have improved: universities then were considered to be in crisis, and confidence in their work was at an all-time low (Acosta 2009). This lack of confidence led to a myriad of policies, and reforming governance played a central role. In general, collegial bodies were declared as obsolete. University executives were considered as the crucial intermediates between public policies and academic work.

Governance has gone through several reforms: structures were redefined, rules were modified, and new processes were introduced. Evaluation—of practically everything that takes place within the university—became central, leading to an increase in the number and quality of databases. Quality considerations concentrated on the outside accreditation of academic majors. As a result, confidence in universities has increased, but, paradoxically, there is scarce evidence that the quality of academic processes and outcomes has increased as well.

Governance has remained principally a political issue. Information is rarely analyzed and is mostly used to prove that universities are complying with the goals set by the federal government. Decision making changed: it did not become more rational (as information is not used) but became more streamlined, as decisions do not require consulting with faculty. With that, the internal balance of power changed. These changes, however, did not produce the changes that New Public Management proclaimed: universities did not become more efficient. On the contrary, the new contract between the state and universities has resulted in an increase in state regulation of higher education, which in turn led to new forms of university management that seek to better regulate academia. The result is an increase of bureaucracy at both levels, not a more efficient, businesslike organization.

Note

1. This chapter was inspired by the presentations of our colleagues Rocío Grediaga, Adrián Acosta, and Romualdo Zárate at the 7th International

Workshop on Higher Education Reform, organized by the Center for Policy Studies in Higher Education and Training (CHET), UBC, Vancouver BC, Canada, October 7–8, 2010. We would also like to thank Garnet Grosjean (UBC) for revising this chapter.

References

Acosta, Adrián. 2002. "Gobierno y gobernabilidad universitaria. Ejes para una discusión" ["University Government and Governance: Topics for a Discussion"]. *Tiempo Universitario*. Venezuela: Universidad de Carabobo, October 7, 2002.

Acosta, Adrián, ed. 2006. *Poder, gobernabilidad y cambio institucional en las universidades públicas en México, 1990–2000* [*Power, Governance and Institutional Change in Public Universities in Mexico, 1990–2000*]. Guadalajara, Mexico: Universidad de Guadalajara.

Acosta, Adrián. 2009. *Príncipes, burócratas y gerentes. El gobierno de las universidades públicas en México* [*Princes, Bureaucrats and Managers. The Government of Public Universities in Mexico*]. Mexico City: Asociación Nacional de Universidades e Instituciones de Educación Superior (ANUIES).

Álvarez-Mendiola, Germán. 2011. "El fin de la bonanza. La educación superior privada en México en la primera década del siglo XXI" ["The End of the Bonanza. Private Higher Education in Mexico during the First Decade of the 21st Century"]. *Reencuentro* (60): 10–29.

Amaral, Alberto, Glen A. Jones, and Berit Karseth, eds. 2002. *Governing Higher Education: National Perspectives on Institutional Governance*. Dordrecht, The Netherlands: Kluwer Academic Publishers.

Ashby, Eric. 1963. "Decision Making in the Academic World." In *Sociological Studies in British University Education*, ed. Paul Halmos (pp. 93–100). Keele, UK: University of Keele.

Birnbaum, Robert. 1988. *How Colleges Work, The Cybernetics of Academic Organization and Leadership*. San Francisco, CA: Jossey-Bass.

Birnbaum, Robert. 2000. *Management Fads in Higher Education: Where They Come From, What They Do, Why They Fail*. San Francisco, CA: Jossey-Bass.

Brunner, José Joaquín. 2006. *Mercados universitarios: Ideas, Instrumentaciones y Seis Tesis en Conclusión* [*University Markets: Ideas, Instrumentations and Six Concluding Thesis*]. Santiago, Chile: Andean Network of Universities. http://www.radu.org.ar.

Casanova, Hugo. 2009. "La universidad pública en México y la irrupción de lo privado" ["The Public University in Mexico and the Upsurge of the Private Sector"]. In *La universidad pública en México*, ed. Humberto Muñoz-García. México City: UNAM, Porrúa.

Casillas, Miguel, Ragueb Chaín, and Nancy Jácome. 2008. "Origen social de los estudiantes y trayectorias estudiantiles en la Universidad Veracruzana" ["Social Background and Trajectories of Students at the Veracruzana University"]. *Revista de la Educación Superior* 36 (142): 7–30.

Clark, Burton R. 1998. *Creating Entrepreneurial Universities: Organizational Pathways of Transformation.* Oxford: Pergamon.

de Boer, Harry, and Jon File. 2009. *Higher Education Governance Reforms across Europe.* Brussels, Belgium: European Centre for Strategic Management of Universities.

de Vries, Wietse. 1996. "Políticas públicas y funcionarios modernos." ["Public Policies and Modern-day Administrators"] *Perfiles Educativos* 71: 54–64.

de Vries, Wietse, and Germán Álvarez-Mendiola. 2005. "Acerca de las políticas, la política y otras complicaciones en la educación superior mexicana." ["About Politics, Policies and Other Complications in Mexican Higher Education"]. *Revista de la Educación Superior* 34 (134): 81–106.

Díaz-Barriga, Ángel, ed. 2008. *Impacto de la evaluación en la educación superior Mexicana. Un estudio de las universidades públicas estatales* [*The Impact of Evaluation in Mexican Higher Education. A Study of Public State Universities*]. Mexico City: UNAM and ANUIES.

DiMaggio, Paul J., and Walter W. Powell. 1983. "The Iron Cage Revisited: Institutional Isomorphism and Collective Rationality in Organization Fields." *American Sociological Review* 48 (2): 147–160.

Edwards, Meredith. 2001. "University Governance: Mapping and Some Issues." Paper presented at the Lifelong Learning Network National Conference, University of Canberra, Canberra, Australia, December 2001.

Fuentes, Olac, Antonio Gago, and Sylvia Ortega. 1991. "El sentido de la evaluación institucional. Un debate" ["The Sense of Institutional Evaluation. A Debate"]. *Universidad Futura* 2 (6–7).

Gago, Antonio. 1989. "Veinte telegramas por la educación superior y una petición desesperada" ["Twenty Telegrams Concerning Higher Education and a Desperate Petition"]. *Universidad Futura* 1 (1).

Gradilla, Misael. 1995. *El juego del poder y del saber* [*The Game of Power and Knowledge*]. Mexico City: El Colegio de México.

Grediaga, Rocio, José Raúl Rodríguez, and Laura Elena Padilla. 2004. *Políticas públicas y cambios en la profesión académica en México en la última década* [*Public Policies and Changes in the Academic Profession in Mexico during the Last Decade*]. Mexico City: ANUIES.

Gumport, Patricia J. 2000. "Academic Restructuring: Organizational Change and Institutional Imperatives." *Higher Education* 39 (1): 67–91.

Ibarra, Eduardo. 2001. *La Universidad en México hoy: gubernabilidad y modernización* [*The University in Mexico Today: Governance and Modernization*]. Mexico City: UNAM and ANUIES.

Keating, Michael S., and David A. Shand. 1998. *Public Management Reform and Economic and Social Development.* Paris: OECD.

Kent, Rollin. 2005. "La dialéctica de la esperanza y la desilusión en políticas de educación superior en México" ["The Dialectic of Hope and Disillusion in Mexican Higher Education Public Policies"]. *Revista de la Educación Superior* 34 (134): 63–80.

López, Romualdo. 2003. *Formas de gobierno y gobernabilidad institucional. Análisis comparativo de seis instituciones de educación superior* [*Outlines of Institutional Government and Governance. A Comparative Analysis of Six Higher Education Institutions*]. Mexico City: ANUIES.

López, Romualdo. 2011. "Las formas de elección de los rectores. Otro camino para acercarse al conocimiento de las universidades públicas autónomas" ["Ways to Elect the President. Another Form of Gathering Knowledge about Public Autonomous Universities"]. *Perfiles Educativos* 33 (131): 8–27.

Marginson, Simon, and Mark Considine. 2000. *The Enterprise University: Power, Governance and Reinvention in Australia*. Cambridge: Cambridge University Press.

Meek, V. Lynn, Leo Goedegebuure, Rui Santiago, and Teresa Carvalho, eds. 2010. *The Changing Dynamics of Higher Education Middle Management*. Dordrecht, The Netherlands: Springer.

Mendoza, Javier. 2009. "Presupuesto federal de educación superior: un nuevo ciclo de negociación para 2008" ["Federal Budget for Higher Education: A New Cycle of Negotiation for 2008"]. In *La universidad pública en México*, ed. Humberto Muñoz-García. México City: UNAM, Porrúa.

Neave, Guy. 1988. "On the Cultivation of Quality, Efficiency and Enterprise: An Overview of Recent Trends in Higher Education in Western Europe, 1986–1988." *European Journal of Education* 23 (1–2): 7–23.

OECD. 2003. "Changing Patterns of Governance in Higher Education." *Education Policy Analysis—2003 Edition*. Paris: OECD.

Pfeffer, Jeffrey. 1981. "Management as Symbolic Action: The Creation and Maintenance of Organizational Paradigms." *Research in Organizational Behavior* 3: 1–52.

Rhoades, Gary, and Sheila Slaughter. 1997. "Academic Capitalism, Managed Professionals and Supply-side Higher Education." *Social Text 51* 15 (2): 9–38.

Secretaría de Educación Pública (SEP). 2010. *Una proporción creciente de los recursos para las Universidades Públicas provienen de fondos extraordinarios* [*An Increasing Amount of Resources for Public Universities Comes from Extraordinary Funds*]. Comunicado 33, March 8, 2010. http://www.presidencia.gob.mx.

Chapter 10

Federal Policies and Governance of Universities in Mexico, 1990–2010

Adrián Acosta Silva

Over the past two decades major changes have occurred in the way government intervenes in the regulation, coordination, and behavior of the national system of Mexican higher education. These changes can be categorized in three areas: (1) the continued emphasis on the assessment and accountability, (2) a new focus on efficiency and quality of higher education, and (3) establishment of a mechanism to coordinate the national and subnational university systems. I argue that this indicates a change in the governments understanding of the role of higher education and explains the introduction of a new policy paradigm and policy instruments (Braun and Merrien 1999). This chapter may help to explain how the change in the "belief systems" has affected actors in the different national contexts, particularly in the area of institutional management and governance of systems and institutions.

In Mexico, three dominant "models" of university governance can be distinguished: (1) the "old" governance model, that was in place from the late 1920s to the end of the 1970s; (2) the "transitional" governance model, developed in the 1980s; and (3) the "new" governance model that emerged during the 1990s and extended into the twenty-first century. The old governance model was based on two basic principles, the obligation of the state to provide public resources to universities, and the autonomy of the university to distribute the resources (Levy 1987). These principles structured institutional management practices for many years, based on a combination of the models of academic, bureaucratic, and political coordination of such resources. The massification of higher education and the economic crisis ended the university's hold on autonomy and brought into question the organization and management practices employed in public universities. These were the conditions that the new governing elites from the Institutional Revolutionary Party (PRI), found themselves in during the 1980s, as they embarked on a mission to define a new agenda and develop policies to steer the course of higher education. The neoliberal era and the perceived pace of political liberalization, combined with the democratization of the Mexican political regime, had an impact on the field of higher education, and enabled government intervention in the sector (Acosta 2004).

The old governance model was preoccupied with the governability of the institution, rather than the institution's performance. The state adopted a watchful, but distant, attitude toward public universities. At that time, the relationship between state and universities was based on trust on the one hand, and the provision of resources and other government support as well as the recognition of universities' autonomy on the other. This formula allowed the universities to benefit from the increase in financial resources and resulting infrastructure that were established to meet the demand of increasing numbers of students, brought about by the massification of higher education during the 1960s and 1970s (Fuentes Molinar 1991; Murayama 2009). In some programs and institutions this was accompanied by an expansion of the number of faculty members and administrative workers.

In general, the old governance model relied on the following elements:

1) Relationships were based on political negotiations rather than on established policies;
2) There was weak state interventionism with a high degree of university autonomy;
3) A concern for the overall legitimacy, efficiency, and stability of universities rather than educational governance (the institutional management of actions and results).

The transitional model between the old and the new governance began as early as 1978 with the enactment of the *Law for the Coordination of Higher Education*, and the constitutional recognition of autonomy in the third constitutional article.[1] On the basis of these two legislative instruments, the federal government and the higher education institutions, through the National Association of Universities and Institutions of Higher Education (ANUIES), began to negotiate on a national system for the planning of higher education and the consolidation of self-governing practices of public universities. This double regulatory effort was hampered from the outset by an "essential tension" (Kuhn 1991, 46), between the freedom of universities to define their expansion policies on the one hand, and the need of the state to coordinate the actions among autonomous universities on the other. These conditions gave rise to the National Permanent Planning System of Higher Education (SINAPPES), a complicated regulatory mechanism that involves the participation of different government agencies and different higher education institutions at different levels of competence (Rodríguez 2007). Not unexpectedly, three decades after its creation, the results are judged inadequate and, in many ways, contradictory (Kent 2009). Reasons for this apparent lack of success are explored below.

The "new" higher education governance model was based on the assumption that the policies would

1) Increase the role of the federal government in the design, operation, and implementation of public policies with the objective of bringing coherence to the public higher education system by increasing federal control and supervision.
2) Recognize that, as the core of higher education, public universities were part of the problem rather than the solution, so they were considered a priority focus for the new policies.
3) Acknowledge that university governing bodies (university councils) felt burdened by federal demands, so developed types of institutional adaptation designed to thwart public policies.

Implementation of "new governance" policies had a direct impact on government administration and university management. New management schemes, styles, and patterns were introduced and took root in institutions. Politicization and bureaucratization became the central mechanisms of the schemes of coordination of administration and academic life. However, in each case, attempts to introduce new management procedures turned into a complex mixture of academic and bureaucratic interests that created new tensions and conflicts.[2] In these circumstances, one can begin to see the emergence of a new institutional complexity, marked on one hand by a confrontation between different logics of institutional performance, and, on the other, by the influence of external factors that restrict and shape the institutional behavior at different levels.

In this altered context, the management and administration of resources became a strategic area for institutional action. An emphasis on control and regulation created tensions, interactions, and conflicts that overpowered the relations among the different university sectors (de Vries and Ibarra 2004). The strengthening of the policy management structures of the universities became the method of transformation, following Burton Clark's (1998) model of the "innovative university" or "entrepreneurial university." The strengthening of the structures of centralized management and strategic decisions for the institutional change increased tensions in university governance. The university central government's choice to federal policies depend on whether they choose to follow the structures constituted formally in each university, thus generating a growing tension between legitimacy and legality of the decisions with the efficiency of policy management.

Federal Public Policies in Mexico, 1990–2010: General Effects on University Governance

The federal policies of higher education in Mexico during the last 20 years (1990–2010) can be described as *modernization policies* (Kent 2009). In university governance terms, modernization means: (1) the intervention of federal government agencies into ordinary and nonordinary university budgets; (2) design and implementation of several programs about merit pay mechanism for university professors, accreditation studies programs, institutional evaluations, and advisory of general institutional performance of public universities; and (3) decreased autonomy and academic freedom (Acosta 2009).

Our project, which produced the data we draw on here, was named "The Governance of Public Universities in Mexico." Funding for the study was provided by the National Council on Science and Technology (CONACYT), the federal organization that funds scientific research in the country. Our task was to review five institutional cases (Universidad Veracruzana [UV]; Benemérita Universidad Autónoma de Puebla [BUAP]; Universidad de Guadalajara [UG]; Universidad Autónoma de Ciudad Juárez [UACJ]; and Universidad de Sonora [USON]), between 1990 and 2010, to identify three specific focal points: (1) the relationships between institutional, academic and administrative actions, and the federal programs; (2) institutional university changes in management fields; and (3) changes in the procedures and rules of political sphere on university structures (for comprehensive information on the study see Acosta 2009, 21–62). According to the central hypothesis of the project, I argue that these factors determine the orientation and the quality of processes of institutional change in the public universities in the study.

Any process of institutional change is determined by external as well as internal factors. Among the external factors are public policies. How these policies are designed and implemented must be highlighted, as they play a role in the process of reconfiguration of institutional structures and practices. The logic that underpins federal policies combines a demand for financial accountability with claims of administrative efficiency. It further suggests that governmental control of academic autonomy will stimulate the production of indicators, processes, and quality assessment procedures. In our study, federal policies acted as restrictions, as they had a tendency to establish "policy networks" of different magnitude and consistency.[3] The "internal" political dimension involves the stakeholders and highlights the political strengths that trigger the modification of the structures of governance and institutional governability in each university. This "inner life" defines the magnitude and orientation of the changes in the political sphere of the universities, since it concentrates and sorts out, formally and symbolically, the political practices of a university (political rules, procedures and leadership, and political styles).

The Effect of External Forces on University Governance

For historical reasons in Mexico and Latin America, public policy has been understood fundamentally (and almost exclusively) as government action. The centrality of the state, and the role of the government machinery in responding to citizens' demands (through unions, political parties, and different types of associations), fostered dependence of social and civil organizations on the state. Dominated by patronage, privileges, or patrimonial practices, these actions strengthened a political formula based on corporate arrangements and an economic formula that legitimized state intervention in the market. The constitution of nationally popular authoritarian or semidemocratic regimes began to operate under the authority of a clearly "state-centralized" matrix (Messner 1999), in which the functions of social welfare were segmented rather than universalized. This "government" profile of public action in a context of low autonomy of social organizations and politics, explains the concentration of power and resources (financial, symbolic, and material) within the state elites. However, public action was "colonized" at different times by social and political forces. Some of these forces emphasized decisions, others issued ultimatums (external or internal to the government that include the demands of international organisms as well as the strength of the national and civil society), some put more emphasis on institutions, while others emphasized social classes and pressure groups. In the absence of an institutional democratic framework of power relations, the political or economically organized forces were those that determined, up to a certain point, the action of the state.

As a result of the economic crisis of the 1980s, the restructuring and adjustment processes of the national economy of the region, and the movement toward the democratization of the political regimes, the relations between the state and the broader society changed dramatically. After the reforms of the "first" and "second" generations, the topic of public coordination went from the centrality of the state to schemes controlled by the management of public policies, or new public management (Aguilar Villanueva 2006). Political restructuring was accompanied by a gradual dismantling of traditional corporate enclaves, and new social and political organizations appeared in the field of public action. After a cycle of mobilizations and conflicts of different types and scope, the democratization of the Latin American political regimes led to a change in traditional political management and the emergence of pluralist dynamics in the policy-making process.

Trust is a particularly pertinent topic to be considered in education policy making. According to the Mexican experience of recent years—as well as for higher education at the international level—mistrust has been the driving force of most of the policies and public programs implemented in higher education (de Boer 2002). The importance attributed to assessment and quality policies, located at the center of the new model of public interventions in the sector, arose mainly from a need to monitor and control the administrative and academic practices of public universities. This explains the overregulation phenomenon that characterized the public higher education system in Mexico in the early 1990s.

The distinction between ordinary and special public financing began in the 1980s during a time of economic and financial crisis in universities, which allowed the strengthening of federal funding to universities. This implied a strengthening of the intervention and regulation capacities of the federal government and its respective agencies in the field of university higher education, science, and technology (Acosta 2002). The 1990s witnessed a consolidation of this tendency to concentrate federal power. As a result, the traditional autonomy of the university changed, weakening the capacity of universities to determine their own orientation and processes, and strengthening the government's ability to manage the system using the strength of the "check-book."

The effects of these changes on governability and university governance schemes foreshadow a permanent tension in that, while the academic and administrative capital of public universities show a growing tendency, there is stagnation, or even a reduction of university social capital. For example, while programs are authorized, and a greater number of qualified or renowned professors are incorporated (see the Academic Personal Improvement Program [PROMEP] Profile and the National Researcher System [SNI]),[4] the number of research publications increases, and greater quantities of International Organization for Standardization's (ISO) national and international certified administrative processes are boosted; yet, the trust between professors and students and the authorities seems to weaken. Under these circumstances, the notion of a "university community," which operates with academic autonomy and which, for a long period of time, has promoted interuniversity cooperation practices, has been replaced by practices that favor competition rather than cooperation; thus, trust, the university's social capital, tends to weaken.

Universities in the Age of Quality and Assessment

One of the features of the "new policies" in Mexico's higher education is clearly federal government activism. At the end of the 1980s and beginning of the 1990s, within the context of Salinas's presidency (1989–1995), a symbolic, political, and practical need for a more active federal role in the transformation of higher education institutions was identified. This need was felt particularly in the public university sector. Until Fox's presidency (2000–2006), federal education agencies had launched a set of initiatives directed to produce changes in public universities. Acting with the power of the purse, rather than ideological provisions, policies, or regulations, the federal government established many of the rules under which changes and budgets were allocated to each portfolio. At the same time, the government used the general paradigm of accountability to introduce the concept that universities are "institutions of public service" (Braun and Merrien 1999, 13–14). As part of what may be called government neo-interventionism in the field of higher education (Acosta 2002), different mechanisms were established to assess, test, and improve the quality of processes and outcomes.

This new federal interventionism has many effects. One of them is the modification of the notion of university autonomy. After a long period of self-governance, autonomy of management and budget decision making, and academic self-determination, became synonymous with university autonomy (Levy 1987). A significant transformation of this autonomy occurred at the beginning of the 1990s based on changing budget conditions and implied transformations in the university organization and management. One major change had to do with technical, academic, and financial decisions taken by each university. The diversification of federal financing gave rise to a professional bureaucracy dedicated to the management of resources. This bureaucracy began to influence the decision making of the university rectors, increasing the tension with the traditional university government bodies. However, the forms of coordination imposed or negotiated with the public universities implied a "soft" reform of the autonomous practices of public universities that introduced overregulation of academic and administrative work to university organization and academic staff.

However, the major impact of this new interventionism has to do with the way federal resources shape or induce changes in the behavior of academics. This is an area of immense interest that needs be explored further. The demands to increase the quality of university higher education is interpreted from the federal bureaucratic language, as the demand for full-time qualified academics holding graduate, preferably doctorate degrees.[5] This demand led to the creation of ad hoc programs in public universities, directed toward improving the academic qualifications of their academic staff. This stimulated a flourishing market of specializations, and short-term master's and doctorate degrees offered by private universities of each region. These postgraduate programs are designed to accommodate the time constraints and capacities of the "clients," in general professors teaching at local public universities. This resulted in the proliferation of academic programs of questionable quality that have a secure and growing market, since full-time professors in public institutions are now required to have a graduate degree.

Another dimension of this "new university autonomy" in the academic field has to do with the behavior of the professors and researchers in the universities. During the implementation of merit pay policies, the professors established strategies to access resources associated with these programs. This generated practices of simulation, cooperation, and productivism by universities to accumulate scores according to the indicators proposed by the programs. In these circumstances, the "bribery for incentives" set up a scenario in which strictly academic exchanges were subordinated to the pragmatic interest of accumulating the highest indicator score in the quickest time possible (Acosta 2004). The original process of accumulation of academic capital does not suffice to transit the merit pay programs, thus we can observe a growing tendency toward productivism managed by the individuals themselves. Little by little, the university began to feel the effects of the "all mighty bureaucracy," the old Weberian curse.

Another consequence of the new state interventionism is an obsession for control of inputs, processes, and results of government actions in higher education. This obsession and its respective institutional translations led to a dramatic increase in the time required to fill out forms, reports, institutional evaluations, self-evaluations, indicator production, documents, meetings, workshops, and seminars. Highly sophisticated programs, methodologies, and focuses support the activism of the government and university bureaucrats and are driven mostly by local and international consultants (Ibarra 2005). Much of this has to do with accountability, (the paradigm used by the federal government to advocate its activism), with the bureaucratic control over universities and academics.

In this context, amid the effects of public policies, a contrasting framework of different specific-institutional contexts has emerged (Álvarez and de Vries 2010). Therefore, while federal government agencies have increased their degree of influence in the decision making of the universities, the "degree of academic, financial and administrative freedom" of universities has diminished proportionally. While the demand for accountability has resulted in rigorous management of institutional information, it has also meant that the construction of data and information needs to be specific to universities. The return of strategic planning to the field of university management has also meant a strengthening of the ranks of the middle- and upper-level bureaucracy, which is in contrast to the academic level. These tensions and contradictions provoke a climate of mistrust between bureaucrats and academics, leading to an increase in "transaction costs" involved in the implementation of federal programs across the country. In other words, widespread mistrust is a side effect of government action on university management.

State Public Universities: Transition from Traditional Arrangements to Federal Rules

There is an increase in resistance to the changes based on quality policies that employ measures of efficiency, legitimacy, stability, without the intervention of university management. The pressure and demands of the federal government upon public universities, encoded in terms of a new public policy paradigm, established a set of limitations, and incentives to foster institutional university change.

Beyond the contradictions, inconsistencies, or inefficiencies of the federal policies, the effects on management style and governance of public universities are important to analyze. Overall, in Mexico's public universities, policies and politics determine the styles of management as well as the operational modes of the university governance. The central logic behind these transformations is a pragmatic approach, adaptable to the demands and proposals of federal programs. Incentives can involve additional financial resources, institutional recognition through multiple accreditations, and quality certifications of academic programs, teacher training programs, and research processes. This involves the creation of different structures to support the central management of universities, particularly the strengthening and expansion of the bureaucratic apparatus and increases in staff to support the rector and key administrative leadership positions. The "strategic" and "integral" management of resources and decisions has changed the traditional governance bodies of public universities, which now play a more passive role in determining institutional priorities regarding the development of policies and resource allocation.

In this framework, a new group of administrators and institutional practices emerged as strategic stakeholders of the policy and university management: the experts of university management. They have become experts in process with specific expertise in handling instruments, tools, and relations to provide university rectors with the power to negotiate and communicate with federal agencies, local and private funds, and recognition providers related to accreditation and quality assessment. They have the "management power," which makes them similar to bureaucrats and traditional university politicians and they occupy leadership and institutional management positions in various areas of the administrative structure of university government. The expansion of the university bureaucracy and the differentiation of a managerial elite in the institutions are indications of the importance that these new stakeholders have acquired in the life of the university and, more generally, of the rise of a new managerial class. The changes have meant a silent but steady erosion of the meaning and scope of autonomy of public universities. It is a low-conflict transformation, but certainly powerful in the sense that, in a relatively short time, universities have learned to play under new rules of assessment and competitiveness, by adapting quickly to comply with programs and standards that are not subject to the decision of the traditional organs of university governance such as academic councils, and board of trustees. Money, recognition, and prestige now govern the changes in institutional behaviors.

In the five cases examined in the study: UV, BUAP, UG, UACJ, and USON, it was possible to discern differences in the institutional responses toward change. The differences were caused by the local environments of the universities, as well as their sociohistorical trajectories and characteristics of their internal political games, their rules and the structure of political action, both in formal and informal environments. While in two cases (UG, BUAP), certain "post-bureaucratic" management models were consolidated, and political governability models were structured. In another case (USON), it was possible to see how new management methods met with resistance in the traditional university governance structures. In two other cases (UV, UACJ), there was a split between the management styles and traditional political modes of the structures of the university government.

In regard to institutional performance, it is difficult to demonstrate a direct relationship between the administrative and organizational reforms of university governance and the improvement of institutional academic performance. It is possible, at the system level, to observe a period of expansion and diversification of the national system of Mexico's higher education however, it is difficult to define clearly whether this was due to new federal policies or if it was a response to the limited growth of student numbers, or to the effects of the extension of the obligatory nature of basic education decreed in 1995 (which involved incorporating high school studies into the Mexican basic education cycle). Moreover, the expansion of higher education was mainly due to the explosive growth of private educational institutions. This unregulated expansion was a response, on the one hand, to the demands of a new consumer market, and from the inability of the public sector to absorb the demand on the other. This hypothesis could explain the systemic effects of public policies in the last number of years.

At the level of public universities, there are not many elements that show a positive association between university reforms and improved institutional performance. We notice a deliberate government attempt to improve the infrastructure, human resources, expansion of college enrollment, and the collection of data as indications that the intervention is working. We still do not have a qualitative comparison to determine whether students that graduate from public universities have more professional success now than in earlier periods, or if college students have developed better learning habits than previous generations.

Conclusions

It is undeniable that Mexico today has better-funded public universities than in the decade of the 1980s, however, they are now forced to comply with the demands and goals of the federal government. We also have more- and better-qualified faculty members today. The number and percentage of full-time professors has increased, and there are academic bodies at different levels and degrees of consolidation in all public universities.[6] However, we do not know if this has significantly raised the quality of teaching, research, and student services in Mexican public universities. Today, we have more scientists (in terms of belonging to the NSI) than ever before in the history of Mexican higher education, and more college professors registered in the database of PROMEP. But, we do not know how those figures affect university teaching, or how they contribute to the development of new researchers (Álvarez and de Vries 2010). The university's role in cultural extension and diffusion— both historical functions of Mexican public universities—have also become neglected because of federal policies.

Based on the evidence above, I contend that efforts by the government to create a new style of educational governance at the university level have been largely unsuccessful. Attempts to incorporate New Public Management theory in Mexico's higher education system have had contradictory and uncertain results. We can, however, observe a trend toward greater federal government control over institutional performance of public universities. But, greater government control does not necessarily mean better coordination of the system. The addition of new stakeholders in the management of resources and programs (House of Representatives, private consultants, and accreditation bodies) have politicized and bureaucratized the management of public resources. And, it remains unclear whether this reform process has improved the performance of institutions in the Mexican higher education system.

NOTES

1. Both the *Law for the Coordination of Higher Education* and the third constitutional article configure the normative framework of the higher education

system in Mexico. The law attempts the coordination of federal government into the public universities system, and the article recognizes the autonomy of universities and the relationship between the state and the higher education system.
2. For "complex mixture," I refer to the themes and critical issues of institutional agendas in public universities: budgets negotiations between federal government and universities leadership, academic changes, labor relations, institutional accountability, evaluation process, merit pay programs for academic personal, and changes of universities governance.
3. "Policy networks" means the building of advocacy coalitions in each institutional case to engage in the reform process and to implement change and adaptation decisions following the rules of the policies of federal agencies. In some cases, university leadership adjustment was easily undertaken according to the new rules of the game (Veracruzana, Ciudad Juárez). In other cases, the public universities made "negotiation adjustments" with federal agencies (Sonora, Puebla). In some cases (Guadalajara), the implementation game implied a new form of university leadership, created according to the critical reform process of the new federal policies (Kent 2009; Acosta 2009).
4. PROMEP began at 1996 and focused on academic qualifications and performance of full-time professors in public universities. SNI was established in 1984 and focused on the scientific and research production of all higher education institutions in Mexico.
5. In fact, one of the six-year strategic subprograms has been the "Perfil Promep," designed to recognize individual professors with graduate degrees from different universities. And the "Desired Profile" of this program considers a doctorate degree as the "maximum degree of qualification." The professor evaluated at this level will receive a "one-time" financial support of 40 thousand pesos, to be used to buy computer equipment, office furniture, or literature.
6. In PROMEP terms, there are three types or levels of "academic bodies" in public universities: (1) *consolidados* (consolidation level), (2) *en proceso de consolidación* (toward consolidation process), and (3) *en formación* (at training level).

References

Acosta Silva, Adrián. 2002. "El neointervencionismo estatal en la educación superior en América Latina" ["State-interventionism in Higher Education in Latin America"]. *Revista Sociológica* [*Sociological Review*] 49 (May-August).

Acosta Silva, Adrián. 2004. *Una modernización anárquica: La educación superior en México en los noventa*. IESALC-Unesco/Universidad de Guadalajara, México [*An Anarchic Modernisation: Higher Education in Mexico in the Nineties*]. Guadlajara, Mexico: IESALC-UNESCO/University of Guadalajara].

Acosta Silva, Adrián. 2009. *Príncipes, burócratas y gerentes. El gobierno de las universidades públicas en México* [*Princes, Bureaucrats and Managers. The University Government in Mexico*]. Mexico City: ANUIES.

Aguilar Villanueva, Luis F. 2006. *Gobernanza y gestión pública* [*Governance and Public Management*]. Mexico City: Fondo de Cultura Economica.

Álvarez Mendiola, Germán, and Wietse de Vries. 2010. "Enseñanzas de las políticas para profesores" ["Lessons from Academic Policies in Mexico"]. *Revista Metapolítica*, [*Metapolitica Review*] 70: 73–78.

Braun, Dietmar, and Francois-Xavier Merrien. 1999. "Governance of Universities and Modernisation of the State." In *Towards a New Model of Governance for Universities? A Comparative View*, ed. Braun, D. and F-X. Merrien (pp. 9–33). Higher Education Policy Series 53. London and Philadelphia, PA: Jessica Kingsley Publishers.

Clark, Burton R. 1998. *Creating Entrepreneurial Universities: Organizational Pathways of Transformation*. Oxford: IAU Press/Pergamon.

de Boer, Harry. 2002. "Trust, the Essence of Governance?" In *Governing Higher Education: National Perspectives on Institutional Governance*, ed. Alberto Amaral, Glen A. Jones, and Berit Karseth (pp. 43–62). Dordretch, The Netherlands/ Boston, MA/London: Kluwer Academic Publishers.

de Vries, Wietse, and Eduardo Ibarra Colado. 2004. "La gestión de la universidad. Interrogantes y problemas en busca de respuestas" ["The Management University: Questions and Problems Searching for Answers"]. *Revista Mexicana de Investigación Educativa* [*Educational Research Mexican Review*] 9 (22): 575–584.

Fuentes Molinar, Olac. 1991. "Las cuestiones críticas de la educación superior" ["The Critical Issues of Higher Education in Mexico"]. *Universidad Futura* [*Future University Review*] 3 (8–9).

Ibarra Colado, Eduardo. 2005. "Origen de la empresarialización de la universidad: el pasado de la gestión de los negocios en el presente del manejo de la universidad" ["Origins of University Entrepreneurialism: From Business Management to University Managemen"]. *Revista de la Educación Superior*, ANUIES [*Higher Education Review*, ANUIES] 34 (2): n. 134.

Kent, Rollin. 2009, *Las políticas de educación superior en México durante la modernización. Un análisis regional* [*The Higher Education Policies in Mexico during Modernisation. A Regional Analysis*]. Mexico City: ANUIES.

Kuhn, Thomas S. 1991. *La estructura de las revoluciones científicas* [*The Structure of Scientific Revolutions*]. 8th ed. Mexico City: Fondo de Cultura Económica.

Levy, Daniel. 1987. *Universidad y gobierno en México. La autonomía en un sistema autoritario* [*University and Government in Mexico. The Autonomy into Autoritarian Regime*]. Mexico City: FCE.

Messner, Dirk. 1999. "Del Estado Céntrico a la 'sociedad de redes'. Nuevas exigencias a la coordinación social" ["From Centric-State to 'Networks Society'. New Challenges to Social Coordination"]. In *Reforma del estado y coordinación social* [*State Reform and Social Coordination*], ed. N. Lechner, R. Millán, and F. Valdés. Mexico City: Plaza y Valdés.

Murayama, Ciro. 2009. *Economía política de la educación superior en México* [*Political Economy of Higher Education in Mexico*]. Mexico City: ANUIES.

PROMEP. 2010. *The Teaching Improvement Program*. Mexico: University of Guadalajara. http: cisgi.cucea.udg.mx.

Rodríguez, Roberto. 2007. "La autonomía universitaria: un debate sobre su concepción y su ejercicio" ["University Autonomy: A Discussion Over Its Conception and Practices"]. In *El régimen de autonomía* [*The Autonomy Regime*], ed. Jorge Medina Viedas, Arturo Gómez Pompa, et al. (pp. 51–62). Veracruz, Mexico: Universidad Veracruzana

SNI. 2010). *National Researcher System.* www.conacyt.gob.mx/SNI/Paginas/default.aspx.

Chapter 11

Higher Education Reform in Ecuador and Its Effect on University Governance*

F. Mauricio Saavedra

When studying higher education in Latin America, Ecuador has received very little attention. Researchers have tended to focus on larger countries, such as Mexico, Argentina, and Chile, leaving countries like Ecuador abandoned from systematic research (Jameson 1997). Although Ecuador has been exposed to noticeable changes during the last ten years, there continues to be a lack of research on its higher education system. As such there is little empirical information available. This study is an attempt to contribute to the literature by examining Ecuador's recent reform in higher education.

The study begins with a preamble to situate Ecuador's recent higher education reform and the point in time when this study began. Following this introduction, the purpose of the study, its theoretical framework, and the method of data collection and analysis employed are presented. Subsequently, the findings of the analysis of data are provided followed by a discussion and a concluding section.

Situating Ecuador's Recent Higher Education Reform

Ecuador's recent higher education reform has been a heated and debated process; the current president of Ecuador (Econ. Rafael Correa Delgado), who has openly expressed his discontent with neoliberal policies (Presidencia de la República del Ecuador 2007), initiated the reform in 2007 with a request to examine the higher education system. In 2008, the president began reform discussions with Ecuadorian higher education leaders and with the regulating organization of higher education in Ecuador at that time, Consejo Nacional de Educación Superior (CONESUP). This organization was made up of college and university presidents from public and private universities. Correa assigned a government agency, Secretaría Nacional de Planificación y Desarrollo (SENPLADES), the responsibility for the proposed reform. As SENPLADES began the process by leading discussions concerning the reform, there were objections that led to heated debates between CONESUP and SENPLADES. As a result, SENPLADES (2009) decided to exclude CONESUP and proceeded to create the proposed bill for reform on their own. Meanwhile, CONESUP began to prepare a bill on its own.

In 2009, two bills on higher education reform were submitted to the legislature; one from SENPLADES (2009) and another from CONESUP (2009). The debate concerning the reform or creation of a new higher education law for Ecuador continued, but this time in the legislature. It is at this point in time that my study began to examine the purpose of this reform and its potential effect on Ecuador's higher education system with a particular emphasis on university governance.

Purpose of the Study

I was particularly interested in understanding the drivers that precipitated the current reform, especially in light of the caution by Kenneth P. Jameson (1997, 1999) and Susan Twombly (1998) about the difficulty of bringing about higher education reform in Ecuador that might lead to significant changes in this arena. Given that two separate bills were submitted to the legislature, it was also important to explore how these bills were created and what they were based on as far as data and analysis is concerned. In addition, examining the objectives of the reform could provide a better understanding of the impact of this reform on university governance.

Theoretical Framework

The analysis was framed by academic capitalism theory (Slaughter and Leslie 1997; Slaughter and Rhoades 2004). Academic capitalism was made possible by neoliberalism, which promotes the use of the market via deregulation and free trade and seeks to transfer the control of the economy from the public to the private sector for the sake of efficiency and economic well-being. Given that we live in a knowledge-intensive economy, academic capitalism explains the process by which colleges and universities are integrating into this new economy. The theory indicates that this integration is occurring through a behavioral change on the part of the higher education community where the members thereof (faculty, administrators, academic professionals, and students) form networks within and between the public and private sectors to market knowledge and gain profit from it. Hence, higher education institutions become marketers who capitalize on their captive market, students, offering them various services and products. Faculty, administrators, academic professionals, and students are seen as the ones interested in knowledge to profit from it. This investing, marketing, and consumption behavior creates the new academic capitalist knowledge/learning regime. This new regime, which is interested in the privatization of knowledge and profit, is compared to the traditional public good knowledge/learning regime, which places an emphasis on knowledge for the sake of knowledge, that is, as a public good to which citizens have access (Slaughter and Leslie 1997; Slaughter and Rhoades 2004).

Academic capitalism within higher education describes the behavior of colleges and universities as they approach the market seeking to increase their revenues through education-oriented activities and other services. Academic capitalism recognizes that colleges and universities also embrace the market within the area of research by developing partnerships with business and industry to market technology transfer activities (i.e., licensing, patents, and products based on market demands). Hence, according to academic capitalism proponents, higher education institutions are shifting from a public good regime to a private good regime where basic research and social benefits are no longer the focus of higher education. This shift from the public good to the private good has in turn led colleges and universities to focus on fields of study closer to the market and on fields related to science, technology, engineering, and math (STEM), and to recruiting students with greater academic ability and greater willingness and ability to pay for higher education (Slaughter and Rhoades 2004).

Academic capitalism was used for this analysis for two reasons. First, SENPLADES (2009) emphasized that higher education in Ecuador, up to that point, had not been seen as a public good but rather as a business where students had been highly marketized; a system that lacked access and quality of education. SENPLADES (2009) pointed out that higher education in Ecuador was in this condition due to (1) abandonment of the higher education system by government, (2) marketizing students, and (3) using universities as a platform for political interests. SENPLADES argued that this was the result of lack of regulation. Jameson (1997, 1999) and Susan Twombly (1998) appear to agree in that both pointed out the absence of a significant change in Ecuador's higher education system due to lack of interest in this area by the government. Jameson (1997, 1999) argued that the higher education system in Ecuador in the 1990s was a reflection of the neoliberal political economy employed during that time. As such, he noted a decline in public funding for education, an absence of government leadership in this area, a lack of accountability and quality on the higher education system, and an increase in universities developing independent sources for finance. Susan Twombly (1998), building on the work of Jameson (1997), emphasized the low quality of the system overall and the lack of concern for higher education by the central government.

The second reason for using academic capitalism in this study is that the central government of Ecuador involved in this process has publically indicated their contempt for neoliberalism and their desire to move toward more social policies (Presidencia de la República del Ecuador 2007). Therefore, this study analyzes the current higher education reform in Ecuador with an academic capitalism lens to examine the extent to which the new policies are dismantling the previous system and doing away with marketization and whether these policies provide the necessary support from the central government for this change to be effective. As such, an antineoliberal higher education system should translate into increased access and low-cost tuition and fees for students, as well as an attempt to increase quality within the system. This study explores whether this is indeed the case.

Data Collection and Analysis

This study employed a phenomenological and a case study approach (Creswell 2007; Merriam 1998; Yin 2003). As such, following approval by the University of Georgia Institutional Review Board (IRB), I collected data to address the purpose of the study. The sample included seventeen individuals from three different populations: university presidents and other university officials, representatives from central government, and higher education leaders. Criteria for the first targeted population included university presidents, representatives of their university, or personnel who had some sort of influence in the governance and decisions made at their university; those who were not influential or involved in the administration of their university were excluded. Criteria for the second group included representatives from central government who had been or were involved in the process of Ecuador's higher education reform; representatives who had not participated in such process were excluded. Criteria for the third targeted population included higher education leaders who were either involved in the process of Ecuador's higher education reform, or, had some sort of influence in Ecuador's higher education system; those who were either unaware or uninterested in Ecuador's higher education reform were excluded.

Data were collected during the month of July in 2010 via interviews. A small number of participants were contacted via e-mail to arrange convenient interview times prior to July 2010. The majority were contacted by phone during the month of July. After scheduling an appointment with a participant, the purpose and goals of the study were explained and a consent form was provided for the participant to read, examine, and sign. Five semistructured questions were employed to obtain information about the topic of this research:

1) In your opinion, what was the main reason for this higher education reform to take place?
2) What are the main objectives of the current reform?
3) What type of data and what type of analyses were used in the creation of the proposed bills for reform?
4) What impact, overall, will this reform have on the higher education system in Ecuador?
5) What impact will this reform have on university governance?

The interviews were audio recorded, transcribed, and subsequently analyzed; there were no follow-up meetings after the interviews and all participants were guaranteed confidentiality. The analysis of the data was performed by reviewing and coding the transcribed data, and grouping similar data into common patterns and themes.

In addition to the interviews, I conducted an extensive document analysis. The various documents and information related to the topic of this study were examined focusing on content and discourse analysis. I also examined the documents relating to the latest higher education law in Ecuador, which was approved on October 4, 2010, and was officially registered on October 12, 2010.[1]

Findings

As previously explained, the two bills (one from SENPLADES and the other one from CONESUP) were submitted to the legislature by the end of 2009 where the debate concerning the creation of a new higher education law continued. By the time I began to do the interviews, the legislature had put together a proposed law for reform, which basically favored the articles offered by SENPLADES's bill. However, this proposed law had gone through a first debate and was about to go through second debate. It is this proposed law that the participants refer to in the interviews.

Interview participants were classified into four groups: representatives of private universities, representatives of public universities, representatives of central government, and higher education leaders. Results indicated that the opinions of those from public universities and those of central government could be clustered on one end of the continuum as favoring the reform and the articles in the proposed higher education law. However, those from private universities were located on the other end firmly against the articles being offered in the proposed law, while the opinions from higher education leaders appeared to be somewhere in between.

Representatives of government and representatives of public universities argued that the current reform came about due to quality concerns within the system and with the intent to improve higher education. One government representative explained:

> It could be said that the beginning of all this process is an anomalous situation that came about with a university, which had many complaints about the way degrees were being granted and the system of study they were employing at that moment. So, the National Assembly, obviously with all of the reports and documents related to the problem that had risen, decided to close down this university, but, in the decree of closure, they warn that there are other universities that could be in the same situation or that could be going through similar issues. Thus, the National Assembly, that is the congress, establishes a constitutional mandate, called *Mandato Catorce* (Mandate Fourteen), which forces CONESUP and Consejo Nacional de Evaluación y Acreditación (CONEA) to do an exhaustive evaluation concerning the way universities were functioning in the country. As such, it gives the timeframe of a year to do such evaluation and within the year 2009 this evaluation takes place where expected but also unexpected results were obtained in that we did not know that some universities were doing so badly because they were not fulfilling the purpose for which they were created. Thus, this triggers the beginning of this process of reform.

While a representative of a public university pointed out:

> The higher education system in Ecuador has too many weaknesses. To me, the main reason [for this reform to take place] is the need for Ecuador to place itself within a productive route towards a system of knowledge production and the weakness that the current higher education system has to be able to collaborate with the country for it to go in this direction.

Another representative of a public university said that "basically, this process of reform points to elevating the academic level of the Ecuadorian university."

Private universities, however, argued that the reform came about for political reasons and for central government to gain control over the system. They saw government as inexperienced and incapable of bringing about an effective reform that would improve the system. In addition, they pointed out that public and private universities, through CONESUP, had already been working on a reform and that the central government took advantage of this situation to bring about a reform of their own. A president of a private university clearly stated:

> I think the main reasons [for this reform to take place] are political and come from a socialist orientation from the whole government in order to control the whole system. This reform, to me, is not the result of an analysis, but rather, it comes from an ideology.

One representative of a private university pointed out:

> It doesn't matter if one is with Correa (the president of Ecuador at the time) or against Correa. The president's intention could be very good; to change many things that are not working well in the country. Unfortunately, the people who are in practice doing this, the people from SENPLADES, are people who do not have any experience in education and are centralized planners. Planners who think, as used to be the case with the Soviet Union, that they can do it [planning] from a desk. Thus, they make, what seem to be good proposals, but at the same time are impossible to fund.

Most universities both public and private indicated that they were interested in a reform; however, private universities emphasized that the articles being proposed were not favorable toward their institutions.

Concerning the information employed for the creation of the bills presented to the legislature, it was argued by government representatives from SENPLADES that their bill was based on qualitative data (opinions of various groups within the country), on whatever information they could find concerning the higher education system in Ecuador, and on the national development plan, which is a national plan for good living presented by SENPLADES in 2009. SENPLADES emphasized that available information concerning higher education in Ecuador was scarce. A representative of government explained:

> We used all of the information available, that is, surveys of living conditions, employment surveys, data from the universities themselves, interviews, secondary information through other institutes and other universities, external universities that located Ecuador in a global context, information from OREALC, from UNESCO, and we examined the topic of science and technology to see how we were doing in that area. Then, with this information, with the poor information we had, we were able to interpolate and able to see, and also, a legal analysis. Then we began to see legally how it had worked and what the problems were... Then, came the process of seminars, the process of *Mandato Catorce* (Mandate Fourteen), which we pushed... then came the process of building the new proposed law for

reform... and it was articulated to the perspective we had concerning the national development plan and the role of the university in it.

The bill from CONESUP, however, was formulated in response to SENPLADES' bill and was based on the Ecuadorian constitution of 2008, previous experience concerning the system, and a comparative analysis of higher education law among countries in Ibero-America. A representative from CONESUP indicated:

> CONESUP, that is, the system, the actors of the system, the universities, put together a proposal of law for the reform that, first of all, was based on the constitution; that is, on the governing bodies, the new CONESUP, and the new CONEA according to the constitution of 2008. CONESUP, first of all, took into consideration the constitutional principles and, in second place, mustered the positive and negative experiences of a higher education law that has been in effect until now, which has strength because it was worked on until the year 2000. It is not about putting together a totally new law, but rather a new law that would take into consideration the good experiences and also the bad experiences, of course, in order to correct them and give the system a new view. Thus, taking into consideration a law that has been in place nine years within the system of higher education, we made adjustments, reforms, updates, deletions, additions, etc. to present a law that could be beneficial for the system. Contrary to the bill proposed by SENPLADES, which until now causes a reaction and a rejection by the higher education community because we consider that it goes against the constitutional principles, then, it has an orientation towards managing power from government, and it is not clear and coherent in the academic aspects. These are the basic principles: breaches the constitutional rules, central power from government against governing policies of the higher education system, and a diffused and confused academic organization. This is our point of view, which is shared by many universities and university presidents.

The findings indicated that representatives from public universities, overall, believed that the reform would have a positive effect on Ecuador's higher education. A representative of a public university expressed:

> I think so [concerning whether the reform would have a positive effect on the country's higher education], in certain aspects [this reform] has placed the finger on the wound (this is an expression in Spanish that could translate into has hit the nail on the head). The purpose [of the reform] is to improve and basically [improve areas] that have to do with quality and academic rigor. That it [the reform] contributes to promote research in the universities.

Representatives from private universities however, strongly argued for a negative effect of the reform on Ecuador's higher education. One representative indicated that "if the question is whether this proposed law for reform is going to improve education, the answer is no. This proposed law is going to worsen higher education." Another representative pointed out:

> What do we know [when asked about the impact of the reform]? In this country we do not know anything, but, it [the reform] is not going to improve the system, that is the important thing. There is no reason for it to improve [higher education in Ecuador]; the proposed law for reform does not say anything about the student. This is a matter of regulation: 221 articles. Also, they [central government] do not realize that, let's see, at least, [they should] follow the tradition of a country so small and so diverse as it is the case of Ecuador, which is unique in the world, and, let the universities also be as diverse as the country where they live. But no, what they [central government] want is to control, to have control, what for?

The main aspects private universities were against within the new proposed law for Ecuador's higher education were those related to governance. Higher education leaders, however, pointed out that the new reform would have both positive and negative effects on the higher education system. One higher education leader said "I think that what SENPLADES is proposing is too strict, but, we cannot leave [higher education to its own] with total liberality either."

As it relates to university governance, public universities argued that the proposed law would not have any effect on their institutions because they already had this practice set in place. However, central government officials (SENPLADES) argued that the proposed law would do away with politicization in university governance in public universities, thereby improving the decision-making process for these institutions. Private universities, however, were somewhat divided: one group argued that there would be no effect for the same reason mentioned above for public universities, while another group argued that the new law would be devastating for their institutions due to economic, political, and personal interests of students. They argued that institutional efficiency and prestige would be affected by bringing in bureaucratization and politicization via the new proposed higher education law. As a representative of a private university explained:

> The impact of the proposed law for reform will be terrible on university governance because...among [our] professors...we have [some] very good speakers. People who can convince, persuade [others], and bottom line leaders; leaders for politicking, let's say. Hence, anyone can say I will cut tuition and fees to half; choose. So, this person convinces the students and professors, or, with offers he/she convinces professors who are full-time to support his/her proposition; anything to win. He/She wins, and in the moment that they cut tuition and fees to half, these universities will deteriorate and/or go bankrupt.

Examining University Governance in More Detail

Given the topic of this study, it was important to examine university governance in Ecuadorian universities in more detail. This section begins with a brief overview, extracted from participant interviews, in regard to university governance in Ecuador prior to the reform. Subsequently, this section examines the reform concerning university governance through the new higher education law approved and officially registered in Ecuador on October 12, 2010.

According to Secretaría Nacional de Educación Superior, Ciencia, Tecnología e Innovación (SENESCYT) (2011), there are a total of 78 universities in Ecuador, out of which 29 are public. University governance varied depending mainly on whether the university was public or private. Overall, it appears that university governance in public universities has been highly politicized with decision making heavily weighted toward the political party controlling the campus. As a result, students who did not subscribe to a political party on campus did not participate on the decision-making process via university governance. This also had an impact on faculty, who had to adhere to a certain party to be able to participate within administrative positions in their respective university. Some of the participants pointed out that among the threats of this political power within university governance in public universities is the fact that a service employee (i.e., a janitor) had the ability to get rid of the president of the university by exercising his/her vote.

Private universities, however, had a businesslike model where, usually, the owner of the university was the president of the institution and where students and faculty were assigned to the academic council rather than being elected. Participants representing the central government argued that because private universities feared that groups of faculty or students might ask for things that the university could not afford, they would simply choose a couple of deans and few students for the university council to be able to say that they were represented, but, overall, they tried to avoid matters related to university governance. Decision making within this model, relied heavily on the CEO of the university.

Governance between the state and the universities was decentralized with very little accountability, which is what the reform sought to change. All public universities and some private universities received funding from the government. Funding was provided via a funding formula, which was based on the number of students, needs of the university, type of undergraduate degree by field, type of graduate degree by field, number of hours worked by faculty, type of degrees held by faculty, administrative efficiency, and for being an Ecuadorian university. The latter applied to public or private universities that had been created in Ecuador.

Higher Education Reform in Ecuador and Its Effect 171

As already explained, the two bills (one from SENPLADES and the other one from CONESUP) submitted to the legislature in 2009 were combined into a proposed law that underwent a first and second debate in 2010. In this same year, after reaching consensus, the legislature sent this proposed law to the president of Ecuador for revision. The president partially vetoed the document and returned it to the legislature with notice that they had 30 days to review and revise the document to take into account his proposed changes. For various reasons, the legislature never came together to revise the suggested changes and the document was subsequently approved through the ministry of the law. Because the legislature failed to review the suggested changes in the allotted time, all of the president's changes were automatically approved as part of the new law on higher education for Ecuador. The new higher education law was approved on October 4, 2010, was officially registered on October 12, 2010, and it has been in effect since then (Asamblea Nacional República del Ecuador 2011).

The new higher education law, in addition to emphasizing access and the right to free higher education as far as baccalaureate programs in public universities, mandates that all universities, whether public or private, adopt the following governance structure:

1) All universities must have a governing board for decision making, made up of university officials, faculty, students, and alumni. The percentage for student participation in the governing board must be between 10 and 25 percent of the total percentage of faculty members who are eligible to vote. The percentage for alumni participating in the governing board must be from 1 to 5 percent of the total percentage of faculty members who are eligible to vote. If decision making includes administrative matters, then service employees and workers must also participate (1 to 5 percent of the total percentage of faculty members who are eligible to vote). Faculty will be represented by those elected and the percentage should be decided by each institution.

2) The *rector* (university president) and *vice rector* (vice president) will be elected through secret vote, and hold the positions for five years. They can be reelected for one additional term. In the election, the students' vote will weigh 10–25 percent of the total percentage of faculty members who are eligible to vote. The vote of service employees and workers will weigh 1–5 percent of the total percentage of faculty members who are eligible to vote. The weight from faculty representation will be determined by each institution.

3) Qualifications for the position of rector or vice rector include that the applicant respectively must hold a PhD/Doctorate degree.

4) In addition, to be elected as rector, the person must have: five years of experience in higher education administration, publications within the

last five years, five years of experience as a faculty member, and must have accessed the faculty position through a competition process based on merit.
5) Universities will be accountable to a new regulating organization SENESCYT, representative of central government who will enforce the new law making sure universities (both public and private) are complying with such regulations. This new organization will not only be in charge of higher education, but will also oversee the areas of science, technology, and innovation.
6) All universities must account for expenditure of funds provided by the government (gratuity for public universities and use of public funds for student scholarships for privates).
7) All universities must invest a minimum of 6 percent of their budgets in research, publications, and for preparing their faculty to obtain a PhD/Doctorate degree.
8) There will be a new funding formula based on quality, efficiency, equity, justice, and academic excellence, which will contain the following parameters: number of students and cost per academic program and level; number of faculty members; degree type held by faculty members; academic experience of faculty members; academic classification and type of institution and academic program; efficiency in instruction and research and relationship with the national and regional development; overall efficiency; and administrative efficiency. SENESCYT has not yet defined the way efficiency will be measured.

From the statements above, it appears that the new higher education law might have an impact on private universities if the university president must be elected. The requirement of a PhD/Doctorate degree to be eligible for university president or vice president will perhaps have an impact on most universities, because, for the most part, university administrators do not currently hold a PhD/Doctoral degree and there are no PhD/Doctoral programs available in Ecuador at the current time; the highest degree available in the different fields is usually that of master's. It is interesting to point out that faculty members in Ecuador, in their vast majority, do not hold a PhD or Doctorate degree. As such, the new higher education law is allowing university presidents and vice presidents five years from the time the law was approved to comply with the PhD or Doctorate requirement and seven years for faculty members to obtain such a degree. In addition, given the new law, faculty and to a certain extent administrators (university presidents, vice presidents, and deans) can no longer just be hired by an institution. Now, in both public and private universities, they must first enter the system via the academia through a competition process based on merit. Finally, it is interesting that the new regulating organism (SENESCYT) is placed within the areas of science, technology, and innovation. From this, one can infer that given the emphasis of science and technology, the new regulating organization might give priority to STEM fields within higher education, especially due to the common discourse of economic development and growth.

Discussion and Conclusions

There is a shift in Ecuador's higher education system from decentralization, deregulation, and lack of accountability to a centralized and highly regulated system where university governance is imposed rather than exercised. Presidents from private universities argue that universities are losing autonomy while government is gaining power. Government representatives, however, argue that if universities were autonomous they would be exercising governance, which according to government representatives, many of the private universities were not doing. Representatives of private universities, however, argue that by the addition of new regulation, the central government is not letting universities govern themselves.

Using the lenses of academic capitalism to examine the extent to which the new policies are dismantling the previous system, one notices the effort from central government to create an antineoliberal higher education system by providing access and subsidizing the cost of baccalaureate programs in public universities. Also, it was previously argued that an antineoliberal higher education system should also increase quality[2] within the system. For the findings, it appears that by regulating university governance the central government is attempting to increase quality within the system through regulation. This is supported by the emphasis on mandating PhD/Doctoral certification and research production. Hence, subsidizing the cost of baccalaureate programs in public universities and attempting to increase quality in the system through regulation would support the central government's discourse about shifting higher education from being a private good to a public good. However, this drive for quality increase seems to have overregulated the system, especially as it relates to university governance. For example, the requirements for a rector, who must not only have five years of experience in higher education administration, but also in teaching and research with a record of publications, as well as having accessed the faculty position through a competition process based on merit might be difficult to achieve, especially when one considers that for the most part research and administration are two separate areas within higher education, each of them requiring a different type of training, set of skills, and experience.

Also, forcing universities to elect the rector who meets the aforementioned requirements might not be the most efficient way to choose the appropriate person for the position. For example, a university cannot go on a search and choose the best candidate to lead its institution because, according to the new law, the candidate for rector must have first entered the institution as a faculty member through a competition process based on merit, and, must be elected.

Given the high priority on centralization, regulation, accountability, and control in the new law, it would be beneficial for Ecuador to examine Mexico's higher education system. Since the 1990s, Mexico has employed policies aimed at significantly improving the quality of education. Two decades later evidence indicates that rather than improving quality, these policies have increased bureaucracy and the financial burden on the system (Álvarez-Mendiola et al. 2010).

Central government's concern for quality in higher education seems to be based on their recognition of the importance of research production for economic growth and the development of the nation. Hence, through the regulation of the new higher education law, central government would appear to desire the establishment of a higher education system comparable to systems in other countries where higher education has been considered a significant contributor to technological advancements and innovation, economic growth, development, and global competitiveness. The discourse from government during my study was on the importance of focusing on applied research via higher education and linking it to industry to gain the aforementioned results. As such, an interesting paradox could develop from this situation. The central government in its attempt to increase the quality of the higher education system in Ecuador through the new laws to support economic growth and development, might at the same time be setting up a system for academic capitalism to take place through applied research and industry through technology transfer, which might contribute to support for neoliberalism, the policy central government is trying to counteract. It will be very interesting to follow Ecuador's new higher education law and assess its impact on the system a few years from now.

Notes

* I would like to thank economist Franklin Saavedra Polanco for his support while in Ecuador in regard to organizing and setting up the respective interviews and collaborating with this study.
1. This law was approved after I had conducted the interviews.
2. In this case, quality appears to be measured by certification, experience, and merit.

References

Álvarez-Mendiola, Germán, Adrián Acosta-Silva, Wietse de Vries, Rocío Grediaga-Kuri, and Romualdo López-Zárate. 2010. "Mexican Higher Education

Governance: What has Changed after Two Decades of Quality Oriented Policies?" Paper presented at the 7th International Workshop on Higher Education Reform, Vancouver, BC, October 7, 2010.

Asamblea Nacional República del Ecuador. 2011. *Trámite de Las Leyes: Ley Orgánica de Educación Superior* [*Processing of the Laws: Law of Higher Education*]. Quito, Ecuador: National Assembly, Republic of Ecuador. http://www.asambleanacional.gov.ec.

CONESUP. 2009. *Autonomía Universitaria: Legislación Comparada de Nueve Países de América Latina y España* [*University Autonomy: Comparative Legislation of Nine Countries in Latin America and Spain*]. Quito, Ecuador: National Council of Higher Education.

Creswell, John W. 2007. *Qualitative Inquiry and Research Design*. 2nd ed. Thousand Oaks, CA: Sage Publications.

Jameson, Kenneth P. 1997. "Higher Education in a Vacuum: Stress and Reform in Ecuador." *Higher Education* 33 (3): 265–281.

Jameson, Kenneth P. 1999. "Moving 'Social Reform' to Center Stage: Lessons from Higher Education in Ecuador." *Higher Education Policy* 12 (2): 123–140.

Merriam, Sharan B. 1998. *Qualitative Research and Case Study Applications in Education*. 2nd ed. San Francisco, CA: Jossey-Bass.

Presidencia de la República del Ecuador [Presidency of the Republic of Ecuador]. 2007. "Discurso de Posesión del Presidente de la República, Econ. Rafael Correa en la Mitad del Mundo" ["Inaugural address of President of the Republic, Econ. Rafael Correa in the Middle of the World"]. Quito, Ecuador: UN Document.

SENESCYT [Ministry of Higher Education, Science, Technology and Innovation]. 2011. *Manual del usuario: Consolidación de Línea de Base Sistema Nacional de Información de la Educación Superior del Ecuador* [*User's Manual: Baseline Consolidation of the National Higher Education Data System of Ecuador*]. Quito, Ecuador: SENESCYT.

SENPLADES [Ministry of Planning and Development]. 2009. *Cadena Nacional de Educación Superior* [*Nationwide Broadcast on Higher Education*]. Quito, Ecuador: Ministry of Planning and Development. http://www.senplades.gov.ec.

Slaughter, Sheila, and Larry L. Leslie. 1997. *Academic Capitalism: Politics, Policies, and the Entrepreneurial University*. Baltimore, MD: Johns Hopkins Press.

Slaughter, Sheila, and Gary Rhoades. 2004. *Academic Capitalism and the New Economy: Markets, State, and Higher Education*. Baltimore, MD: Johns Hopkins University Press.

Twombly, Susan B. 1998. "Reform by Remote Control: Evaluation and Accreditation of Ecuadorian Higher Education." *La educación* 129–131 (1–3): 201–219.

Yin, Robert K. 2003. *Case Study Research: Design and Methods*. 3rd ed. Thousand Oaks, CA: Sage Publications.

Part IV

East Asia and Australia

Chapter 12

Incorporation of National Universities in Japan: An Evaluation Six Years On

Motohisa Kaneko

Introduction

In the wave of reforms implemented by government and higher education institutions in many OECD countries, Japanese national universities were incorporated in 2004. One of the key elements of the new scheme was the "mid-term targets" to be achieved in the subsequent six years, which function as a contract between the government and each university. The levels of achievement are to be evaluated in the sixth year, and the results reflected in the next middle-term targets and corresponding government funding. As of 2010, the first cycle of this process has been completed. What were the intended effects of the original design? How did it work in reality? Why are the outcomes different from the expectation? These are the questions that I address in this chapter.

Incorporation of National Universities: Background, Design, and Expected Consequences

Japanese National University as a State Facility Model

I begin with a simple classification of the relation between government and university. There are three main types or models of university dependent on historical background.

First, a State Facility Model, which is the traditional model of German universities and most of the university systems in Continental Europe. Following the Humboldtian ideal, universities of this type are governmental organizations as regards organization and physical infrastructure. They are seen as a guild of academic members who participate in a wide range of decision making.

Second, a Private University Model, which comprises private institutions of higher education in the United States, and other countries. It owed much in organizational and curricular terms to the endowed colleges of Oxford and Cambridge. In the prototypical case of the Yale Corporation, a board of trustees with a trust fund owns and manages the university, and so with others of its kind.

Third, a Government-Commissioned Model, exemplified by US state universities and most UK universities. These institutions are distinct from the government in governance, but still heavily dependent on government subsidies.

The national universities are organized, like the German and other European universities according to the *State Facility Model*. Universities of the State Facility Model are established by the state as a facility of the government. Although the universities are not exactly part of the of government bureaucracy, they are a function of government, fully supported by the government. However, the academics are autonomous in decision making, not only in academic matters but also in administrative matters. The heavy involvement of academics in decision making follows the tradition of the medieval guild.

From its beginning, the State Facility raised difficulties. There was conflict between the state and the academy. Before World War II, there were cases where government forced the resignation of professors for their political opinions. In the postwar period, with this backdrop clearly in mind, professors exhibited a strong sentiment against government control of national universities. Later the conflict became financial, not merely political. Academics in the national universities were frustrated by the tight financial control by the Ministry of Education. These factors created a sentiment for independence.

Further, there was resentment about disparity between national and private institutions. Provided with generous government funding, national universities enjoyed much better infrastructure for education and research. At the same time, the national universities charged tuition at about half the level of that in private institutions. From the perspective of private institutions, there was little justification for such differentiated treatment.

Finally, there were claims that the national universities were managed inefficiently (see Homma, chapter 13). It has been argued that, protected by state support, the universities were and are exposed to little competition. Moreover, since the internal control of the national university is in the hands of the professors, there has been little mechanism to assure accountability. Against this backdrop, pressure for fundamental reform mounted in the 1990s (Kaneko, 2004).

The factors mentioned above coalesced to bring about the decline of the role of the state in higher education. In response to the difficulties, various countries instituted reforms, which can be generalized under the concept of marketization. Marketization in higher education refers to the introduction of various market mechanisms to higher education. A concept used in close relation to this concept is "Quasi-Marketization," which refers to the schemes where the government acts as one of the consumers of the services that higher education institutions provide. In the discussion that follows, I use the term "marketization" in both senses.

Marketization transforms national universities into independent entities. In the current State Facility Model, the national university has two sides. On one hand, it is a part of the government organization. Its budget is specified in the national budget, and the purpose of the expenditure is specified in detail in the lines of budget. Faculty members and administrators are government employees. The facilities are the property of the government. The academic side of operation, on the other hand, is governed by the faculty members.

After the recent reforms, government and the university are two separate legal entities. This separation raises two questions. First, how will the national university be governed as an independent entity? Second, how will the relation between government and the university be regulated? Obviously, the government loses its direct power to control the university, and yet the government must provide support to the university. The support and the performance of the university have to be balanced, and proper incentives for efficient use of resources must be built into this regulation. In a way, the new model becomes a contract between the government and the university.

These questions suggest that incorporation of national universities is critically dependent upon the design of governance of institutions and the device of latent or overt contract between the government and the university.

Design and Expected Consequences

While the creation of the National University Corporation (NUC) scheme was a direct product of political and economic factors, the design of the scheme was based on a body of logic (Kaneko, 2009). Basically, it was influenced by concepts of New Public Management or Institutional Economics that gained momentum in past two decades. At the core of the concept is the relationship between the "principal" and the "agent," and the explicit contract between the two. The scheme of Independent Administrative Institution is built on this concept: the government as the principal commissions an Independent Administrative Agency to achieve a public purpose. The terms and conditions of the contract are specified in the midterm goals and plan; subsequently the level of achievement will be evaluated, and the results will lead to consequences in the form of either financial rewards or punishment, or possibly even discontinuation of the contract.

The usual argument is that a separation of principal and agent causes the agent to become more "efficient." The agent, free from the strict control by the government must face competition with other agents, but is able to exploit local knowledge and initiate innovations. Moreover, it is given an incentive to gain efficiency through explicit goals. Armed with these mechanisms, the government is able to gain efficiency in provision of its services and become more accountable.

To realize the assumed function, the contract must be clearly stated and include an instrument to measure the level of achievement. It is also necessary that the chief executive of the agent should be designated as personally responsible for the contract, although the institution as a whole functions as an agent of the government. The chief executive then directs the organization toward achievement of the set goals, and the members of the executive board assist the chief executive.

As one of the variations of the Independent Administrative Agency, the same argument should be applied as the justification of the construct of the NUCs. From this perspective it is natural that the midterm goals and plan, and the corresponding evaluation, should become the core of the new relation between the government and the NUC. It is also understandable that the president of NUC has to be given unusually strong power.

The underlying logic of incorporation of national universities can be summarized in a diagram presented as Figure 12.1, where incorporation induces changes at each institution to produce desired effects.

The core of incorporation lies in the following three factors. First, the relations between the government and the national universities are regulated by the midterm goals and plans that are agreed upon by both parties. The

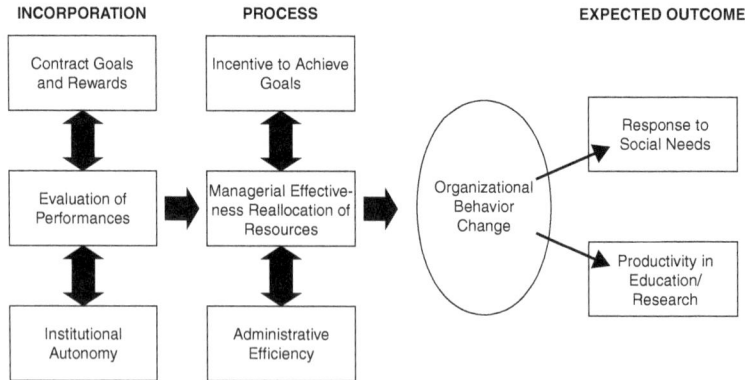

Figure 12.1 Design and Expected Consequences of Incorporation.

government acts as the principal, and each university as an agent, to produce services in education and research. Provided with those goals and plans, the government give subsidies to the institutions. In this sense, the relation is regulated by an implicit contract. The level of achievement of the goals is evaluated at the end of the midterm period, and the results are used to set the next midterm goals and corresponding government subsidies. Meanwhile, institutions are given basic autonomy both in governance and finances. Each institution is presided over by the president as the CEO, and the council appointed by the president makes basic management decisions.

These reforms at the system level are expected to induce significant changes in each national university, particularly in the following three aspects: First, each institution is given specific goals to achieve. Rewards and/or penalties are contingent upon achievement of the goals and create strong financial incentives for the entire institution. Second, the president and his council are provided with considerable power in the governance structure. They reallocate resources both in terms of faculty and administrative staff to achieve the stated goals. Third, the administrative processes are liberated from minute bureaucratic control by the government. This change will free administrators and faculty members from procedural works to invest a greater portion of their time in the work directly related to education, research, and social services.

These three factors would affect not only the behavior of faculty members and administrators, but also the behavior and culture of the organization. In the end, this would result in enhanced productivity in research, education, and other areas. Moreover, these changes would be achieved in the direction that the society expects from the national universities. In this way, incorporation would bring about better national universities, but to what extent, was it realized in the subsequent years?

Implementation

The *NUC Law* was enacted on April 1, 2004, whereupon all 80 national universities were registered as NUCs. The change can be summarized from three aspects: the contractual relation between the government and NUC, evaluation of performance, and enhanced institutional autonomy and power given to the management.

Relation between Government and National Universities

Under the Law, each NUC constitutes a legal entity under civil law. As a legal entity it is able to sue other legal entities and can in turn be sued by others. It owns its own assets, which are called the capital of the corporation, consisting mainly of the buildings and lands that were contributed by the government at the time of incorporation. In principle, it is able to borrow funds, issue bonds, or invest in other entities, but the government maintains strict conditions and restrictions.

The relation between the government and each NUC, which is legally independent from the government, is mainly regulated by midterm (six-year) goals and the corresponding midterm plan, which functions as a contract between the two.

The law stipulates that the Ministry of Education must assign each NUC with midterm goals that specify what is to be achieved within the period of six-years to enhance the level of education and research, and improve efficiency in management of the institution. Based on these goals, the university must prepare a midterm plan to achieve the specified goals, which then must be approved by the government. Reflecting the criticism that this clause gives the government overwhelming power over the NUCs, both Houses passed resolutions that required the government to respect autonomy of NUCs. In practice, the Ministry of Education asked each NUC to draft its midterm goals, and then approved them without substantive changes.

Toward the end of the six-year period, the newly established Council for Evaluation of National University Corporations ("NUC Evaluation Council" hereafter) will evaluate the levels of achievement of the goals with the assistance of National Institute for Academic Degrees. The law states that, depending on the results of evaluation, the government will examine the needs for continuation of the institution and prescribe the necessary actions to be taken by the institutions. The last clause implies that the results may be related to government subsidy to the institution. The resolution of both Houses draws attention to the possibility that this mechanism may lead to an encroachment of academic freedom, and, therefore, request that the government act with caution. Further details in either the method of evaluation or the consequences of evaluation are not yet worked out.

In the old system, the finances of national universities were constituted as part of the government budget; they were classified into separate budget lines, and the expenditure had to be made for the designated purpose of each line. Tuition collected at the national universities was treated as revenue for the national treasury. On the expenditure side, the national universities had to follow the budget and various government regulations when spending the funds. Moreover, the number of personnel employed by universities was under the strict control of the government. However, necessary costs for operation of the university were in principle assumed to be borne by the government.

The *National University Corporation Law* stipulates that the NUCs are financially autonomous entities with their own budgets. After incorporation, the government subsidy was given to each university as a lump sum, without any division by line item. With this, the NUC was, in principle, given basic autonomy in the expenditure of the budget.

With the enactment of the *NUC Law*, the government contributed most of the facilities, lands, and buildings to the NUCs. The evaluated prices of those facilities constituted the capital fund of each NUC. In contrast with the old system in which the budget for a fiscal year had to be executed in the designated year and accounted for within the fiscal year, the NUCs were allowed to carry the balance to the next accounting period. Within a limit, each university is free to make investments: it can borrow money either from government or from commercial banks, and it can also issue a bond with the permission of the government.

At the same time, the *NUC Law* stipulates that the finances of NUCs will be accounted for according to the NUC Accounting Standards, which are similar to the accounting standards required for business corporations. In the old system the budget was divided in line items, and the accounting procedure simply implied executing the budget according to the budget without any infringement on governmental regulations. In the new system accounting takes the form of double-entry bookkeeping. Financial reports must include a Balance Sheet, Profit-Loss Statement, Cash Flow Statement, and other necessary statements.

One of the critical issues in this reform was the level of government contribution to the NUCs. While the law does not provide for specific mechanisms to determine the level of government contribution to the NUCs, the 2003 Report of the Expert Committee for Incorporation of National Universities outlined the basic principle. First, the necessary amount of total cost was calculated for individual areas of study employing a formula that involves such indices as the number of students, that of teachers, and other expenses and their corresponding unit-costs. From the required amount, the institution's own revenue is subtracted to derive the necessary amount of government subsidy. In other words, this method assumed the basic principle that the government had the responsibility to secure the necessary level of funding for each institution.

Evaluation and Incentives

The above discussion indicates that the backbone of the scheme of NUC lies in the cycle encompassing Goal-Evaluation-Reward. That is, the success of the scheme is critically dependent on the power of the evaluation methods as the key of the cycle.

The Independent Administration Agency Law stipulates that the government can take a range of actions, including discontinuation of the function of the institution after deliberation on the results of evaluation. This principle applies to NUCs.

The process involves a wide range of practical questions. The central issue is that the midterm goals, and accordingly the corresponding process of evaluation, have to cover the whole activity of a university. At the same time, the results of evaluation should be given a reasonable level of reliability. Since the results entail significant consequences for the NUCs, including budget allocation, a lack of reliability could lead to a number of problems affecting the credibility of the scheme as a whole and the collapse of the incentive system that the scheme was supposed to create.

The *NUC Law* stipulates that the evaluation of performance in achieving the midterm goal is undertaken by the NUC Evaluation Council under the minister of education, with technical assistances by the National Institute for University Evaluation and Academic Degrees (NIAD). The NUC Evaluation Council was established at the same time of incorporation, and started discussion on the detailed procedures for evaluation. Through this process, the council seems to have encountered a number of difficult issues.

Because the midterm goals encompass the whole area of university activities, and the government subsidy is given in a lump sum, evaluation exercise needs to cover the whole area of activities. That implies that the NIAD have to evaluate the level of research and education in every field of academic specialty, in addition to the various services activities and efficiency of institutional management. Moreover, it has to be completed for every NUC and at the end of the six-year term. This would be a formidable task.

Because of its pivotal role in the construct of NUC, the evaluation should be the most comprehensive and, probably one of the most ambitious, in the world. It is comprehensive in three ways.

First, it involves both the judgment on achieving the goals specified in the midterm plan on one hand, and evaluation of the absolute levels of education and research on the other. While the logical construct of incorporation requires only the judgment of whether the midterm goals have been achieved, it does not necessarily require judgment on the absolute levels of academic abilities. The government and NIAD argued, however, that to make judgment on goal-attainment, one needs the basis of evaluation on the levels.

Second, it requires both self-evaluation by the university and objective evaluation by NIAD. The Incorporation Law requires that the incorporated universities not be subject to arbitrary control by the Ministry of Education. In other words, the midterm goals are set as an agreement by both the Ministry of Education and individual universities. This principle applies to the evaluation procedure. Self-evaluation is also indispensable for practical reasons. Since the evaluation has to be undertaken for all of the 80 national university corporations at the same time, NIAD is not able to start gathering information by itself.

Third, its scope covers both education and research, at the institutional as well as the school level. While evaluation of research might be feasible if provided with enough time and resources, judgment on education might face serious difficulties. One may remember that in UK, where research assessment exercise has been undertaken for some time, assessment on education has not yet been fully implemented (Center for National University Finance and Management, 2007).

It is evident that such a comprehensive evaluation entails enormous costs. Another series issue is how the results will be linked to definition of the next midterm goals. This critical point is still unclear.

Probably the most significant aspect is the relation to government subsidy. While the *NUC Law* stipulates the framework of the NUCs and their relation with the government, it does not specify the financial obligation on the part of government to support the NUCs. As a result, there is a substantial range for alternatives in the level and methods for financial support of the government. That, however, will be a decisive factor for the nature of the NUC in significant aspects. There are three sets of important issues revealed in the process of implementation.

The original design laid out in the 2003 Report of the Expert Committee for Incorporation of National Universities assumed that the government would be responsible for securing the necessary level of revenues, calculated on a formula for each institution. In other words, the government would maintain the "Compensation Principle," implying that the government would fully compensate for the gap between the calculated cost and the income in each university. This principle had to undergo a series of significant alterations in the following periods.

In the fall of 2003, when the *NUC Law* was being prepared and the national universities started preparation for incorporation, the Ministry of Finance released its own plan for funding the NUCs. This plan did not follow the expert committee recommendations that proposed a set of the formula to derive the amount of government contribution to each institution. Instead, the Ministry of Finance indicated that each NUC would be given the amount that the institution received in the previous year irrespective of any change in the numbers of students and faculty members. A fixed rate of across-the-board reduction in government expenditures would apply to the allocated amount. In the case of NUCs, the rate would be 1 or 2 percent. The Ministry of Education, under the political climate of government restructuring had no other option but to oblige.

In the short run, this may not make much difference from the original design with respect to the amount of subsidy, but it implied a significant shift in the principle of government contribution—not only were any prospects for increasing the allocated budget closed, but also the compensation principle was abandoned.

Prior to the reform, each national university was given the budget separated into line items. Because the formula to calculate the allocated budget was known, it was clear how much each faculty received in the budget. Under this circumstance, the faculties had a strong basis for demanding allocation. However, the university administration was given very little room to maneuver.

Since NUCs receive their government subsidy in form of a lump sum, university administrators are given a considerable degree of discretion. In distributing the fund to faculties and other constituent units, most universities set the basis at the previous year and then deduce institutional fund by applying the same rate across-the-board. Through this measure, most institutions increased the resources at discretion of the institutional level. Some institutions introduced redistribution schemes to provide incentives related to achievements in research. These reforms appear to indicate that the management at the institutional level is increasing resources at their discretion.

Meanwhile, the disappearance of line items in the budget implies that each institution has to have sufficient ability in financial management to improve efficiency on the one hand and to avoid risks on the other. The Accounting Standards for National University Corporation was designated exactly for that purpose. For most of the administrative sections, however, it was difficult enough to introduce the new bookkeeping system. Moreover, the organization of universities is extremely complex, with numerous subunits overlapping—a nightmare for accurate accounting. It is, in a sense, a nightmare for cost accounting. Moreover, each unit has its own source of income through research funding.

Legal Status and Governance

By stipulation of the law, each national university corporation has a president, an executive board, an academic senate, a management council, and auditors. In this scheme, the president assumes the ultimate power and responsibility for decision making and execution, while important decisions have to go through deliberation of the executive board. The academic council, upon request by the president, deliberates on academic matters and reports to the executive council and the president. Meanwhile, the management council, more than half of the members of which should be selected from outside the university, gives advice to the president. The auditors are selected by the university, but appointed by the minister of education and report directly to the minister.

The president, who was elected by the academic senate in the old system, is now elected by the Committee for Selection of the president. The committee consists of the same numbers of representatives from the management council and the academic senate; the president and the members of the executive board may join as the member. The elected, in principle, is then appointed as president by the minister of education. The length of term and the exact procedure taken for election are decided by each university. The committee also has the power to relieve the president of his/her duties through a similar procedure to election.

The scheme of incorporation does not necessarily require a change in the status of the employees. However, the cabinet, which was politically committed to the restructuring plan of the government organizations, pushed forcefully for a change in employment status. Meanwhile, the resistance from the national universities failed to gain momentum. Consequently all the academic and administrative members of the NUCs changed their status from government employees to employees belonging to one of the NUCs. The pension and health-care funds, however, remain equivalent to that for government employees.

For each NUC, the first task for transition was to organize the basic governance structure. According to the *NUC Law*, each NUC set up their executive board, academic council, and management council.

The number of members of the executive board is stipulated by an ordinance issued by the government based on the size of the institution. Various surveys indicate that by far the majority of board members were recruited from the professoriate, most of them being former vice presidents and faculty deans. In many NUCs, mostly those of a larger size, the boards included a nonacademic, who is assigned to oversee managerial and financial matters. Many board members carry the title of vice president.

As stipulated by *NUC Law*, the academic board consists mainly of faculty members. In most universities, its size, while not stipulated by any ordinance, tends to be smaller than the former university council that it replaced. In most universities, the members are elected in faculty meetings. The new council retained the conventions and procedures of the old council.

The size of the management council is the subject in discussion in each NUC. In most cases they included executives from local business firms. It is also common to include a member from the local media. Some NUCs have appointed former government officials.

Associated with these changes is the transformation of the faculty administrative committees. Under the old system, various administrative committees were organized under the university council. These committees, consisting of only faculty members, were given the power and responsibility for execution of various functions, such as entrance examination, coordination of curriculums, academic calendars and distribution of scholarships. Under the new system, many of these committees were moved under the executive board and chaired by the assigned board member. Also, some administrative staff became members of these committees. This represents a shift from the old practices of participatory administration to a system where the executive council exerts stronger powers in decision making and execution.

Because of the strong power given to the president, its selection process bears not only symbolic but also practical significance to the governance of the NUC. While the *NUC Law* required that the president be selected by a president selection committee consisting of equal numbers of representatives from the academic and management councils, it does not stipulate the details of the procedure. Depending on the design of the procedure, it may well lead to a significant departure from the tradition of participatory governance.

As it turned out, most NUCs bypassed this problem by implanting the participation of faculty members in the new selection process. In most cases, the president selection committee decided to include a "reference ballot," in which individual faculty members cast a vote for their preferred candidate. The details of selection of the candidates and the specific rules for the reference ballot differed substantially by institution.

Closely associated with this is the procedure for dismissal of the president. The law stipulates that, in the extreme case of loss of confidence in the president, the committee can initiate the process of dismissal of the president. As described above, the president of an NUC is given broad-ranging power—he/she does not have any supervising body comparable to a board of governors or board of trustees. Even though the minister of education appoints the president upon request by the selection committee, it is unlikely that the minister would dismiss a president except for extreme cases of infringement of legal requirements.

Since the *NUC Law* leaves the details to the institutions, each individual institution established its own procedures. If, however, a significant number of the faculty members started demanding the dismissal of a president, the procedure may not able to provide a satisfactory solution. This issue boils down to the rather unusual design of governance of NUC in the sense that the president exerts a power in both decision making and execution, without any effective supervising body above him or her. This arrangement derives from that of the Independent Administrative Agency (IAA), which is meant to achieve gains in efficiency to achieve a goal set by the government.

This logic may be difficult to apply to higher education institutions that pursue a wide range of goals in the long run. Moreover, under the framework of midterm goals and evaluation, it is likely that if a president, who agreed on midterm goals upon appointment, leaves the position after the midterm period, they will not receive any punishment or rewards resulting from the evaluation of the achievements for that period. In this sense, the contract does not provide the correct incentive.

The third issue is the relation between the governance at the university level and that at the faculty level. While the *NUC Law* specifies the governance structure for the whole university, the relation between the university-level decision making and that at the faculty level is left to the discretion of individual universities.

Most of the NUCs left the arrangements basically unchanged. It is the faculty meeting, usually attended by all the academic members, that makes basic decisions at the faculty level. The dean of each faculty is elected among the professoriate. Under this construct, it is logically possible that a faculty makes a decision that contradicts that of the whole university. Moreover, the deans work as the representative from their faculty and not as members of university-level administration. In effect, almost all NUCs maintain a meeting of deans, which, while lacking clear status in formal organization, works as an important vehicle for managing the entire university.

Evaluation

It becomes evident from the above discussion that incorporation introduced a range of radical changes in the ways that the national universities operate. How was it received by the universities, and what are the problems? There are three major issues here.

Instruments for Evaluation and the Link to Rewards

The first issue is the effectiveness of the evaluation-reward scheme. The discussion above suggests that the whole construct of the incorporated university is critically dependent on the evaluation of the university achieving the goals specified at the beginning of the term. The first midterm period, which ended in March of 2010, and the second midterm goals and plans had to be specified before the end of the term. Therefore, the evaluation of the present cycle took place in fiscal year 2009.

It was shown already that the evaluation system is indeed very comprehensive and thorough. Through the evaluation exercise, a composite index was derived for each NUC. The composite index was then translated into the amount of reward/penalty through a formula, which was determined by the Ministry of Education.

As it turned out, the ministry chose not to make the amount of reward/penalty too large. A review of the Composite Index and Financial Reward/Penalty as a percent of the total subsidy indicates that Nara Institute of Science and Technology for example was given the composite index of 70.00, and an additional reward subsidy representing 0.419 percent of total government subsidy. However, Hirosaki University was given the lowest index, and as a penalty, their government subsidy was reduced by 0.417 percent.

On the whole then, the financial consequences of evaluation are relatively minor. The reward or penalty was at most about 0.5 percent or one-two-hundredth of the government subsidy. In absolute terms, the largest change for any university was about 20 million Yen, or about US$250,000. Moreover, for about half of the NUC, which ranked somewhere in between, the percentage was about 0.1 percent. The reward/penalty regime turned out to have no major consequences. Considering the enormous cost, direct and indirect, evaluation incurred at the individual university level and at the NIAD, the level of actual financial consequences was disproportionately small. One could argue that the efficiency of the evaluation exercise was very low.

Since the power to stipulate the method to derive the amount of reward/penalty is vested with the Ministry of Education, and the ministry does not reveal the rationale for the specific formula, it is difficult to analyze the reason behind this formula.

Regarding evaluation, there are several points to be made. First, even though the evaluation was undertaken using a very comprehensive and thorough system, one could argue that there are numerous points where the validity of evaluation can be challenged. However, if the financial consequences would have been too large the evaluation scheme itself might have faced a serious problem. In that case the integrity of the whole scheme might have collapsed.

Second, even though the composite index was derived as weighted sum of evaluation results in research, education, and other areas, the effective weights were different from the designated one. This difference came about because the effective weight is determined not only by the formal weight, but also by variances of the ratings at each area. If the variance is large, then the effective rate should be large. This is particularly important when one considers education relative to research. Since research is relatively easy to rate on a firm basis, the rating of research has a large variance. With education, the variance is small because of the lack of a definite basis for evaluation. Altogether, the composite index favors research, but it runs counter to the original purpose of the evaluation scheme.

The third point is a rather fundamental one. Even though the evaluation scheme is designated to measure the degree of improvement rather than the absolute level of achievement, the results show that, in general, the large and prestigious institutions are rated higher. One can argue that those institutions had been in a favorable position for some time due to their resource allocation whereas small local institutions are left with limited resources.

Managerial Effectiveness

The second issue concerns the improvement in effectiveness of institutional management. It was stated above that by introducing the Incorporation Law the governance structure would be drastically changed to enhance the power given to the top administrators, particularly the president and the board members.

In 2006, two years after incorporation, an opinion survey was conducted by the Center for National University Finance and Management to seek the opinions of the presidents of national university corporations regarding the consequences of incorporation. The results indicate that the presidents regarded incorporation as having positive effects on the whole. In fact, approximately 95 percent of the top officials reported that incorporation had positive effects in enhancing efficiency in management. Also, they found that it had positive effects on enhancing uniqueness of each institution, organizational vitality.

It should be noted, however, they are less sanguine as to the effects on the level of research or education. In fact, the actual effect of increased power given to the top administrators, in not clear. A survey by the Center for National University

Finance and Management showed that in general, the amount of budget reserved by the central administration increased substantially. It is not clear how much was spent for redistributing the money to shift the pattern of internal allocation of resources. From the annual reports of the NUCs, it is difficult to determine whether internal incentives were increased to enhance prioritized goals.

The lack of radical change in resource allocation is closely related to the location of power in the universities. Under the Incorporation Law the president is elected by the election committee composed of representatives of faculty members and lay members. The board of directors of Tohoku University, one of the seven former Imperial Universities, decided in early 2005 that the next president would be elected by the president selection committee itself, not allowing direct involvement of the faculty members. Still, most NUCs selected presidents through popular election by faculty members and sometimes included administrative staff.

This pattern reflects strong belief among faculty members that they should be involved in selecting the president. One can argue that in so far as the president is selected by faculty members, it will be difficult for the president to initiate changes that may run against the interests of faculty members.

Administrative Efficiency

In terms of administrative efficiency, it was expected that by removing strict government regulations, administration would become more efficient in various ways.

From this point of view, incorporation seems not only to have failed to produce the expected effects, but also resulted in rather negative consequences. A survey of administrators, conducted by the Center for National University Finance and Management in the spring of 2010, found that administrators are at best neutral in evaluation of the consequences on efficiency of administration and resource uses. More than half of the respondents disagreed with the statement that incorporation made administration more efficient. About half of the respondents did not consider that the scheme with specified goals and evaluation of achievement was functioning the way it was designed to. However, an overwhelming majority of the administrators agreed with the statement that workloads have increased after incorporation.

The process of organizational transformation accompanying incorporation was considerable, but, considering that the survey was conducted six years after incorporation, this response cannot be considered to reflect temporary problems. One might argue that the results indicate that, while new schemes for managerial control were introduced, various practices and regulations from the time before incorporation are still alive. Under these circumstances, administrators have to work with two principles at the same time.

As a consequence, the administrative works is heavily inclined toward fulfilling various types of regulations and administrative requirements. The same 2010 survey of university administrators, indicates that 42 percent of administrators in national institutions are assigned to "organizational and personnel management" compared to 26 percent in local public, and 24 percent in private institutions.

However, the proportion of those assigned to "academic affairs and student services" was only half of the corresponding figure for private institutions. It is apparent that incorporation has not succeeded in enhancing administrative support for education and research.

Conclusions

The NUC policy on Japanese universities was designed to follow the requirements of new public management. The implementation, however, was influenced by political factors and inertia at the institutional level. Contradiction and ambiguity there abounded.

One can attribute these problems to gaps between design and implementation. There may have been significant problems in the original design itself. In any case, the reform has not yet achieved what it was originally expected to do.

Moreover, the current movement toward radical restructuring of government organization and reduction of government outlays has started to threaten the basis on which the original NUC design was built. If it continues in that direction, the NUC scheme may lose its original characteristics.

Despite these problems, I argue that incorporation should not be considered a failure. In various ways the changes were necessary, even though the design of the change was premature in its commitment to certain versions of the doctrine of the "new public management."

The issue lies now in how the scheme of incorporation can be linked to academic and administrative behavior so as to bring about higher efficiency in education, research, and other activities. The mechanism by which this link might be established is more complex and difficult to achieve than earlier assumed.

References

Center for National University Finance and Management. 2007. *Kokuritu Daigaku Hojin no Zaimu Keiei ni Kansuru Jittaichosa* [*Report of the Survey on Finance and Management of National University Corporations*]. Tokyo, Japan: Center for National University Finance and Management.

Kaneko, Motohisa. 2004. "Japan's Higher Education: The Past, Its Legacies and the Future." In *Past and Future of Asian Higher Education*, ed. Philip G. Altbach and Toru Umakoshi. Baltimore, MD: Johns Hopkins Press.

Kaneko, Motohisa. 2009. "Incorporation of National Universities in Japan: Design, Implementation and Consequences." *Asia Pacific Education Review* 10 (1): 59–67.

Chapter 13

Current Challenges Facing Japanese Universities and Future Perspectives

Masao Homma

Background

Over the past 30 years I have served in the Japanese Ministry of Education, Culture, Sports, Science and Technology (MEXT), ending with an assignment as director general for policy coordination and educational reform. In 2001, I was appointed registrar of Kyoto University. After the corporatization of national universities in 2004, I became vice president in charge of administration, personnel, external relations, and the alumni organization. Kyoto University is one of the oldest imperial universities and recognized as a cradle for original and creative research, with six Nobel Prize laureates in Physics, Chemistry and Medical Science.

During my time at Kyoto University (January 2001-March 2006), I acted to create a new 40-hectare campus with a graduate school of engineering in a western suburb of Kyoto City. I negotiated with industrial corporations such as ROHM, a semiconductor manufacturing company, and FUNAI, an electric appliances company, eventually succeeding in convincing them of the merit of donating buildings and facilities for joint research with industries and international conferences.[1]

Corporatization was expected to provide national universities with more freedom in allocating resources, among them the annual government subsidy. At the same time, faculty and administrative staff were deprived of civil servant status and treated as employees in private companies. National universities were to manage their own affairs and account for spending on teaching, research, and service to society. Taking advantage of this newly acquired freedom, I devised and implemented, after consulting with several "think tanks," a wholesale reform plan for obsolete administrative structures and for an inefficient personnel system.

On leaving Kyoto University, I worked for the National Institute for Academic Degrees and University Evaluation as professor/director in charge of international relations until March 2007. I then served as vice-chancellor of Ritsumeikan University, responsible for new strategy and internationalization till 2010, when I became vice president of the Ritsumeikan Asia Pacific University (APU) responsible for administration and finance.[2]

Ten years from inception, APU has grown today into a university with 6,300 students. Of these, 46 percent are international students from approximately ninety-eight countries representing all five continents. Nearly half of the faculty are internationally trained and recruited from across the world. Those admitted with an English-language background receive an intensive Japanese-language training course for the first two years and then attend Japanese taught courses. Those admitted with proficiency in Japanese do the reverse. About 40 percent of the international students seek to work in Japanese companies after graduation, and the job success rate has been nearly 100 percent. During the first year, international students live together in a university dormitory, often with Japanese colleagues. They work together in a wide variety of cultural and sports events, and in social service activities. The majority have succeeded in nurturing communication skills and leadership quality as well as understanding of diverse cultures, religions, traditions, and history.

This chapter relies largely on my experience as senior management officer of both national and private universities in the past 14 years.

Major Challenges Facing Japanese Universities

Shrinking Higher Education Market: A Stiffer Competition for Students

Japan's higher education market peaked in 1991 when about 2 million youth of the "baby boom" generation became 18 years old. Today, it has shrunk to about 1.2 million. Even so, mostly because of the government's deregulation of university accreditation, some 250 new universities have come into being, bringing the total number of universities to 778. Access rates have continued to rise, reaching an all-time high of 56.8 percent in 2010, although the number of new entrants remained static at about 600,000. Unlike other OECD countries where mature students, those over 25 year of age, account for 26 percent on average, the figure for Japan is a mere 2.7 percent. However, foreign students account for 3 percent of the total student body. Thus mature students and foreign students do not compensate for the absence of young Japanese students.

Thus, the competition for new entrants, a major source of income for private universities, has become more intense. Private universities enroll about 80 percent of total students, while national and local government universities 16 percent and 4 percent respectively. The Promotion and Mutual Aid Corporation for Private Schools of Japan claims that about 40 percent of private universities do not fulfill their statutory quota of admission places. These institutions therefore face a future of repeated financial crisis and eventually bankruptcy.

Diversification of Students

As a result of a sharp increase in the number of universities and a rise in the access ratio during the past two decades, the proportion of students admitted through noncompetitive procedures, which might be based on a recommendation letter from high school or on nonacademic achievements, such as volunteer activities or good sport performances, has exceeded the government's restriction of keeping it at 50 percent of applicants in substantial terms.

A decline in academic competence and in motivation to study is an inevitable result of de facto free admission in an increasing number of faculties and universities. This imposes a great burden on university learning and teaching. Moreover, in an affluent and mature society, such as Japan, a powerful ethic to study hard, get a good university credential, join a well-known company, work hard, and succeed in professional life, once dominant among young people, is lost for most of today's youth.

To make university learning more effective, many universities are introducing supplementary measures such as first year, or even pre-entrance, supplementary, or "remedial" courses and lessons in academic writing, foreign languages, or mathematics. More and more universities are employing retired high school teachers to help those students with difficulties in adapting to university study.

Despite these measures, the dropout rate has continued to rise in recent years to an average of 12 percent. A considerable number of dropouts are citing difficulties in catching up with academic courses and a lack of sense of belonging in university as reasons for not continuing. In any case, such a high rate of dropout suggests failure as an educational institution, and a loss of important financial resources. In Japan, 80 percent of operating costs of private universities derives from student tuition fees.

Bankruptcy of Universities: Reality or Nightmare?

Government forecast of the number of 18-year-olds in 2030 is one-third less than the current cohort of 900,000. This demographic change will necessarily affect universities, particularly their finance. As mentioned earlier, currently about 40 percent of private universities fail to reach the government-authorized number of places for new entrants. Changing demographics have ramifications particularly for private universities. If the prediction holds, as many as 100 out of a total of 590 private universities could experience financial difficulties resulting from a lack of students, and eventually going bankrupt, even though only a small number of universities (four or five) have so far closed or merged with another university. Government is preparing an emergency "rescue" plan for students of bankrupt universities, moving them to neighboring universities.

The government proposes 10 percent annual cuts in subsidies to national and private universities over the next three years beginning with fiscal year 2011 budget. Although these proposed cuts were withdrawn in the face of vehement opposition from university presidents and Nobel Prize laureates, fearful of damaging already poverty-stricken universities, it seems inevitable that cuts will take place sooner or later, especially in light of high government debt.

If the cuts become a reality, they will have substantial negative effects on all universities, but the effects will be unevenly distributed between national, other public universities, and private ones. National universities are much more dependent on government money than private institutions, with 50 percent of operating costs coming from the national treasury. Private universities, however, only receive 10 percent of operating costs from the public purse.

The cuts are likely to be devastating for national universities, particularly small- and medium-sized local universities where there is little room for further cuts or economization of costs in teaching and research activities, or for seeking donations from local industries. Further, alumni organizations are very weak in Japan, with a few exceptions. In private universities increased tuition fees are not a viable option when they are competing for students.

Effective and Efficient Management and Increased Accountability

In any case, universities, whether national or private, cannot afford largely inefficient and ineffective management led by amateur faculty members. *Selection and concentration of resources* should be introduced if they are to survive. Cuts in staff costs, maintenance costs of buildings and facilities, renewal costs for equipment and computers, and even closures of some departments and affiliated primary and secondary schools might have to be considered.

While subsidies to universities have been shrinking, demands for more accountability for the money spent have intensified in the past 20 years. University performance in education, research, and contribution to society and industry is now open to public scrutiny and skepticism. Industry, once indifferent to universities, has begun to take an active interest in them. The transfer of knowledge from university to industry, and the content and quality of teaching, particularly in undergraduate programs in humanities and social sciences, are at the forefront of their inquiries. Universities are asked to provide clear evidence that university graduates are equipped with competencies and abilities necessary to survive in a globalized world of work.

The Ministry of Economy, Trade and Industry (METI), voicing their concerns about the quality of university graduates, has proposed since 2006 that the university nurture "Basic Social Skills and Competencies" as an essential mission. The Ministry of Education followed suit, proposing "Basic Skills and Competencies as Bachelor." These skills and competencies consist largely of problem-setting capabilities, independent and critical thinking, logical reasoning, communication skills, leadership, and teamwork quality besides skills and knowledge in their specialized field of study.

Recent statistics suggest that the average *weekly* reading and studying time of a university student in humanities and social science subjects is less than one hour. Aiming to improve university education, the government has introduced a wide variety of policy measures beginning in the 1990s, such as faculty development, special subsidies for good practice in education, promotion of syllabus, and course evaluation by students. As a person familiar with teaching and learning, I suggest that these efforts have produced only limited results. For unless and until university teachers are convinced of the importance of their ultimate mission, developing competent graduates, those measures are doomed to failure.

Moreover, university evaluation, first introduced as self-evaluation and as an "encouragement" measure in the 1990s, but not compulsory until 2004, when it became the responsibility of a third party for implementation, has had only limited impact on education. There are always ways for universities to circumvent the process. In the end, university evaluation has led to more bureaucratic work and no substantial improvement in the quality of teaching.

Internationalization of Universities: A False Dream?

Furthermore, government and industry are not satisfied with the amount or the speed of the *internationalization* of university education. There is a perception that university graduates, even from well-known universities, lack communication skills in foreign languages, understanding of foreign cultures and religions, and more importantly overseas experience. The government introduced a *Global 30* program in 2009 and initially selected thirteen universities, seven national and six private,[3] as a potential basis for internationalization. These universities are expected to start at least two entirely English-taught courses, one undergraduate and one graduate, and are committed to accept at least 3,000 foreign students by 2020. The goal set by the government is to triple the number of foreign students from the current level of 120,000 to 300,000 by the year 2020. However, the new government, led by the Democratic Party which came to power in autumn 2009, cut the budget for the *Global 30* program by about half claiming that internationalization of universities is their inherent mission and, as such, something that has to be realized without additional government funding.

University faculty, even those of *Global 30* universities, are not enthusiastic, if not hostile to, about internationalization. For example, at Ritsumeikan, there were heated discussions as to whether the institution should apply for the *Global 30* program in the first place. Financial support from the government, to last for only five years, is far below the actual costs needed for foreign students, considering the cost of constructing dormitories, providing scholarships, and employing English-speaking academic and nonacademic staff. More importantly, the faculty fear that the arrival of significant numbers of foreign students might affect the traditional one-way teaching style. Presently, at Ritsumeikan there are just 1,500 foreign students, or approximately 4 percent of the total student population; once that figure reaches the target of 4,000 foreign students or 11 percent of the student body, universities will no longer be able to ignore them.

Yet, Ritsumeikan is doing well in the sense that it eventually agreed to apply for *Global 30*. Whether it is or is not selected for the program, it decided to go on with its original plan for enhancing international programs, inbound and outbound. A certain number of national universities were half-hearted and even skeptical about applying for *Global 30,* since they worried that once government money stops, so would programs—or internationalization itself.

How Japanese Universities React to Challenge

Management by Academics: Amateurism Doomed to Failure

One of the main challenges facing universities in Japan today is the efficient and effective management. Modern universities can no longer afford to be an "Ivory Tower" or an "Intellectual Community" where distinguished scholars reign but neither govern nor manage. Rather they have become more and more complex entities with multidimensional problems and challenges just as more accountability is expected of them.

Yet universities in Japan have long been and are still managed by academics with little or no professional training in administration and management. University presidents and vice presidents lack basic knowledge of what modern universities should do in a rapidly changing world, particularly when these leaders come from the scientific faculties. Successful business leaders or experienced government administrators are rarely brought in to assume university leadership or take up the posts of finance or personnel directors, and in a limited number of such cases, success is an exception. It is a common complaint that academic management is "*Gakushi* (Bachelor)'s business"—a play on words and reference to Meiji Period's "Samurai (*Bushi*)'s business."[4]

The result is in inefficient and ineffective university management. The situation is, generally speaking, worse in national universities where, even after corporatization, a sense of "crisis" is still lacking among academic and non-academic staffs. There are only half-hearted efforts to adopt efficient management practice, as taxpayers' money flows in abundance regardless of actual performance in teaching, research, and management: it is true that an evaluation by an independent committee is implemented every six years on each university's achievements in light of its self-set plan, but the difference between the "best performing" university and the "worst" one is a mere 600,000 yen (US$70,000) in government subsidy at first six-year midterm plan (2004–2009); many people say it is a kind of a nightmare joke (see chapter 12). Apart from the fact that half of the annual revenue of national universities is subsidy from the government, most of the important senior management posts are filled by ex-officials of the MEXT, which gives national universities a sure sense of security, thus leading to the lack of a sense of crisis.

University management staffs recruited from among faculty members generally lack skills, knowledge, and experience necessary for managing effectively and efficiently. Worse, they lack the will to become professional managers, since they see their jobs as part-time tasks, not their prime concern, a temporary and forced deviation from what they perceive to be their real vocation.

They try to retain their obligation (or privilege) of supervising graduate students or teaching undergraduates even after appointments as vice president or governing board member. Teaching and research are, in their view, the only way to prove they remain academics.[5]

Between 2006 and 2009, I was a part-time member of the governing board of a well-established engineering university in Tokyo. The chairman and two members of the governing board, responsible respectively for personnel and administration, and for finance, were all professors of the university. I once asked them why they, trained as engineers and scientists, had to shoulder such cumbersome administrative responsibilities and their answer was that "there could be no other way." When I suggested to them, "Yes there is another way. That is to appoint well-qualified and experienced administrative staffs as governing board members. There are a few such administrators ready and willing to do your jobs," they became silent. I took the silence as their disagreement, if not distrust, of this suggestion, and perhaps a feeling of uneasiness about administrative staff managing a university.

Ascent of Administrators to Decision-Making Positions

Historically, administrative staff were regarded as incompetent, third-class citizens of the university community who may be good at routine work, but lack the professional knowledge and skills necessary for managing an increasingly complex university. Administrative staff have never been expected to have a say in academic affairs, since administration was seen as belonging exclusively to faculty. In sum, university administration has been long regarded as a boring, nonprofessional job.

But the situation is changing rapidly. The university finds itself faced with developing a "branding" strategy, risk management, organization and retention of alumni, fund-raising, information security, application of ICT to education, promotion of intellectual property rights, university evaluation and accreditation, institutional research, midterm and long-term planning, on-site hospital management, faculty and staff development, diversification of student selection procedures, curriculum reform, and the list goes on. University management and academic affairs both have to rely on the professional skill and experience of administrative staff.

Universities are adopting three approaches: recruiting and training of capable administrative staffs; headhunting professionals from outside, among them industries, banks, central- and local-administrations, and professional organizations; and to lesser degree, training academics as professional managers.

As the difficulty of a university administrator's work becomes known, more competent and motivated people are applying. After corporatization, about one-third of new recruits at Tokyo and Kyoto universities were their own graduates, unthinkable before 2004. These universities attracted 20–30 qualified university graduates for each administrative post under the new dispensation.

As for staff development, universities have invested more resources in training administrators. Many universities have introduced full scholarship schemes to send promising young administrators to good management and business schools in Japan and even abroad. An increasing number of ambitious administrators study at part-time graduate courses of management with or without assistance from their universities.

The Japanese University Administrators Association (JUAM) was founded in 1998 to promote staff development, while Association for Innovative University Management (AIUM) started its activities in 2005 to promote innovations and reforms in management and university teachings.[6] The two associations have altogether about 2,000 university administrators as members. The Japanese Management Association (JMA), with a long history in training business managers at various levels, runs training courses for university staff.

Graduate courses intended for university administrators have been set up by universities such as Oberlin, Tokyo, Nagoya, and Meiji. Ritsumeikan

Education Trust developed a one-year part-time training program for administrators in 2005. The program consisted of graduate-level courses on statistics and social research methods, 30 lectures on higher education policy, analysis of competing universities' strategies and various aspects of Ritsumeikan University management, and analysis and writing a thesis to propose realistic solutions to the perennial problem of their office. They visit universities both in Japan and in the UK and the United States as a part of program, looking for new ideas.

Limitations Inherent to Academics

Managers drawn from academic ranks give priority in decision making to the faculty's vested interests over those of students or taxpayers or the society at large. When faced with restructuring educational programs and courses in response to changing social and industrial needs or academic developments, they resist. Restructuring often means downsizing of existing courses, or even elimination of courses or closure of departments. Faculty naturally dislike this kind of restructuring, although they may understand the need for it. For academics, teaching posts are their raison d'etre and protecting them is their unquestionable mission. Analogously, they oppose reforms that require faculty to adapt to globalization, whether accepting more foreign students and faculty and more courses taught in English, or to show better performance in student learning.

When management is faced with vehement faculty opposition, their usual response is to "postpone" decision. They cannot close their eyes to the reality, nor can they pretend that the problem did not exist in the first place, nor convince themselves that the problem is so innocuous as to require no action. Yet appropriate decisions, however unpopular, must occasionally be made for the sake of the institution.

Medical education programs in Japan have not undergone any major changes over the past one hundred years, even though there have been numerous important scientific discoveries in medical science over the past 50 years, and the need to introduce ethical education in medical training programs has long been emphasized. Overall review and subsequent restructuring of medical education programs seem inevitable. But any attempt to change the basic structure of the programs has met resistance and sabotage from faculty members, afraid of a possible decrease or cancellation of courses they teach, with later cancellation of their teaching posts.

The chairman of a committee for new medical education curriculum, appointed by the Japan Medical Education Society, has had to demand at the outset of committee deliberations that members put aside loyalty to their discipline and place the interests of the mission of medical science, which is to serve the patients and contribute to the best interests of the society, over their professional parochial interests.

This is the sort of problem that the government is faced with every time it reviews the contents and overall composition of the national curriculum in schools so as to make them relevant to social needs. Since teaching hours are fixed at 40 hours per week, new courses or programs can only be introduced at the expenses of existing ones. For example, to introduce additional classes in physical education or music, other classes must be cut. The teachers of the courses likely to be cut will lodge very strong arguments against such cuts. If the government succumbs to these pressures and allows the resistance to win, the nation as a whole will suffer.

The provost or vice president in charge of academic affairs are supposed to see to it that education programs meet the needs of society and industry, but have no power to compel the faculty to review and finally to change the curriculum. Deans or vice deans responsible for curriculum, for their part, are not interested in, or even not aware of the need of systematic and regular curriculum review. In any case, they are only appointed for a limited period of two to three years and only on the part-time basis.

The key is the development of stronger leadership supported by more experienced and well-trained management staff equipped with solid data and facts. Introduction of a strategic plan and a Plan, Do, Check, Act (PDCA) cycle for institutions of higher education, combined with research and publication of changes in universities to the outside world, will aid in enacting policies and procedures for effective higher education in a time of rapid change.

Some Suggestions for More Viable and Competitive Higher Education System

To make Japanese universities more viable and internationally competitive, bold government policies and changed university practice are necessary.

In view of huge government debts, it is unthinkable to increase public investment in higher education in the foreseeable future. Instead the vital question is how to allocate government's limited funds in a more efficient and effective manner. In my view, it is vital to realign the present resource allocation scheme.

First, the size of the system—number of universities, students, teachers, and eventually budget—should be proportionate to the population of 18-year-olds. This implies a 40 percent reduction. The seven Imperial Universities (*Teidai*) including Tokyo and Kyoto could be converted into research-intensive universities by dramatically downsizing or abolishing outright undergraduate courses. New departments and graduate schools would be "international," "comprehensive," "human," "cultural," or "local." Potentially redundant teachers could find a suitable post in a newly created department or school, defined and named in an inclusive manner. The "Liberal Arts College" found in most universities comprises scholars in almost all the major disciplines by definition and its reorganization would be welcome to its faculty. The same applies to reorganization of teacher training colleges, which find teaching posts for only one-third of their graduates. These too should be reorganized into interdisciplinary courses. Moreover, some national universities such as Kyoto Institute of Technology, created in 1899 to cater to local traditional industry's needs in crafting, textiles, silk yarning, ceramics, and dyeing—and Hitotsubashi University, specialized in social sciences—have lost their raison d'être as national universities, as their mission to provide equal access to higher education can be satisfied by private universities.

Second, restrict MEXT officials from accepting public, national university posts as managers. Only if and when they pledge loyalty to the university concerned, and demonstrate their will and capability to plan and implement reform, should they be allowed to assume managerial posts. So far, their loyalty has been to the MEXT. MEXT officials are, generally speaking, capable with wide perspectives. The difficulty is that they lack a will to make structural changes in university management.

Third, bring in professionals at senior levels to improve management and university teaching, whether from government or from industry. A best mix of university academic and nonacademic staffs and outside professionals will be a key to efficient and effective management of university.

Fourth, establish an office for "institutional research" so that any plan to improve management and teaching is based on hard evidence. Universities will not change unless challenges and problems facing the university are shown in visible form. Any reform plan will fail if the debate goes "philosophical."

Finally, and most generally, strengthen the capabilities and qualifications of university administrators.

Japanese universities will not change and adapt themselves to changing social and industrial needs unless politicians and the wider public become aware of the problems surrounding universities. Conditions for a better and more efficient university system are not easily created, and the prospect of reform is remote.

Notes

1. Before my arrival at Kyoto University, there was strong anti-industry sentiment among faculty. That sentiment was in some degree overcome after the university witnessed a successful example of industry-academia cooperation. Kyoto University's efforts to attract donations from companies and founders of

venture business continue and have produced impressive results. For example, the former Chairman of NINTENDO, Yamanouchi, donated a large university hospital ward worth US$100 million, while Inamori, a retired chairman of Kyocera, donated a beautiful building along the Kamogawa River to house *A Center for the Future of Human Minds*.
2. APU is a unique university in the sense that it is a joint venture of the Ritsumeikan Trust, a private institution, local governments of Oita Prefecture and Beppu City, and a group of Japan's top private companies, all of which were keenly aware of the urgent need for creating a truly internationalized university in Japan. The prefectural and city governments contributed altogether more than US$250 million to found the APU and provided land for the campus and connecting roads between it and the city. Such well-known companies as Panasonic, SONY, and Tokyo Mitsubishi UFJ Bank, committed US$50 million for scholarship for international students.
3. The 13 universities are Tohoku, Tsukuba, Tokyo, Nagoya, Kyoto, Osaka, Kyushu (national), Waseda, Keio, Sophia, Meiji, Doshisha, and Ritsumeikan (private).
4. After the Meiji Revolution in 1868, the Samurai clan, having lost their privileges and revenues, often started various businesses. These mostly failed because the owners spent excessive amounts of time and energy on clan politics but paid little attention to matters of business.
5. An example is a former vice president of a prestigious national university, who kept two secretaries to look after his research links even after he was appointed vice president responsible for finance and research. After he was selected president of the university, he in turn appointed a famous anatomist as vice president responsible for finance and then for administration. He is a fine scholar, but has demonstrated little capability as a financial manager or as a tough negotiator with trade union leaders.
6. The author is the founder, president, and editor-in-chief of a monthly magazine entitled *The University and College Management*.

Chapter 14

Intellectuals, Academic Freedom, and University Autonomy in China

Qiang Zha

Introduction

This year marks the centennial anniversary of the Revolution of 1911. Also known as the Xinhai Revolution, it overthrew the last imperial dynasty in China, established a republic, and promoted democracy. However, even with the passing of one hundred years, academic freedom and university autonomy are still viewed as problematic in China, when benchmarked against Western norms and values. To a large extent, Chinese universities remain the state's educational and research arm for national development. Compared to their Western counterparts, Chinese universities appear to be more responsive to national and local development needs, embracing a close articulation between institutional strategic planning and national and local development plans. In fact, the majority of Chinese scholars appear to be content with—and even actively and deliberately seek—a high level of articulation between their academic pursuits and the national interest, rather than seeking to be independent and functioning as a critical voice in national or global affairs.

Many attribute this to what might be described as "politicized" university governance, with leadership mainly resting in the hands of the (Communist Party of China's) Party Committee on the campus, strong government intervention into university affairs, and the consequent emphasis put on administrative power on the campus. Nevertheless, this very kind of scenario was observed in the former Soviet Union, if not even more so, yet a tradition of public intellectuals also took shape there.[1] Some associate the Chinese situation with an overemphasis on collectivism in Chinese society. Indeed traditional Chinese culture features autocracy and hierarchy, emphasizing collectivism over individualism, and putting the group or national interest above that of the individual. Most recently, when an academic integrity crisis emerged with academic misconduct becoming prevalent among Chinese scholars, the government has promulgated a series of policies aiming to clean up academic corruption on university campuses (Ministry of Education 2002, 2006, 2009). To a large extent, the government plays the role of a watchdog for the academic integrity of scholars and universities, unlike in the West, where this role is commonly assumed by academic peers. So, what might be typically termed as "governmental interference" into academic affairs in the Western context appears to be necessary in the Chinese academic context. All in all, when discussing academic freedom and university autonomy, it is quite a different scenario in China.

In this chapter, I describe the status quo of university autonomy and academic freedom in China, and employ the concept of knowledge traditions as the analytical framework to discuss, comparatively, the possible differences in the norms and values relating to academic freedom and university autonomy between China and the West, with particular attention to the role played by the intellectuals in the different contexts. I attempt to answer the question of whether or not it is practicable to adapt the Western norms and values of academic freedom and university autonomy to the Chinese university. This has become a controversial issue in China's academic circles and more widely. The issue is intertwined with the increasingly hot debate on the Beijing Consensus[2] as an alternative model for development.

The Status Quo of Academic Freedom and University Autonomy in China

State control over higher education seems always to have had a place in China, but now it appears under the guise of something that we might identify as academic centralization or nationalization. The state promotes decentralization of steering and management in exchange for institutional performance and accountability on the one hand, and tightens its control over normative criteria for knowledge production on the other. State control, which used to reside mainly in the organizational process, has penetrated the knowledge production process, which is now often driven by a kind of state willpower or managerialism and follows a technical rationale. Put explicitly, knowledge production no longer arises from scholars' individual interest, but has become an integral part of national efforts to fulfill the century-long dream of China's resurgence. Individual scholars who excel in terms of producing valuable and useful knowledge for national development may enjoy a high level of intellectual authority. This type of intellectual authority is clearly not the same as academic freedom in the Western context, but in some ways it provides even more flexibility and greater power than does academic freedom. For instance, the three renowned scientists who shared the same surname "Qian," namely, Qian Xueshen (known in the West as Hsue-Shen Tsien, a physicist and the father of China's space programs), Qian Weichang (or Chien Wei-zang, a physicist and an applied mathematician), and Qian Sanqiang (a nuclear physicist), guided the country's science and technology development priorities and strategies for many years. There are such roles at all levels in Chinese academia and in society at large. More recently, Qian Xuesen captured people's attention around the country with his influential question, "Why have Chinese universities all failed to engender great minds?" His question is echoed in heated discussion and debates throughout the country, something that would be barely imaginable elsewhere. Ironically, shortly before his death, an intellectual who enjoyed almost unparalleled intellectual authority challenged the very academic and knowledge patterns that had granted him this privilege on the grounds that they stifled creativity and individuality.

Nevertheless, this privilege is only granted to a select and "successful" few, and can be removed if they turn against the state. Admittedly, a reciprocal relationship characterizes knowledge-power nexus in many societies. Hans Weiler (2001, 34) depicted a symbiotic relationship between knowledge and power:

> Power legitimates both knowledge and the existing modes of knowledge production while, on the other hand, knowledge is used to legitimate existing arrangements for the exercise of power... The former part in this mutual relationship—the role of political authority in legitimating knowledge—is amply illustrated by the role of the state in sanctioning what does and does not constitute proper knowledge... On the other side of this mutual relationship, knowledge has to be seen as a critical source of legitimacy for the modern state and its often precarious authority.

If this mutual relationship can be perceived as a spectrum, the Chinese scenario leans toward the extreme that power legitimates knowledge—indeed Confucianism itself became the dominant ideology in traditional Chinese society because of state promotion during the Han dynasty—while the Western scenario tilts toward the extreme that knowledge legitimates power. This difference has to do with the contrasting knowledge traditions in Chinese and Western societies. The Chinese knowledge tradition emphasizes learning through observation and experience, while the Western knowledge tradition (exemplified by the Platonic emphasis on logical conception) asserts that knowledge is only created through a sophisticated process of rational deduction and theoretical understanding. This contrast in knowledge views between China and the West will be illustrated further in the following section.

No matter what view of knowledge prevails, academic freedom should be at the very core of the mission of the university. It is essential to knowledge advancement, and best facilitates creativity and innovation. Many would argue that a fully developed higher education system cannot exist without academic freedom. If academic freedom means the free pursuit of teaching and research, as well as decision making based on solely academic criteria, the intrusion of political or other factors into decision making is a concern. Nevertheless, there does not yet seem to be a consensus on this, and as a result there is considerable debate about the appropriate limits to academic freedom. Many have argued that the freedom conferred on academics creates a reciprocal responsibility, which connects the idea of academic freedom to the view of knowledge held by the intellectual. Against this backdrop, the discussion concerning Chinese intellectuals and their academic freedom in this chapter appears to be particularly significant. I argue that the problems with regard to academic freedom and university autonomy in China are profoundly connected to the Chinese knowledge tradition. In addition, the solution may also lie with revitalizing the progressive aspects of the knowledge tradition, and connecting them to the contemporary norms and values.

The Chinese Knowledge Tradition in Comparison with Western Norms and Values

Regarding the paradigm for understanding knowledge creation, Egon Guba (1990, cited in Zeera, 2001, 56) raised three fundamental questions that serve to characterize the paradigms: (1) ontological ("what is the nature of the 'reality'?"), (2) epistemological ("what is the nature of the relationship between the knower and the known?"), and (3) methodological ("how should the inquirer go about finding out knowledge?"). If we use these three questions as a framework to understand knowledge and knowledge production, the Chinese knowledge tradition appears to be very different from that in the West. Certainly, the use of "different" here is in the sense of ideal types, a research method widely employed in comparative education studies, which Max Weber (cited in Hayhoe 2008, 23) defined as "an attempt to analyze historically unique configurations...by means of generic concepts."

By this token, we may compare the different views on knowledge creation or acquisition between Confucius and Plato, two philosophers whose ideas had a long-lasting influence on the development of education norms and values in the societies of the East and the West respectively. Confucius viewed knowledge as starting with "the empirical cumulative understanding of masses of particulars, then linking these particulars to one's own experience, and subsequently to an underlying unity that tied everything together" (Hayhoe 2008, 26). For Confucius, knowledge "remains indissolubly linked to the empirical world" (Schwartz 1985, 95). He maintained that the "Dao (the Way) is not far from man. When a man pursues the Dao and remains away from man, his course cannot be considered the Dao"[3] (cited in Yu 2006, 2). Ying-shih Yu (2006, 2) thus concluded that the "Chinese transcendental world of Dao and the actual world of everyday life were conceived from the very beginning to be related to each other in a way different from other ancient cultures undergoing the Axial breakthrough."

By contrast, Plato saw knowledge as created through dialectical reasoning in the form of questioning/answering and exchanging arguments, and through the perception that requires a rigorous process of deductive logic. For Plato, knowledge rises above the capacity of ordinary human experience, something only reachable for those with the potential to become "Philosopher Kings" (Plato's *The Republic*).

The Confucian tradition then prompted Chinese scholars, first and foremost, to realize their ideals through action and take on a kind of direct responsibility for managing the state. *Great Learning*, one of the Confucian classical texts on higher learning, spelled out an ideal path for Confucian scholars along the following lines:

> Things being investigated, knowledge became complete. Their knowledge being complete, their thoughts were sincere. Their thoughts being sincere, their hearts were then rectified. Their hearts being rectified, their persons were cultivated. Their persons being cultivated, their families were regulated. Their families being regulated, their states were rightly governed. Their states being rightly governed, the whole kingdom was made tranquil and happy.

Thus knowledge was less a matter of understanding the world than of changing it and "a scholar, having completed his learning, should apply himself to be an official" (Confucius, *Analects*, 19:13). This notion appears to be similar to Plato's assertion that the country should be ruled by wise and learned "Philosopher Kings," yet differs in terms of epistemology and methodology or pedagogy. For Plato, education serves to select those who are capable of philosophizing, and is designed to strengthen the character of those who are capable. By contrast, the "concept that everyone is educable, everyone can become a sage, and everyone is perfectible" forms the fundamental dynamism in the Confucian knowledge and education tradition (Lee 1996, 30).

Stressing simultaneously "a person's internal establishment" and "the ideal of external manifestation" (Lee 1996, 37), this tradition was best explained by the Confucian canons of knowledge and the civil examination system, which selected intellectuals to serve as scholar-officials. Put explicitly, the Confucian scholars were expected to combine the roles of acquiring knowledge, cultivating morality, and managing the state. They sought a unity of knowledge and action through their roles as scholar-officials. Rather than seeing themselves as independent social critics, they saw their role as practicing and ensuring benevolent governance. Tu Weiming (2005, 220) observed:

> Confucian followers were primarily action intellectuals, deeply immersed in "managing the world" of economics, politics, and society. Their strategy was to transform the world... through culture, specifically through moral

education. Confucian scholar-officials were perceived of as the conscience of the people, for they served the long-term well-being of the entire country.

Notably, a healthy unity of knowledge and action requires strong backing in the intrinsic "sagehood" of the Confucian knowledge tradition, that is, the Confucian morality, set against the extrinsic distractions of fame, wealth, and rank. As Mencius put it, an ideal Confucian intellectual must abide by the rule that "no money or rank can make dissipated, no poverty or hardship can make shaken, and no power or force can make bend" (Mencius, *Mencius,* IIIB). While there were inevitably cases of corruption and a resultant cynicism, this scholar-official role didn't necessarily constrain the Confucian intellectuals in terms of their morality and capacity for independent thinking. More often, they were seen as upholding social justice and morality with their "iron shoulders."

By contrast, while putting more emphasis on the innate characteristics of human beings, the Western tradition understandably gives a sort of privilege to intellectuals as learned individuals. This issue is intertwined with the historical and persistent tension between academia and government in Western societies that can be traced back to Socratic times, as well as the individualism that has been paramount since the Enlightenment. Yet, simply put, this knowledge tradition is a source for the norms and values that underlie academic freedom and university autonomy in today's Western societies. Its developmental trajectory is described below.

In medieval times, the earliest European university could "play off one authority against another" in the "interstices of power," and find "a modest secure niche" for the professor to teach and the student to learn without much external control over their area of expertise and interest (Perkin 2006, 159). In early-nineteenth-century Germany, this concept was enshrined by the research-oriented Humboldtian university, which upheld the idea of freedom to teach and to learn. The university was thus "considered a special place, devoted to the pursuit and transmission of knowledge. Academe claimed special rights precisely because of its calling to pursue truth. The authorities, whether secular or ecclesiastical, were expected to permit universities a special degree of autonomy" (Altbach 2001, 206). Later in the early twentieth century, the American Association of University Professors (AAUP) took the concept of academic freedom within the classroom and laboratory much further

> as encompassing all issues, not just those within the field of a scholar's expertise...The AAUP also linked the concept to the special protection of expression outside of the university. Professors were considered valuable social critics, and they were accorded special protection for their speech and writing on all topics. (Altbach 2001, 207)

An even broader definition of academic freedom came to being in Latin America, following the university reform movement of 1918, "to the extent that civil authorities were forbidden to enter the property of the university without the permission of the academic community" (Altbach 2001, 207). This led to the birth of the "autonomous" Latin American university. Judged by Western norms and practices, academic freedom and university autonomy in China are often viewed as problematic. Indeed, the Chinese knowledge tradition seems to be rooted in a close linkage to social and political life, and to emphasize the strong and direct responsibility of Confucian intellectuals for ensuring social order and benevolent governance. Unlike the Western tradition, where scholars believe in the power of words and seek to be public intellectuals through engaging in critical debate, the Confucian tradition articulates an ethic of responsibility, and prompts intellectuals to achieve self-cultivation, self-development, and self-realization through action. That often means taking up a government office and testing their knowledge in the practice required for managing that office. In the methodological sense, it should be noted that a knowledge tradition embodies the enduring modes of thinking or the salient features of cultural self-understanding, which would inevitably function to shape the particular contour of development in any given society, including the norms of academic freedom and university autonomy. However, and in functional terms, a tradition could be both a constraining and an enabling force in the development of modern consciousness. Thus, "an investigation of traditions in modernity" should avoid the "dichotomous thinking of tradition and modernity as two incompatible forms of life," to get rid of conceptual naivety and methodological fallacies (Tu 1998, 9-10).

Connecting the Progressive Aspects of the Chinese Knowledge Tradition to Contemporary Values and Consciousness

In this section, I attempt to show that the Confucian knowledge tradition exhibits an integral paradox or contradiction between its pursuit of both the intrinsic value and the external manifestation of knowledge, and argue that the solution should stem from inside the tradition as well, which requires to revisit and revitalize its progressive aspects such as emphasizing humanistic education that fosters character development and the notion of learning for self-cultivation and perfection.

The Twisted Confucian Knowledge Tradition and the Current Academic Crisis

It might be fair to say that the Confucian knowledge tradition built up its unique features with a high-standard humanism and morality, and with an emphasis on the unity of action and knowledge. Max Weber (cited in Ringer 2004, 226) noted: "For twelve centuries...China has made literary education the exclusive measure of social esteem; it has done so far more exclusively than Renaissance humanism and, most recently, Germany has done." Weber explicitly located Chinese traditional education as leaning toward one extreme on a spectrum of educational aims that he sketched out. This was emphasizing the nurturing of humanity, with the other extreme being the transmission of specialized knowledge. Echoing Weber's notion, Mei Yiqi, a renowned scholar who held the longest presidency in the history of Tsinghua University from 1931 to 1948, aggressively advocated liberal education: "What is needed by society is first and foremost talent that has liberal qualities, followed by specialized talent; if an expert without liberal qualities comes to guide the people, the consequence would not be to renovate the people, but to upset them" (cited in Liu 2004, 105). In fact, the Confucian doctrine of "cultivating the self, regulating the family, governing the country, and leading the world into peace," which is quoted above, might be seen as a complete set of principles for humanistic education. *Great Learning* then states the Confucian aims and principles for humanistic education in a more explicit way: "What the Great Learning teaches, is to illustrate illustrious virtue; to renovate the people; and to rest in the highest excellence" (Confucius, *Great Learning*). By this token, in Confucian terms, education is meaningful only when it leads to perfection of the self, or the pursuit of sagehood.

While acknowledging that the "intrinsic significance of education in the Confucian tradition...lies in ultimate human perfection," Lee Wing On (1996, 37) noted that "this is only one side of the coin. The other side places emphasis on the dimension of external manifestation and utility of education, as there is always a correlation between a person's internal establishment and external performance." He interpreted the program of "cultivating the self, regulating the family, governing the country, and leading the world into peace" in *Great Learning* in two ways: "If a person wants to govern the state, he should first cultivate himself; on the other hand, if there is a person who has cultivated himself sufficiently well, he should ultimately seek the opportunity to obtain a government office, in order to extend his good influence" (Lee 1996, 37). This appears to be another principle of the Confucian education and knowledge tradition, which is sometimes expressed in the terse phrase "sage within and king without" (Chang 1976, cited in Lee 1996, 37). Indeed, to become a "king without" is the highest desire for every Confucian scholar. Many have never been able to realize this wish, due to various obstacles along the way, but they have still focused their efforts on self-perfection. Nonetheless, reading what lies between the lines in their writings, one can still tell that this desire remains firm at the bottom of their hearts. Perhaps this Confucian view on education and knowledge can be best captured by the following words of Mencius: "When you obtain your desire for office, practice your principles for the good of the people; and when that desire is disappointed, practice your principles alone" (Mencius, *Mencius*, VIIA).

Closely linked to the Confucian notions of education and knowledge is the notion of hardship in the Confucian tradition, which carries a strong sense of responsibility for collective well-being. Mencius made a strong point that experiencing hardship should be regarded as a blessing in disguise: "When Heaven is about to confer a great responsibility on a man, it will exercise his mind [determination] with suffering, subject his sinews and bones to hard work, expose his body to hunger, put him to poverty, place obstacles in the path of his deeds, so as to stimulate his mind, harden his nature, and improve wherever he is incompetent" (Mencius, *Mencius*, VIB). This notion is certainly evident in Confucius's own words, for example, "An intellectual who is concerned about (the comforts of) his residence is not fit to be an intellectual" (Confucius, *Analects*, 14:3), and "A moral intellectual is one who escapes no danger in face of truth, discards personal interests in front of disaster, practices righteousness at the expense of life, and looks upon death as going home" (Lü Buwei, *Master Lü's Spring and Autumn Annals* [*Lüshi chunqiu*], 12.2).

From this way of thinking about hardship, Confucius strongly encouraged moral responsibility toward others' and for the collective well-being. He said that "a humane person, in wishing to establish self, establishes others; in wishing to enlighten self, enlighten others" (Confucius, *Analects*, 6:30). This may be responsible for a tendency toward pan-moralism in the Confucian tradition, in which the separation of knowledge and action, and a failure to connect one's pursuit of knowledge to the national interest, would be seen as a lack of ethics as an intellectual and could lead to deprivation of one's privileged status as an intellectual. Confucius further highlighted a "sense of shame," if one failed to fulfill one's moral responsibility, like the notion of "original sin" in Christianity. While "original sin" denotes the human inadequacy or even depravity before God, the "sense of shame" entails an individual's deficiency and consequent shame in relation to standards and requirements set by the collective community. This point is made in Confucius's own words in *Analects*: "When the state is orderly, to be poor and base is shameful. When the state is disorderly, to have wealth and high office is also shameful" (8:13).

The sense of original sin is the mindset of an individual facing God, and its biggest challenge comes from disbelief in God. The sense of constant shame stems from an individual's feeling toward the requirements of social standards and conscience. Judged against social standards and norms of various kinds and of different times, one could become attracted to the material world, and thus behave in a utilitarian or superficial way. Indeed, Lee Wing On (1996, 37) noted that "a government office can also be an extrinsic reward associated with fame, wealth, a beautiful wife, and upward social mobility, which have nothing to do with internal sagehood." Like a double-edged sword, the emphasis put on worldly affairs and collective well-being could result in a split Confucian tradition, depending on current social trends. I believe that these should be seen as responsible, at least partially, for the current crisis among the Chinese intellectuals, in particular the crisis relating to their academic integrity. This emphasis, which is embedded in the Confucian tradition, has caused Chinese intellectuals to be particularly vulnerable, compared with their Western counterparts, amid changing social and political contexts.

Since the founding of the People's Republic of China in 1949, Confucianism was largely set aside and replaced by Marxism as the dominant ideology. Soon the Chinese intellectuals felt lost in successive political movements, such as the Hundred Flowers Campaign, the Anti-Rightist Movement, and the Cultural Revolution, to name a few, which often targeted and attacked intellectuals, leaving them to suffer as objects of suspicion and oppression. They became largely voiceless from the late 1950s to the mid-1980s, and some became cynical. The 1980s witnessed something close to a second enlightenment era—if the May 4th Movement of 1919 is regarded the first such era in modern Chinese history—when faculty and students at Chinese universities took a lead in pushing for political liberalization. Nevertheless, the Tiananmen Square Tragedy in 1989 left them little choice but to retreat to university campuses and seek a particularistic identity. The majority of Chinese intellectuals now enjoy using their knowledge and expertise as vehicles to gain power and wealth (Zha 2010). Put another way, while Chinese intellectuals who excelled in their scholarship sought to become scholar-officials in traditional society, they now turn to material wealth to prove their success in a society gradually dominated by commercialism.

This has been particularly true since the early 1990s, when socialist ideals and Marxist principles gave way in face of economic liberation and marketization, and Chinese society has experienced an ideological crisis. Along with increasing wealth, the market economy has also encouraged utilitarianism and a one-sided emphasis on cumulating material wealth. When their academic integrity lost its ideological underpinnings and utilitarianism took over, many intellectuals found themselves blindly attracted to various "shortcuts" to power and wealth. It is in this context that academic misconduct, including manipulating data or plagiarism, has become widespread, even in top universities (*China Youth Daily* 2009; *Science* 2009). In most cases, the Chinese intellectuals tend to target their research at specific projects, instead of pursuing real academic interests, to secure easy and generous funding. Peer review practice has been adopted by most academic journals and grant programs, yet it is no secret that a large proportion of decisions are influenced by the applicants' privileges and reputation or, even worse, by personal relationships. Put explicitly, when the "noble aspect" of Confucian morality fell by the wayside, the utilitarian mentality became dominant. In sum, since 1949 society has fostered an education inspired by Marxist principles of dialectical materialism. When this mindset was combined with the increasing commercialism of recent years, the humane aspects of Chinese traditional culture have more or less disappeared. Now the escalation of utilitarianism among Chinese intellectuals and on university campuses has had serious repercussions for creativity and innovation, and might be seen to be jeopardizing China's ambition of upgrading its higher education system, in particular its efforts at creating world-class universities. Until Chinese scholars can show themselves to be accountable and exercise reciprocal responsibility, they may not be entitled to the kinds of autonomy and academic freedom that have been part of the Western tradition.

Connecting the Progressive Aspects of the Confucian Knowledge Tradition to Contemporary Values and Norms

As socialism and Marxism have lost much of their grip and legitimacy, the Chinese government is now working diligently to emphasize nationalism as an ideological substitute. Confucianism and traditional culture, "as new symbolic capital in the discourse of nationalism," have made a comeback and are helping to fill the ideological vacuum. "Lately, the Chinese government has drummed up an endorsement of Confucianism" (Liu 1996, 202). While it is doubtful if Confucianism can recover its status as the dominant ideology, this move could open up the opportunity of connecting the progressive aspects of the Confucian knowledge tradition to contemporary norms and values. Notably, neo-Confucianism has become popular as a global discourse, and neo-Confucianism stresses individualism.

For example, in spite of its apparent inclination toward collective well-being, Confucianism actually advocated maintaining a balance between the value of the collective and of the individual, and did call for attention to and respect for the individual. Returning to knowledge and learning, the notion of learning for self-cultivation and perfection signifies clearly the individualistic orientation. Lee Wing On (1996) noted "It originates from Confucius' dictum in the *Analects* (14:25), which was expended to criticize the attitude of learning for the sake of pleasing others or showing off to others" (33). Indeed, the mentality of individualistic orientation and determination is manifested in many sayings by Confucius and Mencius: "Among any three people walking, I will find something to learn for sure. Their good qualities are to be followed, and their shortcomings are to be avoided" (Confucius, *Analects*, 7:21); "Like building a mound, if one more basketful of earth is needed to accomplish it and I stop: that is because I choose to stop. Like (building a mound) on level ground, although only one basketful of earth has been dumped on it and I keep on: that is because I choose to go forward" (Confucius, *Analects*, 9:19); "If I reflect on myself and find that I am not right, then won't I even fear facing a bum off the street? But if I reflect on myself and find myself to be right, then even if it be an army of one hundred thousand, I will go forward!" (Mencius, *Mencius*, IIA).

Notably, Confucianism valued the individual, not in the sense of emphasizing his/her rights or the awareness of a civil society, but the individual's unexcused responsibility for moral action. Nevertheless, neo-Confucianism has expanded and become rich in its appreciation of individualism (de Bary 1983; Lee 1996). Neo-Confucianists

> attacked bureaucratic scholarship and the vogue of learning for sitting civil examinations in the Song dynasty... A major task of the neo-Confucianists in the Song dynasty was to revitalize the significance of the intrinsic value of education. This was a prime motivation for them to establish *Shuyuan* (academies) in order to counter-balance the public schools which prepared students for extrinsic rewards—success in civil examinations. (Lee 1996, 33–34)

The *Shuyuan* stressed a liberal tradition with an independent ethos that was tolerant of different schools of thought. They also promoted a humanistic education that fostered character development, as opposed to the pragmatism of the civil examinations system. Education in *Shuyuan* is considered important for its intrinsic value, and oriented "towards the deep approach rather than the surface approach to learning" (Lee, 1996, 34). Its approaches suggest that "seeking knowledge (learning) and thinking are two sides of the coin" (Lee 1996, 35), and emphasize "studying extensively, enquiring carefully, pondering thoroughly, sifting clearly" (*Doctrine of the Mean*, XX.19) in the learning process. In sum, this emphasis on learning for the sake of one's self clearly signifies the individualistic orientation in the Confucian knowledge tradition (Lee 1996). When "learning becomes an inner-directed process" (Lee 1996, 34), "We are, therefore, intrinsically free" (Tu 1998, 14).

An urgent task now for Chinese intellectuals seems to be revitalizing these progressive aspects of the Confucian knowledge tradition, and connecting them to contemporary values and consciousness, which include liberty, equality, respect for individual dignity and individuality, and democratic polity. In particular, the notion of "sage within and king without" might need to be separated, maintaining only the core that stresses self-cultivation, that is, learning for the sake of one's self, and pursuing knowledge for knowledge sake, which may contribute to the formation of a much-needed critical self-consciousness among contemporary Chinese intellectuals. At least, the undertaking of king without doesn't have to mean taking up a government office,[4] but can be applied to many other possible activities such as knowledge mobility and social advocacy, that is, those bearing clearer features of an open society. An open society would better accommodate academic freedom, and, in turn, better facilitate creativity and innovation in pursuing knowledge.

Concluding Thoughts

Until now, it appeared impractical to transplant and copy Western style and practices of academic freedom and university autonomy in the current Chinese context. This is not even an issue that is completely at stake in political reform, which, though, certainly has a crucial effect. It seems that it should start with a transformation of the Confucian knowledge tradition. At least, this transformation should commence in parallel with democratization of China's political system and society.

The discussion above points to the intrinsic significance of the Confucian tradition for pursuing knowledge, and for learning, where the fundamental value lies first and foremost with self-cultivation and the pursuit of human perfection. The neo-Confucianists carried this notion much further. Zhu Xi, for example, put great emphasis on "being true to oneself," "rectifying the mind and making the will sincere," and "taking self-cultivation as the starting point for reaching out to others" (de Bary 1983, 22–24). "The purpose of learning is therefore to cultivate oneself as an intelligent, creative, independent, autonomous, and what is more, an authentic being" (Lee 1996, 34). Thus, the Confucian knowledge tradition could have provided fertile soil for the establishment of academic freedom and of university autonomy as a protection mechanism. Its core values, if revitalized appropriately, could connect to contemporary values and consciousness elsewhere.

However, the Confucian knowledge tradition carries an integral paradox or contradiction. As Lee Wing On (1996, 37–38) notes that "the aspiration for extrinsic rewards coexists with the ideal of external manifestation of a person's internal establishment in the Confucian tradition...although they look contradictory to each other." Precisely in this sense, the Confucian knowledge tradition requires some serious transformation to get rid of the tendency of adopting a utilitarian or surface approach to knowledge, which can be both misleading and corruptive. If such a transformation were properly accomplished, the Confucian knowledge tradition would not only shine in the Chinese context, but also contribute to communization and transcendence of the much wider intellectual communities in today's globalizing world. Essentially, neo-Confucianism has become part of the global discourse, and its renaissance and transformation in the homeland would certainly symbolize and strengthen its dynamism and influence more widely.

For example, Tu Weiming (1998, 4) challenged the "Enlightenment faith in progress, reason, and individualism," arguing, "In the context of modern Western hegemonic discourse, progress may entail inequality, reason, self-interest, and individual greed." The transformed Confucian knowledge tradition may help to usher in a basic sense of duty and responsibility among intellectuals around the world, which, in turn, may serve to transcend the mentality of criticism for criticism sake among many Western intellectuals. Similarly, the Confucian faith that "a humane person, in wishing to establish self, establishes others; in wishing to enlighten self, enlighten others" may present, when augmented by another Confucian rule that "do not do unto others what you would not want others to do onto you" (Confucius, *Analects*, 15:24), an alternative or idealistic approach for protecting and institutionalizing academic freedom, that is, self-mastery versus legal sanction. This approach could become crucial, for now the university everywhere "has become, or is in danger of becoming, an integral organ of the state or the corporate economy and so of losing its autonomy and academic freedom" (Perkin 2006, 161). In other words, legal sanction may not be sufficiently strong to guarantee academic freedom and university autonomy in today's circumstance. Against this circumstance, Tu Weiming (1998, 14) illustrated the Confucian notion of freedom as "embodied in our responsibility for ourselves as the center of relationships," and asserted, "That alone deserves and demands respect."

Notes

1. Tu Weiming (2005, 221) observed: "Etymologically the English term 'intellectual' originated from the idea of the intelligentsia in Tsarist Russia. A salient feature of the Russian intelligentsia was its spirit of protest. As a rule, members of the Russian intelligentsia were critics of officialdom, and they were frequently persecuted as dissidents. Their relationship to the political establishment was always adversarial. This distinctive characteristic of the intellectual remains strong in Russia to this day. One loses one's reputation and status as an intellectual if one joins the establishment or if one no longer challenges the authority of the government."
2. A popular intellectual trend, in China and also elsewhere, is to suggest that, especially in the wake of the global financial crisis, China's economic model, "the Beijing consensus"—as opposed to the "Washington Consensus"—could supplement or even replace the US model. To some extent, it articulates both anxiety over the full-blown absorption of China into the global "world-system" and the desire for resistance. While this notion is subject to challenge and remains contested, an increasing number of Chinese intellectuals appear to endorse the view that Western-style governance and democracy need to be contextualized.

3. When quoting Confucius, Mencius, and other classics, I freely adapt the translated versions of Khu and colleagues (1996); Lau (Trans. 1970, 1996); Lee (1996); Legge (Trans. 1966); Tu (1998); Yu (2006), plus my own interpretation.
4. In 2008, Chinese universities conferred over 50,000 doctoral degrees, outnumbering those conferred by the American universities and becoming the world's largest system of doctorate education. However, more than half of the Chinese doctoral degree recipients ended up at jobs within the government bureaucracy at national or provincial levels (*Phoenix Satellite Television*, cited in Zha 2011).

References

Altbach, Philip G. 2001. "Academic Freedom: International Realities and Challenges." *Higher Education* 41 (1–2): 205–219.
China Youth Daily. 2009. "Gong zong jian yan: zhiding yange de zhiye caoshou guiding he falv guiding" ["The Public Suggests to Make Strict Laws and Bylaws on Professional Ethics"]. April 28, 2009. http://www.cyol.net.
Confucius. 1996. *Analects*. Trans. John B. Khu, Vicente B. K. Khu, William B. S. Khu, and Jose B. K. Khu. Beijing, China: World Affairs Press.
Confucius and Mencius. 1966. *The Four Books: Confucian Analects, the Great Learning, the Doctrine of the Mean, and the Works of Mencius*. Trans. James Legge. New York: Paragon Book Reprint Corp.
de Bary, William Theodore. 1983. *The Liberal Tradition in China*. Hong Kong: The Chinese University of Hong Kong Press.
Hayhoe, Ruth. 2008. "Philosophy and Comparative Education: What Can We Learn from East Asia?" In *Comparative and International Education: Issues for Teachers*, ed. Karen Mundy, Kathy Bickmore, Ruth Hayhoe, Meggan Madden, and Kathy Madjidi. Toronto, ON: Canadian Scholars Press Inc.
Lau, D. C. 1996. *Lü shi chun qiu zhu zi suo yin [A Concordance to the Lüshichunqiu]*. Taipei, Taiwan: The Commercial Press, Ltd.
Lee, Wing On. 1996. "The Cultural Context for Chinese Learners: Conceptions of Learning in the Confucian Tradition." In *The Chinese Learner: Cultural, Psychological and Contextual Influences*, ed. David A. Watkins and John B. Biggs. Hong Kong: Comparative Education Research Centre, University of Hong Kong.
Liu, Baocun. 2004. *Daxue linian de chuantong yu bianqe [The Traditions and Changes of University Ideas]*. Beijing, China: Educational Science Press.
Liu, Kang. 1996. "Is There an Alternative to (Capitalist) Globalization? The Debate about Modernity in China." *Boundary 2* 23(3): 193–218.
Mencius. 1970. *Mencius*. Trans. D. C. Lau. Harmondsworth, UK: Penguin.
Mencius. 1998. *Mencius*. Trans. David Hinton. Washington, DC: Counterpoint.
Ministry of Education of China. 2002. *Guanyu jiaqiang xueshu daode jianshe de ruo gan yijian [Several Opinions on Strengthening Academic Integrity]*. Beijing, China: Ministry of Education. http://www.edu.cn.

Ministry of Education of China. 2006. *Guanyu shuli shehui zhuyi rong ru guan jin yi bu jiaqiang xueshu daode jianshe de yijian* [*Opinions on Establishing Socialist Values of Glory and Shame and Further Strengthening Academic Integrity*]. Beijing, China: Ministry of Education. http://www.moe.edu.cn.

Ministry of Education of China. 2009. *Guanyu yansu chuli gaodeng xuexiao xueshu bu duan xingwei de tongzhi* [*Notice of Server Penalty on Academic Misconduct in Higher Education Institutions*]. Beijing, China: Ministry of Education of China. http://www.moe.edu.cn.

Perkin, Harold. 2006. "History of Universities." In *International Handbook of Higher Education. Springer International Handbooks of Education 18*, ed. James J. F. Forest and Philip G. Altbach. Dordrecht, The Netherlands: Springer.

Plato. 1945. *The Republic*. Trans. Francis MacDonald Cornford. London/Oxford/New York: Oxford University Press.

Ringer, Fritz K. 2004. *Max Weber: An Intellectual Biography*. Chicago: University of Chicago Press.

Schwartz, Benjamin. 1985. *The World of Thought in Ancient China*. Cambridge, MA: Harvard University Press.

Science. 2009. "Retractions Put Spotlight on China's Part-Time Professor System." *Science* 323, March 6, 2009, 1280–1281.

Tu, Weiming. 1998. "Beyond the Enlightenment Mentality." In *Confucianism and Ecology: The Interrelation of Heaven, Earth and Humans,* ed. Mary Evelyn Tucker and John Berthrong. Cambridge, MA: Harvard University Centre for the Study of World Religions, distributed by Harvard University Press.

Tu, Weiming. 2005. "Intellectuals in a World Made of Knowledge." *Canadian Journal of Sociology* 30 (2): 219–226.

Weiler, Hans. 2001. "Knowledge, Politics, and the Future of Higher Education: Critical Observations on a Worldwide Transformation." In *Knowledge across Cultures: A Contribution to Dialogue among Civilizations,* ed. Ruth Hayhoe and Julia Pan. Hong Kong: Comparative Education Research Centre, University of Hong Kong.

Yu, Ying-shih. 2006. *Address on the Occasion of Receiving the John W. Kluge Prize*. Washington, DC: Library of Congress. December 5, 2006. http://www.loc.gov.

Zeera, Zahra A. 2001. "Paradigm Shifts in the Social Sciences in the East and West." In *Knowledge across Cultures: a Contribution to Dialogue among Civilizations,* ed. Ruth Hayhoe and Julia Pan. Hong Kong: Comparative Education Research Centre, University of Hong Kong.

Zha, Qiang. 2010. "Academic Freedom and Public Intellectuals in China: A Century of Oscillations." *International Higher Education* 58 (Winter 2010): 17–18.

Zha, Qiang. 2011. "Is There An Emerging Chinese Model of the University?" In *Portraits of 21st Century Chinese Universities: In the Move to Mass Higher Education,* ed. Ruth Hayhoe, Jun Li, Jing Lin, and Qiang Zha. Hong Kong: Comparative Education Research Centre, The University of Hong Kong and Springer.

Chapter 15

Higher Education Reform in Indonesia: University Governance and Autonomy

W. James Jacob, Yuanyuan Wang, Tracy Lynn Pelkowski, Ravik Karsidi, and Agus D. Priyanto

Introduction

Comprised of over 17,000 islands that form an archipelago reaching from Southeast Asia to Australia, Indonesia has perhaps the most diverse and difficult higher education environment when it comes to issues of access, equity, and delivery of curriculum.[1] Meeting the needs of such an enormous country spread across so many islands, with hundreds of distinct ethnic groups and indigenous languages, poses a formidable challenge for higher education policy makers and planners.

There is also great diversity in religion at the higher education level to the point where, arguably, two higher education systems exist—the secular and the religious. Both the Ministry of National Education (MONE) and the Ministry of Religious Affairs (MORA) play significant roles in Indonesian higher education. In the world's most populous Muslim country, many Indonesian higher education institutions (HEIs) are sponsored by Islamic organizations. Academic hospitals are sponsored in this way: some medical staff are based at the hospital, and others are members of Faculties of Medicine in public universities. There are also several Christian HEIs in Indonesia. In recent years there has been a trend toward providing interreligious dialogue, curriculum development, comparative religious instruction, and increased tolerance in Indonesian higher education.

As in other developing Asian countries, Indonesian higher education has experienced dramatic developments driven by economic growth. Most Indonesians regard higher education as a means of upgrading their socioeconomic mobility and contributing substantially to economic growth. Thus, strategies for further development of higher education have been increasingly important for government policy makers. Current development initiatives aim to strengthen HEIs with an emphasis on providing greater access and strengthening the quality of instruction.

In this chapter, we discuss key political, economic, and market trends over the past 15 years. Our research team identified three central trends in the development of Indonesian higher education: emphasis on quality, autonomy, and distance education. We then introduce our qualitative study in which we interviewed one hundred experts on the Indonesian higher education subsector. Based on participants' responses, our findings section summarizes perceived challenges and opportunities related to the most prominent higher education trends. The discussion section weaves together key findings and the three trends identified in the literature. We conclude with recommendations for future research and the realization that Indonesia will increasingly influence regional and international higher education.

Three Trends

The following sections correspond to three relevant trends in Indonesian higher education identified through archival research and discourse analyses. The identified trends are higher education quality, autonomy, and distance learning.

Higher Education Quality

As the demand for HEIs grew throughout the latter half of the twentieth century, institutional quality became a prevalent concern. The rapid growth of the tertiary education system outpaced the qualification levels of instructors, and capacity to conduct vital research was minimal at both public and private institutions. According to Anthony R. Welch (2006), private institutions established in the 1960s were unofficial and unaccredited, while tax regulations allowed schools to establish themselves without the procurement of basic facilities. Compared to the public sector, low investment and low per-pupil spending rates permit private schools to be characterized as having lower-quality teachers, poor facilities, and students who are not academically inclined. Moreover, appropriate staff-student ratios have become more problematic with the high enrollment rates of private institutions, although this depends on the fees charged by the institution.

In response to a growing concern over institutional quality, the New Paradigm in higher education management, established in 1994, focused on the five pillars of quality, autonomy, accountability, accreditation, and evaluation (Brodjonegoro 2002). The five pillars have been addressed through the establishment of new government bodies. The Director General of Higher Education (DGHE) developed the Board of Higher Education (DPT), which includes three councils focusing on education, research, and development.

Accreditation of HEIs in Indonesia is administered by the National Accreditation Board for Higher Education (BAN-PT: Badan Akreditasi Nasional Perguruan Tinggi), also established in 1994. BAN-PT is an external accreditation body "authorized to formulate and implement the accreditation of academic programs of public and private institutions independently" (Nizam 2006, 39). BAN-PT provides the public with a means to evaluate the quality of a school, although not all institutions are required to be accredited. The BAN-PT process classifies undergraduate institutions into four levels from A (satisfactory) to D (unsatisfactory); post graduate programs are rated as U (excellent), B (good), or T (fair). Other quality control measures included the Quality for Undergraduate Education (QUE) initiative from 1998 to 2004 that was supported by the World Bank, as well as Government Regulation 61/1999 introduced in July 1999, which enabled a select number of state/public universities to be considered autonomous institutions under the "State Owned Legal Entity Universities" initiative (BHMN: Universitas Badan Hukum Milik Negara).[2]

The QUE project was a competitive merit-based grant open to both public and private institutions. According to Nizam (2006), QUE was a successful reform that resulted in institutional accountability and cost-effective planning on the part of HEIs. The QUE model has recently been modified and adopted by other government and private funding programs. Performance indicators used to determine eligibility for grant funding are specified by grantees. In addition to competitive grants and ranking systems designed to improve accountability, the focus on institutional autonomy, as initiated by BHMN, is also a key trend in Indonesian higher education.

Quality assurance remains an important topic for lawmakers, government planners, and higher education administrators nationwide. Training programs at all levels, for senior administrators, faculty-wide administrators, support staff, and lecturers is an ongoing initiative at most Indonesian HEIs. For example, from 2009 to 2011, the Consortium of Indonesian Universities-Pittsburgh (KPTIP: Konsorsium Perguruan Tinggi Indonesia-Pittsburgh) held a series of higher education management training seminars on quality assurance, good governance, and autonomy.

Higher Education Autonomy Initiatives

Higher education autonomy remains a delicate political topic in Indonesia. Moves toward autonomy by MONE policy makers and higher education administrators are often met with opposition from media, public, and students. Tuition fees are often closely linked with most autonomy initiatives. Tuition increases to help cover operating costs and capital investments are often viewed as unfair by students, especially those from low socioeconomic status backgrounds. The university autonomy law dates back to legislation in 1999, which allowed select public universities to establish tuition fees to better meet their financial needs. HEIs were encouraged to fully or partially fund increasing operating costs and institution-related investments through special fees and donations.

A World Bank-funded project—Managing Higher Education for Relevance and Efficiency (IMHERE)—supports provision of an enabling environment for increased HEI autonomy and practices of good governance. IMHERE also supports quality, equity, and access opportunities for students. The eight-year-funded initiative began implementation in 2005.

Established in 2008, the *Law on Educational Entities* required all HEIs to incorporate as legal entities and take full or partial responsibility for their academic and resource capacities; previously, all funds related to public HEIs were centrally managed. In April 2010, however, the legislation was struck-down as unconstitutional by the Indonesian Supreme Court. Critics maintained that the law commodified higher education and benefited the wealthy far more than the masses. Within such a delicate higher education environment, many administrators remain committed to finding new ways to raise revenues to meet the inevitable increasing costs of higher education. Such ventures include establishing entrepreneurial activities and partnerships and pursuing additional funds within the legal framework higher education autonomy (Hapsari 2010; Jacob 2010).

Higher Education Distance Learning

In Indonesia, increased access to higher education for previously underrepresented students cannot be achieved without mastering several forms of distance education. In the current higher education context, technology constraints and access limitations require a variety of online and print-based delivery mediums (Luschei et al. 2009). Keith Harry and Hilary Perraton (1999) argue that changes in technology provide greater distance education opportunities. To a certain extent, distance education, shaped by technological opportunity and advancement, has provided a means of recruiting more students, and shifted the boundaries of on-campus and off-campus education. But limitations in technology and access to online instruction remain and are only exacerbated, in rural and remote island locations.

Aminudin Zuhairi, Effendi Wahyono, and Sharon Suratinah (2006, 96) argue that "the development of distance education [is] the result of an attempt to meet the national education needs." Paulina Pannen (2003) reiterates the importance of distance education provision in overcoming geographical and socioeconomic constraints. The advancement of technology contributes to the development of distance education in Indonesia, encouraging more institutions, especially at the tertiary level, to participate. Distance education in higher education enhances access opportunities for the large number of high school graduates excluded from conventional universities due to geographical or socioeconomic constraints (Pannen 2003; Pannen and Abubakar 2005).

Some of the leading Indonesian distance higher education organizations include the Indonesia Open University, Southeast Asian Ministers of Education Organization (SEAMEO), Indonesian Distance Learning Network (IDLN), MONE's Center for Communication and Information Technology for Education (Pustekkom), and many HEIs with individual distance education delivery networks and outreach programs to branch campuses. International HEIs also play an increasingly prominent role in providing higher education to students with especially strong English skills and an ability to afford international tuition rates.

The continual improvement and further development of distance education in Indonesia is a priority of government policy makers and planners. Distance education can provide a platform of greater higher education capacity delivery. It is a means of achieving greater equity in higher education, especially among several of the most disadvantaged groups regardless of their geographic location, social and economic status, gender, and ethnicity.

In the following section we detail the challenges and opportunities facing Indonesian higher education, based on the results of an empirical study[3] conducted by the authors.

Challenges in Indonesian Higher Education

Financial Challenges

Most senior administrators in our study expressed concern about raising student enrollments and student-instructor ratios without corresponding funding increases. The student-instructor ratio is a real concern, as enrollments remain high compared to the average number of faculty members at each university. One administrator suggested that "it is common for our university to have 50–100 students per faculty member" (IN55–6). This unbalanced ratio of students to faculty creates a difficult environment for instruction and limits instructors' abilities to provide multiple methods in teaching with such large classes.

Financial challenges are also experienced by students, who have seen an increase in student fees and tuition. Tuition is only one funding stream for Indonesian HEIs and often it is not enough to meet growing financial demands of providing services. Two of our participants observed:

> While our government has asked us not to raise tuition costs, we are faced with the burden of upgrading our infrastructure, technology capacities, and teacher qualifications. Each of these initiatives requires adequate funding. We are often left on our own to seek new ways to procure funds. Many of our challenges require innovative ways for securing additional funding. Among these new funding streams are entrepreneurial ventures with the private sector. (IN01-6)
>
> We are given the charge from our government to strive for academic excellence. Our rector has even challenged us to reach world-class university status. But all of these worthy goals require substantial investments, including substantial financial investments. (IN08-6)

The challenge to meet increasing financial demands is an issue of concern for Indonesian higher education administrators. This is especially true during the current global economic crisis, which has in a number of ways resonated through the higher education subsector in Indonesia. Several respondents felt that greater financial autonomy was required to be able to meet the financial demands facing HEIs in the present environment. Others expressed a desire for greater autonomy from the government. A former rector discussed the importance of autonomy:

> Financial autonomy is required for us to meet the financial demands facing our universities in Indonesia. It is especially true to have greater fiscal autonomy when the government has indicated they will be reducing the amount of overall funding to our university in the near future. (IN66-6)

There is evidence of greater autonomy being encouraged from within MONE. In July 2011, several rectors were presented with awards for demonstrating excellence in entrepreneurialism for their efforts to procure higher education institutional funding through nontraditional and innovative methods and ventures. Undoubtedly greater financial autonomy will be necessary to sustain revenue generation in an era where reduced government support appears to be the norm, and will continue well into the future.

The Need for Greater Quality Assurance

Most Indonesian HEIs struggle to align the curriculum with the market economy. With the rapid rate that technology and other industries change, it is difficult for HEIs to keep pace with these changes. Out-of-date textbooks and, perhaps more often, a human resource base of unqualified or underqualified instructors, presents less than optimal learning opportunities within HEIs. Many higher education lecturers are academically underqualified. It is common to find entire departments where the instructors have no more than a master's degree. In many cases, undergraduate degree holders are providing instruction to higher education students. This creates the need to upgrade the academic qualifications of current faculty members. One participant agreed: "We are in the process of trying to upgrade the qualifications of our faculty members so that they are better prepared to teach our students. Too many of our instructors are under-qualified to teach our students" (IN76–6).

Quality assurance training is not only needed at the instructor level, but it is also needed at the administrator level. There are few established higher education management training programs in Indonesia. This was reinforced by a participant who remarked: "Higher education leadership and management training is a particular need among all HEIs. It is a current focus of MONE and also leading funding agencies" (IN73–6). A rector concurred: "We hope to establish the first doctoral program in higher education management," and "we hope to be able to establish this new program with our international partner the University of Pittsburgh" (IN01–6). Many participants identified the need for quality training in one or more of the following areas: leadership, financial management, academic writing, research and development, good governance, facilities management, student affairs, as well as establishing international partnerships, internship programs, industry advisory councils, sustainable university autonomy, and the use of advanced technologies.

The number of Indonesian islands spread across such a vast region of ocean creates a unique higher education delivery challenge for policy makers and higher education providers. Providing a quality education in this diverse geographic context is particularly difficult, especially in the remote and distant island regions of the country. The best higher education opportunities are generally near the major urban centers on Java or Sumatra, where the top-20 ranked universities are located. One interviewee emphasized the importance of increasing both the quantity and the quality of higher education in the regional centers throughout the country:

> I think there is a stronger interest in higher education. We are struggling to make that. One of the great challenges in Indonesia is the quantity and the quality of higher education in the provinces, the regions of Indonesia. I mean in the city center, in the major city center, we have good universities. But the big demand is to [provide] quality and quantity of higher education in the provinces. (I14–6)

The inequality of educational opportunities is exacerbated by the distance between the major urban centers and the primary islands. Technology has the ability to reduce these distances, but there are also challenges associated with the distribution of technology. Quality Internet connections are not always available in even the best universities, let alone in remote HEIs. Yet, many respondents expressed optimism that technology was an essential way to help provide greater access to higher education opportunities for students in rural and remote island locations.

Technology Challenges

Many technology challenges exist within the Indonesian higher education subsector. Among the most prevalent challenges are the need for greater access to electronic academic journal databases, finding optimal distance education delivery models, providing greater access to the Internet, and training instructors and students on how to use the currently available technology.

Many participants recognized the need for greater access to the best academic journal databases in the world. A primary reason that this remains a challenge to most HEIs is the cost for providing access to students and faculty members. "With our very modest budget, we have to be very selective in what databases and journals we subscribe to on an annual basis," a head of a university library said (IN59-6). The secretary of the Consortium for Indonesian Universities-Pittsburgh responded "We are doing all we can to find additional revenues and partnerships because our universities have relatively limited library budgets. This is a challenge each of the 16 universities in our consortium have" (IN69-6). "One way to help overcome this challenge is to establish library partnerships with some of our international partner universities. Hopefully we can find ways to help share these resources with other universities in Indonesia as well as with willing partners of ours overseas."

Distance higher education models are common practice throughout Indonesia, but there remains a need to improve the delivery of programs. More could be done to improve distance education courses and opportunities for students. Multidelivery mediums are essential for meeting the unique and diverse requirements of higher education students throughout the country. One participant explained: "The optimal use of technology can substantially enhance student learning in the classroom" (IN83-6). Optimal delivery mediums that could be further developed in HEIs might include one or more of the following: synchronous, asynchronous, facilitated learning opportunities, and hybrid instructional modules and courses. And, with videoconferencing and social networking technologies becoming more accessible and user friendly to a wider user base nationwide, distance education opportunities also increase.

Higher Education Opportunities

Focus on Building Indonesia's Human Resource Capacity through Higher Education

There is a growing need to upgrade the skills of lecturers, administrators, and staff members nationwide. This provides not only a challenge for the government but also a unique opportunity to shape how this national reform effort will be undertaken. There are not enough instructors with doctorate degrees. DGHE is investing significant funds to help upgrade the skills and qualifications of higher education administrators and faculty members. Sandwich programs that allow faculty members and doctoral students to study at a foreign university for a period of three to six months enable them to work side-by-side with faculty members from some of the top universities in international settings. Where some programs are actually decreasing the amount of funds they provide to Indonesian graduate students studying abroad (I10–6), DGHE and bilateral organization initiatives seem to be on the rise to help meet the national goal of upgrading the qualifications of higher education faculty members and administrators.

Restructuring teacher education programs is a key reform effort for the government and is considered by many to be a national need and emerging trend. One participant explained that specialized teacher education institutions have recently been, or are in the process of being, restructured into comprehensive universities. This is one of the ways in which the government is able to upgrade the qualification of teachers in primary and secondary schools (I01–6). He continued:

> They were initially founded as teacher training institutions that focused on 100 percent teacher training. Over time, these institutions diversified their curriculum and became more comprehensive. Probably the biggest major is still teacher education, but it's probably not more than 50 percent. This is what's happening in Indonesia. They want to upgrade the qualifications of the teachers (there are still many teachers who don't have the equivalent bachelor's degree [in the subject area they teach]). So these teacher training institutions, many of them have two- and three-year certificate programs rather than bachelor's degree programs. The [government is striving to have] the bachelor's degree become the required minimum qualification standard for all teachers, both at the primary and secondary levels.

HEIs play a crucial role in meeting the pre- and in-service training needs of teachers throughout the country. Many current teachers attend school part time in an executive delivery format where they enroll in classes held on weekdays after work, or on the weekends.

Establishing Sustainable Partnerships with Foreign HEIs

About one-third of respondents indicated that the Indonesian government is interested in developing sustainable partnerships with HEIs in foreign countries, such as the United States, Australia, China, Singapore, and Malaysia. One respondent suggested: "Indonesian universities set their missions in a global context and raise the level of teaching by sending more young Indonesian educators to foreign countries" (I09-6). Another respondent stated that "these partnerships are different from those of the mid 1990s, which focused upon the access of Indonesian students to foreign (predominantly US) universities and individual projects conducted between the faculty of US and Indonesian universities" (I06-6). Others suggested: "These partnerships show the efforts of the Indonesian government in building long-term sustainable linkages between its HEIs and those in foreign countries" (IN45-6; IN75-6). Partnerships can be powerful marketing tools. For example, the ability of Sebelas Maret University to partner with the University of Pittsburgh in the development of its PhD Program in Higher Education Management enables it to gain several advantages rather than establishing the program on its own. Joint instruction, videoconference seminars, faculty exchange experiences, and curriculum development help participating faculty members from both universities combine limited resources to offer the nation's first doctoral-level Higher Education Management Program.

Aligning the Curriculum with Market Needs

There is an increasing need for administrators of Indonesian HEIs to help bridge the gap between what is taught in the classroom and what their students will experience firsthand in the job market upon graduation. This curriculum gap was mentioned by a majority of participants (80 percent), who recognized that the job market is continuously changing. Some fields are particularly vulnerable to market changes, and if higher education instructors and the curriculum they provide to their students do not remain up-to-date their students will not be prepared for entry-level jobs upon graduation. The role that internships can play in preparing students for the workplace was summed up by two participants:

> Most of our students in engineering need to supplement their university education with extracurricular learning opportunities. Internships are particularly important in this regard. We would like to establish a stronger internship program at our university for all of our students, one that will help bridge the gap that exists between our curriculum and the job market demands. (IN43-6)

> Internship opportunities are standard for all of our students, however, they are not often long enough. Too often the employers of our interns do not recognize the potential value of having our students intern for a time period at their companies. We would like to change this so that they can see exceptional value in our university interns serving in their companies. We recognize that internship providers are those who will potentially hire our best university graduates. (IN02–6)

Other participants recognized the need to establish Industry Advisory Councils to help link industry leaders—employers from both the public and private sectors—with Indonesia's HEIs. "This is an essential need in our country," one rector responded, "we need to do more to involve industry leaders with our curriculum, providing instruction, and actively participating with our faculty members in funding research and development opportunities" (IN67–6).

Increase in Privatization of HEIs

Several participants acknowledged that for the most part growth in the number of HEIs since independence has been largely in the private sector. There continues to be a steady increase in the number of religion-oriented private universities—both Christian and Islamic HEIs (I03–6; I09–6). Even in the public sector, there is a steady influx of private influence, especially regarding financial investment in higher education. One participant said that "private money is made available where there isn't adequate public funding. Religious foundations, such as Islamic and Christian-oriented foundations, remain significant sources for financing Indonesian higher education" (I08–6).

Goal to Achieve World-Class Status

Becoming a world-class HEI is a goal for many Indonesian higher education administrators. But achieving this goal is a difficult process, and will take time for a higher education system regarded by many as still in its infancy. One participant mentioned that Indonesian universities are eager to be recognized as world players in higher education and have a strong interest in professionalizing their faculty:

> They are eager to rise to a level where they can become equal partners in higher education rather than part of a developing immature system. They have a desire to increase their status and increase their professionalism. One of the things I heard consistently was that they are trying to find what distinctive traits they can bring to the conversation. So they are trying to identify areas that are both of value to Indonesia and places where they have distinctive strengths. (I05–6)

The influence of the top global higher education ranking systems has a direct impact on aspirations of Indonesia's top universities. Three global ranking systems are watched closely by policy makers and Indonesian higher education administrators: the *Times Higher Education* (*THE*) World University Rankings; Shanghai Jiao Tong University Institute of Higher Education's *Academic Ranking of World Universities* (which is also referred to as the Shanghai index or Shanghai rankings); and the QS World University Rankings. Currently, there are no Indonesian universities ranked among the top one hundred world universities in the three global higher education rankings. Recognized by many participants as the top national HEI, the University of Indonesia remained unranked in 2010 among the top two hundred universities and among the top five hundred universities of the *Academic Ranking of World Universities*; it ranked 236th overall by QS World University Rankings in 2010. In this regard, Indonesian HEIs remain very much on the periphery compared to the world's elite universities in terms of international recognition and rankings (Marginson 2007; Marginson and van der Wende 2006). Still the top universities in Indonesia remain significant when it comes to finding employment at national and local levels (OECD 2004).

Conclusions

In this section, we link several of our findings with the three trends identified in our initial discourse and analyses on the need for improvement in higher education quality, autonomy, and optimal distance education.

Quality assurance remains at the forefront of higher education initiatives at MONE, for multi- and bilateral aid organizations, and most higher education administrators. In July 2011, the University of Pittsburgh partnered with Sebelas Maret University to establish the first Higher Education Management Doctoral Program. The program will be based at Sebelas Maret University in Surakarta, Java, and provide higher education management training on topics such as quality assurance, strategic planning, human resource management, and institutional resource planning. The program will provide higher education training to administrators at all levels and include enrollments from the 16 Indonesian universities of the KPTIP as well as other HEIs throughout the country.

Our study indicates that many higher education administrators remain committed to finding alternative ways of procuring funds, to offset increasing higher education costs and compensate for decreasing funds provided by the government. Higher education administrators who want to help their institutions improve in areas of quality of research and teacher qualifications recognize the need for upfront investments in training and research capacity

(Maulia 2010). Higher education capacity building at all levels—human resource, institutional, and infrastructure levels—comes with a financial price tag. Thus, administrators are forced to search for alternative ways of creating revenue. This endeavor should not happen in a haphazard manner but be led by a carefully orchestrated strategic planning process. Alternative revenue generating initiatives are most successful when aligned with the respective higher education institutional missions and also in alignment with market needs (Jacob 2010). Higher education administrators are aware of previous concerns of the public with corruption and the commercialization of higher education; they desire to practice principles of good governance while at the same time being able to meet the increasing costs associated with providing top quality higher education (IN07-6; IN15-6).

Some HEIs, such as the Indonesia Open University in Jakarta, provide higher education opportunities to individuals who have access to the Internet (Luschei et al. 2009). Yet, access to the Internet remains a major challenge for millions of Indonesians, particularly those in rural and remote island locations. For those with Internet access, instructors can improve their skills and abilities by designing and using technology in the classroom, and subsequently offering optimal distance education courses to those most in need of this higher education resource. Distance education, using the Internet, can provide a potential bridge to overcome the technology challenge identified by so many participants in our study.

Another trend we observed was the presentations to higher education administrators and faculty members, by former higher education leaders on ways to prevent student uprisings and terrorism from occurring on Indonesian university campuses. These presentations were organized in coordination with MONE and delivered in July 2011 (IN66-6). It has long been recognized that HEIs worldwide serve as centers of student demonstrations and protests against government policies. This has also been the case in Indonesia, where students often support and lead political movements (Romano 1996; Hamad et al. 2001; Almasmari et al. 2011). Aware of the recent government turmoil experienced in predominantly Arab Muslim countries of the Middle East and North Africa Region, government officials in Indonesia recognize the importance of the role that HEIs play in political demonstrations and in leading political movements.

To sum up, Indonesia is Southeast Asia and Oceania's most populous nation with a vibrant higher education system. While its HEIs may not rank among the top institutions on the world stage, they have great potential for growth and increased recognition in the future. Because of its unique geographic situation—an archipelago with thousands of islands—Indonesia is positioned to become a world leader in distance higher education delivery. In fact, to meet the growing demand for increased knowledge acquisition and professional training, Indonesia's HEIs must develop and provide optimal distance education programs. Quality remains a central issue that current and future policy makers and planners must face. An insistence on quality is what will help catapult Indonesian HEIs to the forefront in coming decades. Three challenges emerge from participant responses relating to financial, quality assurance, and technology issues. Understanding how to overcome each of the challenges will assist Indonesia to become a regional leader in higher education. Opportunity trends include the development of the human resource base through higher education, the establishment of sustainable partnerships with foreign HEIs, and the need to better align the curriculum with market needs. Combined with continued growth in the private higher education sector, and a goal to improve Indonesia's elite HEIs to strive for world-class status places, Indonesian higher education is at a crossroad with many opportunities. Further research is required to determine how Indonesian HEIs can best maximize the opportunities identified in this chapter. The latent potential of such a large higher education system with such tremendous growth opportunities will enable this crouching Asian tiger to emerge as a respected player on the global higher education scene in the future.

Notes

1. Established in 2007 as part of a higher education management training program of United States Agency for International Development's (USAID) Decentralized Basic Education 2 Project, KPTIP was organized to build partnerships between member universities. The purpose of the consortium is to improve the quality of higher education among KPTIP member universities, strengthen the system of decentralized education in Indonesia, and provide an avenue for member universities to better network and collaborate together. Comprised of 19 universities in Indonesia and the United States, KPTIP sponsors a number of publications, projects, an Academy for Higher Education Management, and training meetings on a variety of higher education topics.
2. BHMN was first piloted in 2000 in four public universities considered to be the most established in Indonesia (University of Indonesia, Gadjah Mada University, Institut Teknologi Bandung, and Bogor Agricultural University). Three other universities joined in subsequent years: North Sumatra University, Medan (2003), Indonesian Institute of Education, Bandung (2004), and Airlangga University (2006).
3. Data for the study were collected using a mixed-methods approach based around a survey instrument. Researchers conducted on-site, telephone, Skype, or correspondence interviews with content area experts (CAEs). Most CAEs included higher education administrators, policy makers, university faculty members, and other practitioners with substantial experience working firsthand in Indonesia. Selection of participants used snowball sampling

techniques based on an extensive literature review and suggestions from identified CAEs. A total of one hundred individuals participated in this study (with an 83.3 percent response rate). The instrument consisted of seven closed-ended background questions and fourteen open-ended questions relating to Indonesian higher education. Examples of qualitative questions asked include "Question 4: What strategies do you think are most effective at upgrading the quality of higher education in Indonesia?" and "Question 6: What are the emerging trends in Indonesian higher education?"

Qualitative data was recorded and transcribed, cleaned, coded, and analyzed using NVivo qualitative analysis software. The following procedure was followed to decode qualitative responses from CAE interviews: (1) participant codes: I03 indicates that the participant is a content area expert and she/he is the third international interviewee or IN23 indicates the participant is an Indonesian CAE and she/he is the 23rd person to be interviewed; and (2) section codes: the 5a of IN23–5a represents the question number response from the 23rd Indonesian CAE respondent. For instance, I03-13 indicates that this data came from the third international CAE interviewed, and the referenced section came from Question 13 transcription using NVivo.

References

Almasmari, Hakim, Joe Parkinson, and Farnaz Fassihi. 2011. "Middle East: Demonstrations Expand Beyond Egypt: From Algeria to Iran, Protests Sparked by Anti-Mubarak Revolt Show Renewed Vigor, as Regimes Scramble to Respond." *Wall Street Journal*, February 14, A14.

Brodjonegoro, Satryo Soemantri. 2002. *Higher Education Reform in Indonesia*. Jakarta, Indonesia: Directorate General of Higher Education, Ministry of National Education.

Hamad, Ibnu, Helmi Qodrat Ichtiat, and Zulham. 2001. "Political Education through the Mass Media? A Survey of Indonesian University Students." *Asia Pacific Media Educator* 11: 55–71.

Hapsari, Arghea Desafti. 2010. "Court Rejects Education Entities Law." *The Jakarta Post*, April 1.

Harry, Keith, and Hilary Perraton. 1999. "Open and Distance Learning for the New Society." In *Higher Education through Open and Distance Learning*, ed. Keith Harry (pp. 1–12). New York: Routledge.

Jacob, W. James. 2010. "Achieving Greater Autonomy in Indonesian Higher Education." Paper presented at the Universitas Sebelas Maret, Surakarta, Indonesia, February 24, 2010.

Luschei, Thomas F., Dewi Padmo, and J. Michael Spector. 2009. "The Open University of Indonesia and Florida State University: Communication, Collaboration, and the Important Work of Training Teachers." *TechTrends: Linking Research & Practice to Improve Learning* 53 (1): 20–22.

Marginson, Simon. 2007. "'One Little Piece of Endless Sky...' Global Flows and Global Field: Imagining Worldwide Relations of Power in Higher Education." Paper presented at a seminar titled Geographies of Knowledge/Geometries of Power: Global Higher Education in the 21st Century, February 5–7, 2007, Gregynog, Wales.

Marginson, Simon, and Marijk van der Wende. 2006. *Globalisation and Higher Education*. Paris: OECD.

Maulia, Erwida. 2010. "Govt to Retain Universities' Autonomy." *The Jakarta Post*, April 13.

Nizam. 2006. "Indonesia: The Need for Higher Education Reforms." In *Higher Education in Southeast Asia*, ed. UNESCO (pp. 35–68). Paris: UNESCO.

Organisation for Economic Co-operation and Development. 2004. *Quality and Recognition in Higher Education: The Cross-Border Challenge*. Paris: OECD.

Pannen, Paulina. 2003. "Distance Education Public Policy and Practice in Higher Education: The Case of Indonesia." *Brazilian Review of Open and Distance Learning* 3 (4).

Pannen, Paulina, and Abubakar. 2005. "Designing e-learning: Shouldn't We Be Ready?" Proceedings of the Second International Conference on eLearning for Knowledge-Based Society, August 4–7, 2005, Bangkok, Thailand.

Romano, Angela. 1996. "Dinamika Aktivitas Kaum Intelektual di Indonesia" ["The Dynamics of the Intellectual Community's Activity in Indonesia"]. *Bambang Suteng Sulasmono* 10 (1): 8–19.

Welch, Anthony R. 2006. "Blurred Vision? Public and Private Higher Education in Indonesia." *Higher Education* 54 (5): 665–687.

Zuhairi, Aminudin, Effendi Wahyono, and Sharon Suratinah. 2006. "The Historical Context, Current Development, and Future Challenges of Distance Education in Indonesia." *Quarterly Review of Distance Education* 7 (1): 95–101.

Chapter 16

"Transforming Australia's Higher Education System": New Accountability Policies for a Global Era?

Lesley Vidovich

In Australian higher education, the establishment of a powerful, new, and controversial national regulatory body—the Tertiary Education Quality and Standards Agency (TEQSA)—emerged from the federal government's radical policy shift outlined in *Transforming Australia's Higher Education System* (2009). With TEQSA's main brief to monitor the quality of Australian higher education, it became one of the government's key "solutions" to the policy "problem" of enhancing Australia's positioning in the competitive global knowledge economy. In addition to accrediting institutions, TEQSA's role is to monitor teaching and learning standards as well as research standards, and therefore it represents a significant development in enhancing the accountability of universities to central government. In the period before TEQSA was fully operational, major concerns were voiced from the sector that TEQSA policies would create a stranglehold of "red tape" around universities, undermining their autonomy. This chapter analyses the tensions around TEQSA accountability policies, many of which are reflected and refracted through higher education policies in other countries. Examining global-national-local dynamics of accountability policies in relation to Australian higher education provides an opportunity for "policy learning" internationally. The discussion draws on the conceptual lens of trust to examine the implications of accountability policies that appear to undermine the very risk-taking and innovations which purportedly characterize a global knowledge era.

Introduction: Global-National-Local Dynamics

In its landmark report, *Tertiary Education for a Global Knowledge Society*, OECD stated: "the widespread recognition that tertiary education is a major driver of economic competitiveness in an increasingly knowledge-driven economy has made high quality tertiary education more important than ever before" (OECD 2008, 13). In Australia, TEQSA was established to enhance the accountability of universities to the Federal Government for achieving high quality outcomes "in the national interest." The creation of TEQSA was part of a larger policy ensemble, *Transforming Australia's Higher Education System* (Australian Government 2009), which was designed to forge a radical shift in the engagement of the Australian university sector with an increasingly competitive and globalized marketplace for knowledge and skills. TEQSA legislation was delayed several times due to the high level of contestation from the sector (universities), although TEQSA is expected to be operational in 2012.

Globalization forms the broader framing for this analysis of new accountability policy in Australian higher education. It is a complex and contested phenomenon that points to the greater interconnectedness of the world—economically, socially, culturally, and politically (Bottery 2006). Simon Marginson (2007) argues that globalizing processes in higher education can be better understood by conducting "situated case studies" that are nestled within their own localized context. This analysis of TEQSA policy in Australian higher education can be seen, then, as a case study of wider patterns of changing accountability policies across many countries. The author has argued elsewhere (Vidovich 2009) that in the last decade we have witnessed a "policy pandemic" of new accountability policies in higher education across the globe. This term was derived from Ben Levin's (1998) concept of "policy epidemic," but it takes the disease analogy one step further to denote accelerated uncritical policy "borrowing" sweeping across continents and countries with very different historical, cultural, political, and economic traditions and circumstances. In counterbalance to "policy pandemics," it has also been argued that a greater emphasis on critical "policy learning" (in contrast to uncritical "policy borrowing") is required to support the development of policies that are more relevant to the unique localized settings of different jurisdictions (Lange and Alexiadou 2010; Vidovich 2009). That is, "policy learning" emphasizes the "agency" of policy actors in determining site-specific policies and practices.

"Agency" in negotiating locally relevant policies is a concept that we are hearing more about in recent times, after a period when globalization was understood in more simplistic terms of a top-down omnipotent force overwhelming all before it. In the field of higher education, Simon Marginson and Gary Rhoades's (2002) "glo-na-cal agency heuristic" has been influential in highlighting the dynamic two-way exchanges between global, national, and local (university) levels in contemporary higher education policy processes. Their heuristic foregrounds the agency of individuals and organizations at all levels in actively engaging with apparent "global" trends.

This chapter is framed by the "glo-na-cal agency heuristic" and focuses on the dynamics of accountability policy processes extending between global, national, and local levels. Although the primary focus is on national level accountability policy in Australian higher education, two-way interactions are also considered with the "global" level (international developments) and the "local" level (university responses). Examining global-national-local dynamics in relation to Australian higher education accountability policies provides an opportunity for "policy learning," both in Australia and in other national contexts.

The Australian Higher Education Policy Setting

Australia is a federation with a division of powers between the Commonwealth and state governments set in the constitution at federation in 1901. Although the states have legal responsibility for education, in the last 30 years (corresponding with the ascension of globalization and neoliberal ideology), the Commonwealth has increased its steerage using financial policy levers, purportedly to serve the national interest. The Commonwealth has the "power of the purse" in Australia as it raises income tax, creating a vertical fiscal imbalance, so that states become reliant on the Commonwealth for funds. Although state governments still take a major role in setting schooling policy, higher education is largely dictated by the Commonwealth government (also referred to as the federal or national government).

There are now 39 universities in Australia enrolling approximately 1 million students. Universities Australia is an association representing all universities, but the sector is also divided into subgroups (some more formal than others). The groupings with a secretariat are Group of Eight (research-intensive), Australian Technology Network (former institutes of technology), and Innovative Research Universities (established as alternatives to "traditional" universities in the 1960s and 1970s). In addition, there are nonaligned universities (largely former colleges) as well as private universities and providers. CEOs of universities are referred to as vice chancellors. There has been over 100 percent growth in university student enrollments in the last two decades, but in the same time period teaching staff has increased by only 33 percent (with more than half of those being casual). It is interesting to note that administrative staff has increased by substantially more (42 percent). In the decade between 1995 and 2005 (under a conservative coalition government), Australia was the only OECD country in which government funding for higher education remained static. There was a growing reliance on international students (especially from the Asian region) for income by most Australian universities. At the time of writing however, there was a significant decline in international enrollments, with both the United States and United Kingdom attracting larger market shares. The expansion in student enrollments coupled with underfunding (including understaffing) and enhanced international competition points to potential concerns about "quality" in Australian higher education.

When a new Labor government was elected in Australia at the end of 2007, one of its first acts based on its election platform of an Education Revolution was to initiate a major review of higher education. The Review Chair was a well-respected former university vice chancellor, and the report (Bradley 2008) recommended radical transformation of Australian higher education. The government's policy response to this Bradley Review was a ten-year reform agenda entitled *Transforming Australia's Higher Education System* (2009) where the government accepted almost all of the review recommendations, including injection of A$5.4 billion over four years into the Australian university sector, despite the global financial crisis. The government stated that this policy ensemble "is essential to enable Australia to participate fully in, and benefit from, the global knowledge economy. Funding that meets student demand—coupled with ambitious targets, rigorous quality assurance and full transparency—is the only way Australia can meet the knowledge and skills challenges it faces" (Australian Government 2009, 5). TEQSA is a key initiative in this policy ensemble and as an umbrella structure it pulls together new and diverse forms of accountability policies.

Accountability Policy Tensions

Accountability can be defined as the "obligation to be responsive to the legitimate interests of those affected by decisions, programs and interventions" (Considine 2005, 207), but the simplicity of this definition belies the multiple and often-contradictory incarnations of accountability policies. Multiple discourses include quality (with all of its variants such as quality assurance [QA] and quality improvement [QI]), excellence, standards and performance indicators, to name just a few. These are not discrete policy domains, and there is extensive slippage between these various accountability discourses, as evidenced in the OECD's (2008) *Tertiary Education for a Global Knowledge Society*. This two-volume report devotes a chapter to "Assuring and Improving Quality." It opens by citing a number of definitions of quality assurance, leading with "the process of establishing stakeholder confidence that provision (input, process and outcomes) fulfils expectations and measures up to threshold minimum requirements" (Harvey cited in OECD 2008, 261). However, the chapter acknowledges the complexity of the concept of "quality assurance," in part due to "the diverse perceptions of quality itself" (262), and cites the seminal work of Harvey and Green (1993) who distinguished five key aspects of quality as exception (excellence); perfection (zero defect); fitness for purpose (defined by the provider); value for money (efficiency and effectiveness); and transformation (enhancement). The chapter also presents Judith Sachs's (1994) distillation of Harvey and Green's five categories into two broad types of QA for accountability and QA for improvement (sometimes referred to as QI). The OECD report notes that these dual requirements "are tackled quite differently across countries... [and that] deep conflict is embedded in current developments worldwide" (OECD 2008, 265). Although the report identifies three main approaches to quality assurance—accreditation, assessment (evaluation), and audit (review)—hybrid combinations of these are also evident in many countries.

Despite the multiple variants of accountability in higher education across the globe, and an array of policies on quality assurance, empirical research conducted by the author and colleagues in different countries on higher education accountability policies over the last decade has revealed a number of common patterns of embedded tensions. This research spans Australia (Vidovich 2002, 2004), South Africa (Vidovich et al. 2000), England (Vidovich and Slee 2001), Mainland China (Vidovich et al. 2007), Hong Kong Special Administrative Region (Currie et al. 2008), and Singapore (Vidovich 2008). In particular, tensions were consistently noted by research participants between internal and external accountability; outward (horizontal) and upward (vertical) accountability; accountability that assesses processes and outcomes; and accountability that assesses in qualitative and quantitative terms. While internal institutional self-assessment (potentially a form of professional accountability) featured as a first stage of quality assurance mechanisms in higher education in many countries, research participants maintained that it was the publicly visible external audit that was much at higher stakes in terms of funding and reputation. Consequently, a growing emphasis on external accountability potentially undermines the developmental value of internal self-reflection. Within the expanding domain of external accountabilities, research participants reported tensions between outward forms of democratic accountability to the community and upward forms of managerial accountability to governments who seek tighter steerage of higher education. Upward accountability has also been augmented by the influence of international league tables and competition between universities—and countries—to enhance their position in the global marketplace. One might argue that there has been a powerful hybridization of managerial and market accountabilities to forge upwardly directed accountability agendas that potentially threaten the autonomy of universities. Research participants also frequently reported tensions between accountability for institutional processes on the one hand and outcomes on the other. The general trend has been to move from a focus on processes to focus on outcomes, although this is more entrenched in research than in teaching and learning. In relation to assessment of outcomes, research participants point to tensions between more qualitative assessments aligned with professional judgments and more quantitative assessments where a number is assigned (such as a citation index in research or a score on a course experience questionnaire in teaching and learning). Research participants frequently raised issues about the validity and reliability of quantitative measures in such a complex arena as higher education. A narrowing of research and teaching activities to fit with government prescribed quantifiable measures was also a repeated concern of participants.

This empirical research across a number of countries revealed relatively consistent trends toward external and upward accountabilities, and a focus on assessment of outcomes in quantitative terms. This trend represents an increasing emphasis on the prove dimension of accountability (quality assurance) at the expense of an improve dimension (quality improvement or enhancement). While the former is more about centralized government control, the latter is more respectful of university autonomy. These tensions that were identified in higher education accountability policies reflect wider tensions between regulation and deregulation, respectively. The evolution of TEQSA accountability policies has involved the negotiation of these tensions between the Australian government and the higher education sector (universities). TEQSA predecessors in the 1990s and 2000s (Committee for Quality Assurance in Higher Education and Australian Universities Quality Agency) conducted relative "light touch" audits of universities, but by the third decade of quality assurance policy in Australian higher education, the assessment of processes rather than outcomes, in particular, was seen as not rigorous enough to meet the demands of the increasingly competitive globalized context of higher education.

The Evolution of TEQSA Policy (2009–2011): "The Devil is in the Detail"

TEQSA significantly augments the regulation of Australian higher education, heralding new forms of accountability policy. TEQSA accountability is focused on standards, as indicated in the TEQSA Bill (Australian Government 2011) that includes a Standards Framework for

1) Providers (including registration and course accreditation)
2) Qualifications
3) Teaching and learning

4) Research
5) Information.

The government's initial policy statement (2009, 32) indicated that TEQSA would "cut through some of the regulatory complexity and red tape that currently exists." However, TEQSA legislation forged accountability mechanisms that are much more comprehensive, complex, and "high stakes" (for e.g., potential deregistration of institutions and allocation of performance funding) than ever before. This, then, begs the question of why the Australian Government saw the need for new accountability mechanisms. First, reform targets of enhanced participation and equity in higher education created concerns that standards would drop with greater student numbers and diversity. Second, as the reforms were injecting significantly more money into the sector there was a perceived need for enhanced accountability for public funds. Third, with the reforms moving to a student demand system of funding (away from central Government allocation of student places), the minister asserted that "students must be protected in a more market driven system" (Evans cited in Trounson 2010c, 25). Fourth, with anticipated accelerating growth in private providers of higher education, monitoring their standards was seen to be in the "national interest" of preserving the reputation of Australian higher education, locally and internationally.

The two year period between the TEQSA policy announcement in 2009 and the legislation in 2011, was marked by high levels of resistance from the sector to the extent that legislation was delayed. As different issues were negotiated along this policy trajectory, temporary policy "settlements" were reached. One particular development stood out in the evolution of TEQSA policy discourses and details, and that was the strategic appointment of Denise Bradley as the Interim TEQSA Chair in mid-2010. Bradley had chaired the major review of Australian higher education (Bradley 2008) that initiated TEQSA. This appointment could be seen as punctuating the development of TEQSA policy into two phases with different characteristics.

In the early policy development phase from mid-2009 (policy announcement) to mid-2010 (appointment of Interim TEQSA Chair), universities were highly critical of TEQSA. Their primary concerns were about microregulation and overwhelming red tape that threatened to strangle universities and seriously erode their autonomy. Different university groupings (for e.g., Group of Eight) were initially lobbying over policy details in different ways, reflecting their own interests and positioning within the sector. By 2010, the chorus of resistance reached a crescendo with TEQSA being variously described in the media as toxic, intrusive, muscular, and a "Sherman tank." The executive director of the Group of Eight universities indicated that the group had initially been a vocal advocate of TEQSA to "get rid of the shonks and shore up the quality of provision," but TEQSA had turned into a "narrow and highly prescriptive straightjacket for institutions" (Gallagher cited in Hare 2010a). The government faced a "mini revolt" (Healy 2010) by vice chancellors over TEQSA policy and subsequently it announced a redraft and delay of the TEQSA legislation, promising that "the second draft of the higher education standards would look quite different from the first" (Healy 2010, 21). Criticism continued, however, with one vice chancellor asserting that "every extra standard...means another spool of red tape running from Canberra [capital of Australia] around the throat of academics" (Craven 2010, 28). In mid-2010, the debate was markedly diffused with the appointment of Denise Bradley as interim chair of TEQSA—seen by the sector as a welcome "circuit-breaker." The chair of Universities Australia (representing all universities) commented that "all the signs point to the fact that the government has been listening to the concerns of the sector" (Coaldrake cited in Hare 2010b).

In the subsequent policy development phase from mid-2010 (appointment of interim TEQSA chair) to mid-2011 (legislation), Denise Bradley successfully shifted the policy discourses away from microregulation. She forged a commission model for the TEQSA Board that dispersed power more widely than a single CEO who could, for example, operate alone to deregister a university. Bradley also forged discourses of partnership between the government and the sector, and frequently reiterated the negotiated "solutions" to the key sector concerns: "TEQSA would operate with a risk-based proportionate approach using threshold standards" (Bradley cited in Trounson and Lane 2010, 37). Interestingly, the new minister for higher education was also quoted, using exactly the same words, pointing to a harmonization of policy discourses amongst the policy elite. Thus, all universities would not be subject to the same scrutiny, and those at greater risk of falling below the threshold standards (especially the new private providers) would be subject to more frequent and rigorous audits.

A national regulator with "teeth" was welcome by the sector (Lane and Hare 2011), as long as the autonomy of existing universities was not eroded, and the "teeth" were used to "bite" the new private providers. Criticisms of TEQSA policy were moderated after Bradley's appointment, although they certainly did not disappear. One of the key concerns from university vice chancellors as policy details continued to emerge was inadequate consultation with the sector. For example, in late 2010, there was an invitation-only two-day briefing on the new draft TEQSA legislation, and only seven of the thirty-nine vice chancellors were present amongst the thirty delegates, signaling a closed and tightly controlled consultation (Trounson 2010b, 37). Another controversial issue was the measurement of student learning outcome standards and the lack of a valid and reliable measurement instrument. The government's proposed use of the Collegiate Learning Assessment (CLA) test from the United States to measure graduate generic skills drew strong negative sector reactions, as evidenced by headlines in the higher education press: "No end to row over standards" (Trounson 2010d, 29) and "US test of skills a poor fit here" (Lane 2010a, 25). A government spokesperson claimed that the "CLA would allow international benchmarking and pointed to OECD endorsement of the test" (Lane 2010b, 24). The OECD also had its own project called AHELO, signaling much wider (albeit nascent) agendas for the measurement of learning outcomes. As resistance from the sector mounted, the government pushed back its timeline from 2013 to 2014 for development of a CLA-style instrument along with a new University Experience Survey as key elements in accountability for student learning outcomes, and it promised "to consult with universities to build more robust instruments" (Lane 2011, 33). The chair of Universities Australia "welcomed the government's moves to address the sector's concerns" (Coaldrake cited in Trounson 2011a, 35). Under the influence of the Universities Australia chair, sector responses to TEQSA were becoming less differentiated according to university groupings and his central role in the negotiation of TEQSA policy was widely recognized: "Coaldrake's legacy is an unprecedented unity across the sector, leaving it in a strong position to present a united front to Government" (Trounson 2011b, 31). Universities were coming together and harmonizing discourses around their preferred policy options to "tether" TEQSA.

In all, the autonomy of universities was the central issue for the higher education sector throughout the evolution of TEQSA policy in the period from 2009 to 2011, although the target of criticism was more microregulation in the early negotiations and a lack of consultation in the later negotiations. In this period, the sector moved from antagonistic fractured voices about TEQSA policy to a more unified voice and greater participation in the policy processes. The contestation evident in the evolution of TEQSA policy details corresponds to the tensions outlined in the previous section. By the time of TEQSA legislation in 2011, the broad parameters of its accountability policy "settlement" had distilled—with temporary settlements negotiated on specific issues along the way. However, the sector will continue to be "devilled" by the details of TEQSA accountability policy for years to come.

TEQSA Policy Processes Viewed through the Conceptual Lens of Trust

The concept of "trust" is emerging as a potentially useful analytic tool in educational research, although its application is largely in the schooling sector. Anthony Bryk and Barbara Schneider (2002) characterized trust in terms of competence, respect, personal regard for others, and integrity. Mieke van Houtte (2007, 826) later defined it as "confidence that expectations will be met," and he delineated five dimensions of trust as competence, honesty, openness, reliability, and benevolence. Competence, respect, and confidence are key words in these definitions. However, William G. Tierney (2006) observed that there is a lack of either conceptual or empirical work on trust in higher education, and he set about developing a "grammar of trust" consisting of nine frames: a repeated interaction; a dynamic process; an end; an exchange; utilizing faith; taking risk; an ability; a rational choice; and a cultural construction. In the first frame, trust develops through repeated interactions between parties, but conversely, a single interaction can cause trust to be destroyed. In the second frame, trust is a dynamic process through which complexity can be reduced because it can enable expectations about what will occur. In the third frame, as well as being a process, trust can also be an end, in a cyclical manner, whereby the process of trusting can generate an outcome of more trust. In the fourth frame, trust is an exchange or a reciprocal relationship between parties, which goes beyond a particular event. In the fifth frame, trust can be seen as faith that another party will fulfill their part of an agreement. In the sixth frame, trust involves taking a risk that another party will do as expected. In the seventh frame, trust is an ability that is learned over time, rather than being innate. The last two frames, Tierney argues, constitute an overarching language to conceptualize trust, with rational choice focusing on how individuals align themselves to a structure, whereas a cultural construction conceives of more fluid social organizations. He emphasizes a cultural understanding of contexts; that is, how individuals within cultures acquire and change abilities that generate trust. From his "grammar," Tierney defines trust as "a dynamic process in which two or more parties are involved in a series of interactions that may require a degree of risk or faith on the part of one or both parties" (2006, 57).

Discourses of trust were clearly evident in this case study of new accountability policy in Australian higher education. The principal "parties," from Tierney's (2006) definition, in the TEQSA case were the institutions of government (represented by the policy elite of ministers and "purple circle" of advisors) and universities (represented by vice chancellors and their national associations). In the policy statement *Transforming Australia's Higher Education System*, the Australian Government (2009, 9) heralded "a new relationship between Government and Educators: a relationship built on mutual respect, trust and agreed funding compact." In the negotiation of specific TEQSA policies in the period 2009–2011 between the federal government and universities, the issue of trust (including "confidence" as part of the ensemble of discourses around trust) was raised by both "sides":

1) From the government: "It's about trusting universities and providing some additional incentives [performance funding]" (Coutts cited in Hare 2010a).
2) From universities: "The universities themselves must have confidence in their regulator...it is vital that the [TEQSA] chief executive has

the confidence of the sector as a whole, not just one or other faction" (Craven 2010, 28).

Trust was also highlighted by the chair of Universities Australia when he was encouraging the government to release the second draft of TEQSA legislation for sector consultation: "we are hopeful and encouraging the government to release a draft at an appropriate point...which would help build trust and confidence in the process" (Coaldrake cited in Trounson and Lane 2010, 37). The chair of Universities Australia (Coaldrake) was one of two key focal points for building trust, both within the sector and between the sector and the government. The other key focal point was the interim chair of TEQSA (Bradley). As a vice chancellor acknowledged: "Bradley has the respect and confidence of the higher education sector" (Hare 2010c, online). In addition to chairing the major review of Australian higher education in 2008, she was a former highly regarded vice chancellor. Since the 1970s, she had been a member or director of commissions, councils, and prestigious professional organizations, and she was also a foundation director of the Australian Universities Quality Agency (predecessor of TEQSA), pointing to her expert knowledge of quality/accountability policy. Denise Bradley was able to bring this long experience and respect to build a "bridge" of trust between the government and the sector over TEQSA policy. Together, Bradley and Coaldrake facilitated a series of temporary settlements toward embedding TEQSA policy in Australian higher education. There was a noticeable "harmonization" of policy discourses, both within the sector to resist TEQSA and later between the sector and government as policy settlements were beginning to gel.

It is important to reiterate, however, that there were multiple vested interests in the policy, and the dynamics of trust-mistrust relationships were complex and rapidly changing during the policy negotiations. High levels of mistrust "broke out" on numerous occasions, for example, when the vice chancellors staged a "mini-revolt" over microregulation by the government in the first draft of TEQSA legislation, and also when the government proposed direct importation of the CLA instrument from the United States to measure student learning outcomes. Trust was compromised in these instances. In each case, in response to outcries from the sector the government backed off, delaying planned policies, and promised to revise policy details as well as consult more widely with the sector—all strategies designed to reclaim trust.

I have focused here on the dynamics of trust between the principal parties of Australian government (national level) and universities (local level). However, there were also issues around trust—implied if not explicitly articulated—in international (global level) interactions as TEQSA policy evolved. For example, there was apparent trust in the quality of the CLA instrument from the United States to measure student learning outcomes. Similarly, there was implied trust in the OECD as the Australian government was keenly awaiting the results of the OECD's feasibility study on AHELO to inform the Australian approach. Will this level of trust in international developments and confidence that they will be relevant to Australia be misplaced? The OECD has a lot to say about trust in higher education policy processes: "that mechanisms of regular and institutionalized consultation—which are inherent to consensual policy making—contribute to the development of trust among parties, and help them reach consensus" (OECD 2008, 317). This suggests a sanitized conceptualization of policy development that washes away political struggles and contestation over policy as well as the strong possibility of mistrust developing between key policy actors. More specifically in relation to accountability and quality assurance systems, the OECD (2008, 294) emphasized that one of the key challenges is "to build consensus and trust among all stakeholders with an interest in quality." Did this happen in the case of Australia's TEQSA policy? Yes and no. I have indicated above that trust relationships were important in the policy negotiations, and that the government was prepared to modify policy details (albeit marginally) to maintain some level of trust, but all stakeholders were not consulted. These TEQSA policies will significantly impact the work of academics within universities, and surely "all stakeholders" includes academics (and students), but their voices have hardly been heard in this policy process. Arguably, it will be too late once the realities of new and complex forms of accountability hit the grassroots level in universities over the next two or three years. How will lack of consultation with academics affect trust relationships within universities? Longitudinal research as TEQSA policies are enacted will be illuminating.

Conclusion

This chapter offered an Australian case study of changing accountability policies. The focus was on highly contested policies around the establishment of the TEQSA, which threatened to strangle universities in "red tape" and erode the autonomy of universities, purportedly in "the national interest." The sector wanted regulation (to control the threat of burgeoning new providers), but universities did not want to sacrifice any of their existing autonomy. At the heart of the contestation is a push-pull tension between regulation and deregulation. More specifically, tensions embedded in TEQSA policies resonate with those endemic to accountability policies in many countries across the globe. There has been a marked transition from internal to external and from outward to upward forms of accountability, as well as a transition from assessment of processes to outcomes and from qualitative to quantitative measures. In Australia, TEQSA accountability policy represents more regulation for higher education, with the privileging of QA over QI. The interim chair of TEQSA, Bradley, was aware of these tensions and the need for TEQSA to work through them: "balancing quality assurance with quality improvement will be a key challenge" (Bradley cited in Trounson 2010a, 21). Time will tell how well this challenge is met. The period of development of specific TEQSA accountability policies between 2009 and 2011 was marked by a series of "mini revolts" from the higher education sector, followed by the government modifying policy details and time lines to achieve temporary policy settlements along the way toward TEQSA legislation. It seems that the Australian government has largely been successful in achieving its goal of a superregulator, notwithstanding the need for some compromises to gain the cooperation of the sector. However, is this omnipotent accountability mechanism an appropriate policy "solution" to the "problem" of enhancing competitive positioning of Australian universities in a global knowledge economy? I would argue that the autonomy or agency of universities (from Marginson and Rhoades's [2002] "glo-na-cal agency heuristic") to engage with the increasingly globalized field of higher education in their own ways is the key to diversity and innovation characteristic of a global knowledge era. Trust is a central concept here. From Tierney's (2006) definition, trust provides the foundation for risk-taking. Therefore, the impact of any accountability policies that do not protect and foster trust relationships will be to undermine the very risk-taking and innovation that purportedly characterize a global knowledge era.

By examining the global-national-local dynamics of Australia's TEQSA policies, there is an opportunity for critical policy "learning" (Lange and Alexiadou 2010; Vidovich 2009), in contrast to uncritical policy "borrowing." So, what is to be learnt from this Australian case of developing accountability policy in higher education? There is no intention to generalize from the Australian case to other countries, as the "solutions" to policy "problems" are (or at least should be) very context-dependent. I would say, though, that trust is a central and useful concept in understanding the global-national-local dynamics of accountability policy processes. Trust must be nurtured.

References

Australian Government. 2009. *Transforming Australia's Higher Education System*. Canberra: Department of Education, Employment, Workplace Relations and Social Inclusion.
Australian Government. 2011. *TEQSA Bill*. Canberra: Department of Education, Employment, Workplace Relations and Social Inclusion.
Bottery, Michael. 2006. "Education and Globalization." *Educational Review* 58 (1): 95–113.
Bradley, Denise. 2008. *Review of Australian Higher Education*. Canberra: Department of Education, Employment, Workplace Relations and Social Inclusion.

Bryk, Anthony, and Barbara Schneider. 2002. *Trust in Schools: A Core Resource for Improvement.* New York: Russell Sage Foundation.
Considine, Mark. 2005. *Making Public Policy.* Cambridge: Polity.
Craven, Greg. 2010. "Taking the Toxic out of TEQSA." *The Australian Higher Education Supplement*, June 23, 28.
Currie, Jan, Lesley Vidovich, and Rui Yang. 2008. "'Countability Not Answerability': Accountability in Hong Kong and Singaporean universities." *Asia-Pacific Journal of Education* 28 (1): 67–85.
Hare, Julie. 2010a. "Be Careful What You Wish For: More Regulation on the Cards." *Campus Review*, February 15.
Hare, Julie. 2010b. "Bradley, Schofield to Lead Implementation of Quality Agencies." *Campus Review*, July 12.
Hare, Julie. 2010c. "Come Together." *Campus Review*, July 19.
Healy, Guy. 2010. "Canberra Appeasing Unis on Regulator." *The Australian Higher Education Supplement*, May 19, 21.
Lane, Bernard. 2010a. "US Test of Skills a Poor Fit Here." *The Australian Higher Education Supplement*, December 1, 25.
Lane, Bernard. 2010b. "Performance Funding Queried." *The Australian Higher Education Supplement*, December 8, 24.
Lane, Bernard. 2011. "Extra Time Given to Develop Key Learning Gauges." *The Australian Higher Education Supplement*, January 26, 33.
Lane, Bernard, and Julie Hare. 2011. "Regulator with Teeth 'Welcome'." *The Australian Higher Education Supplement*, March 9, 32.
Lange, Bettina, and Nafsika Alexiadou. 2010. "Policy Learning and Governance of Education Policy in the EU." *Journal of Education Policy* 25 (4): 443–463.
Levin, Ben. 1998. "An Epidemic of Education Policy: What We Can Learn From Each Other?" *Comparative Education* 34 (2): 131–141.
Marginson, Simon. 2007. "Global Position and Position Taking: The Case of Australia." *Journal of Studies in International Education* 11 (1): 5–32.
Marginson, Simon, and Gary Rhoades. 2002. "Beyond National States, Markets and Systems of Higher Education: A Glonacal Agency Heuristic." *Higher Education* 43 (3): 281–309.
Organisation for Economic Co-operation and Development. 2008. *Tertiary Education for a Knowledge Society.* Paris: OECD.
Sachs, Judith. 1994. "Strange Yet Compatible Bedfellows: Quality Assurance and Quality Improvement." *Australian Universities' Review* 37 (1): 22–25.
Tierney, William G. 2006. *Trust and the Public Good.* New York: Peter Lang.
Trounson, Andrew. 2010a. "Balancing Act a Challenge for New Tertiary Standards Agency." *The Australian Higher Education Supplement*, July 14, 21.
Trounson, Andrew. 2010b. "Regulatory Briefing for Fortunate Few." *The Australian Higher Education Supplement*, November 10, 37.
Trounson, Andrew. 2010c. "Evans Insists on a TEQSA with Teeth." *The Australian Higher Education Supplement*, November 17, 25.
Trounson, Andrew. 2010d. "No End to Row over Standards." *The Australian Higher Education Supplement*, December 1, 29.
Trounson, Andrew. 2011a. "Risk-based Approach to Regulation." *The Australian Higher Education Supplement*, February 23, 35.

Trounson, Andrew. 2011b. "The Next Man in the Hot Seat." *The Australian Higher Education Supplement*, March 9, 31.

Trounson, Andrew, and Bernard Lane. 2010. "Sector Pins Hope on TEQSA Legislation." *The Australian Higher Education Supplement*, December 15, 37.

van Houtte, Mieke. 2007. "Exploring Teacher Trust in Technical/Vocational Secondary Schools." *Teaching and Teacher Education* 23 (6): 826–839.

Vidovich, Lesley. 2002. "Quality Assurance in Australian Higher Education: Globalization and 'Steering at a Distance'." *Higher Education* 43 (3): 391–408.

Vidovich, Lesley. 2004. "Global-National-Local Dynamics in Policy Processes: A Case Study of 'Quality' Policy in Higher Education." *British Journal of Sociology of Education* 25 (3): 341–354.

Vidovich, Lesley. 2008. "Research Assessment in Singaporean Higher Education: Changing Accountabilities in a Context of Globalization." *The International Education Journal: Comparative Perspectives* 9 (1): 41–52.

Vidovich, Lesley. 2009. "You Don't Fatten the Pig by Weighting It: Contradictory Tensions in the 'Policy Pandemic' of Accountability Infecting Education." In *Re-reading Education Policies: Studying the Policy Agenda of the 21st Century*, ed. Maarten Simons, Mark Olssen, and Michael. Peters. Rotterdam, The Netherlands: Sense Publishers.

Vidovich, Lesley, Magda Fourie, Louis Van der Westhuizen, Heinrich Alt, and Somare Holtzhausen. 2000. "Quality Teaching and Learning in Australian and South African Universities: Comparing Policies and Practices." *Compare* 30 (2): 193–209.

Vidovich, Lesley, and Roger Slee. 2001. "Bringing Universities to Account? Exploring Some Global and Local Policy Tensions." *Journal of Education Policy* 16 (5): 431–453.

Vidovich, Lesley, Rui Yang, and Jan Currie. 2007. "Changing Accountabilities in Higher Education as China 'opens up' to Globalization." *Globalization, Societies and Education* 5 (1): 85–107.

Contributors

Authors

Adrián Acosta Silva, Facultad Latinoamericana de Ciencias Sociales (FLACSO), is professor at Universidad de Guadalajara since 1984, and head of the Department of Public Policy at the CUCEA-Universidad de Guadalajara (2010–2013). His books include *Príncipes, burócratas y gerentes: el gobierno de las universidades públicas en México* (2009) and *Poder, gobernabilidad y cambio institucional en las universidades públicas en México* (2nd edition, 2010).

Germán Álvarez-Mendiola is professor at the Center for Advanced Research and Studies in Mexico. He has acted as advisor to the Mexican Ministry of Education and consultant to other organizations. Among other works, he is the author of *Modelos académicos en ciencias sociales y legitimidad científica* (2004).

Paul Axelrod is professor and former dean (2001–2008) of the Faculty of Education at York University. His published books include *Making a Middle Class: Student Life in English Canada during the Thirties* (1990) and (as coauthor), *Opportunity and Uncertainty: Life Course Experiences of the Class of '73* (2000).

James Cohn is chief academic officer, Quest University, Squamish, British Columbia, Canada. Before appointment at Quest, Jim was for 15 years a teaching participant in the Great Books program of St. John's College (USA).

Wietse de Vries is professor at the Benemérita Universidad Autónoma de Puebla, México. His current research involves international comparisons of student and graduate outcomes.

Masao Homma is professor and vice-president, Ritsumeikan Asia Pacific University. He was director-general for policy coordination and education reform in Japan's Ministry of Education from 1999 to 2004, and registrar of Kyoto University and, after its incorporation in 2004, vice-president. His books and papers on higher education include *The Corporatization of National Universities and Its Impacts on University Reform* (2005).

W. James Jacob is director of the Institute for International Studies in Education at the University of Pittsburgh's School of Education. His research includes higher education organizational analysis in developing countries with geographic emphases in Africa, East Asia, and the Pacific Islands. He is coeditor of Palgrave Macmillan's *International and Development Education* series and associate editor of the journal *Excellence in Higher Education*.

Motohisa Kaneko is professor of higher education at the University of Tokyo. He directed the Center for Research and Development of Higher Education at the University of Tokyo until 2010, and was dean of the Graduate School of Education. Since spring 2010, Kaneko is professor and director of research at the Center for National University Finance and Management.

Ravik Karsiki is rector of Sebelas Maret University, Indonesia.

Alma Maldonado-Maldonado is a researcher at the Center for Advanced Research in Mexico. She was previously assistant professor at the University of Arizona's Center for the Study of Higher Education. Her research focuses on comparative higher education. She recently coedited *International Organizations and Higher Education Policy* (2009).

Ross Paul was president of various Canadian universities (most recently Laurentian and Windsor). His book, *Leadership under Fire: The Challenging Role of the Canadian University President*, appeared in 2011.

Tracy Lynn Pelkowski is an instructor and a doctoral student in social and comparative analysis in education at the University of Pittsburgh. Her research includes work on race and racism in education.

Agus D. Priyanto is director of Sebelas Maret University's International Office, Indonesia. His research emphasizes linguistics and higher education management.

F. Mauricio Saavedra is director of Institutional Research and director of Research for the Social Sciences and Humanities at the Universidad Internacional del Ecuador, Quito. He conducts research on higher education policy and undertakes comparative analyses of Latin American higher education.

Theresa Shanahan is a lawyer, associate professor, and associate dean, Research and Professional Development, at the Faculty of Education, York University, Canada. Her research includes work on law and policy (K-12 and postsecondary education), the political economy of postsecondary education, and university governance.

Nelly P. Stromquist is a professor of international education policy in the College of Education at the University of Maryland. She specializes in international development education and gender, which she examines from a critical sociology perspective. Her most recent books include *Feminist Organizations and Social Transformation in Latin America* (2007), and as editor, *The Professoriate in the Age of Globalization* (2007).

Roopa Desai-Trilokekar is assistant professor, Faculty of Education, York University, whose research touches on internationalization in higher education, policy development, and federalism. She is coeditor of *Canada's Universities Go Global* (2009).

Lesley Vidovich is professor at the Graduate School of Education, University of Western Australia. Her research interest is education policy studies, including higher education and schooling. Her published works center on the education policy domains of accountability, quality, equity, and curriculum. She has conducted international comparative studies that include Australia, Europe, South Africa, North America, China, and Singapore.

Yuanyuan Wang serves as a lead evaluator for Collaborative Evaluation and Assessment Capacity (CEAC) at the University of Pittsburgh. A doctoral student in social and comparative analysis in education at the University of Pittsburgh, Administrative and Policy Studies Department, her research interests include international education, especially the effects of college students' participation in international area studies on their global competency.

Richard Wellen is an associate professor in the Department of Social Science and the Graduate Program in the Faculty of Education at York University. He has written on a number of topics related to higher education, including student finance, student consumerism, intellectual integrity, and changing models of scholarly communication.

Pavel Zgaga is a professor of philosophy of education and education policy at the University of Ljubljana, Slovenia. During a period of social and political transition in Slovenia, he was state secretary for higher education (1992–1999) and minister of education (1999–2000). In 2001, after his return to academe, he cofounded the Center for Educational Policy Studies (CEPS). From 2001 to 2004 he was dean of the Faculty of Education and a member of the Senate of the University of Ljubljana

Qiang Zha is a professor at the Faculty of Education, York University. His research interests include comparative higher/education, East Asian and Chinese higher education, global citizenship education, among others. In 2004, he was a corecipient of the UNESCO Palgrave Prize on Higher Education Policy Research. Professor Zha is in the midst of a large research project concerning "Canadian Universities and International Talent in a New Era of Global Geo-Politics."

Editors

William Bruneau is professor emeritus of the University of British Columbia. His research is divided between European studies and Canadian history, particularly the history of Canadian universities. His recent books include *Counting Out the Scholars* (2002), a study of the development and misapplication of performance indicators in higher education. He is editor of *The Collected Papers of Bertrand Russell*, volume 18 (forthcoming 2013).

Professor Bruneau is past president of the Canadian Association of University Teachers, the largest professorial organization in Canada, and of the UBC Faculty Association. His political experience includes a three-year term as an elected trustee of the Vancouver School Board.

Garnet Grosjean is a lecturer in adult and higher education in the Department of Educational Studies and academic coordinator of the Doctor of Education in Educational Leadership and Policy (EdD) Program at UBC, Canada. He coordinates an intercontinental program on adult learning and global change. His research emphasizes higher education and the changing economy, accountability and performance models, the social organization of learning, and policy and practice implications of experiential learning. Grosjean is a registered Professional Biologist (R.P.Bio) and an accredited member of the College of Applied Biology of British Columbia (1977-present).

Hans G. Schuetze is professor emeritus of higher education policy and research, and senior research fellow at the Centre for Policy Studies in Higher Education and Training, University of British Columbia. He currently practices in a law cabinet in Hannover, Germany, specializing in public law, especially legal issues of education. His research is in comparative adult and higher education; educational reforms and their origin, implementation, and effects; and legal and economic issues in education.

Index

academic capitalism, 7, 141, 162, 163, 173, 174
academic freedom, 11, 13, 16, 18, 19, 21, 47, 50, 56, 59, 66, 68, 73, 82, 102, 104, 150, 184, 209, 210, 211, 212, 214, 215, 219, 221, 222
academic misconduct, 210, 218
accountability, 5, 8, 12, 13, 19, 34, 56, 64, 65, 66, 69, 73, 74, 84, 87, 91, 128, 140, 141, 147, 150, 153, 154, 158, 164, 170, 173, 174, 180, 200, 202, 210, 227, 241, 242, 243, 244, 245, 246, 247, 249, 251, 252, 253, 259, 260
accreditation, 97, 98, 115, 121, 136, 138, 140, 142, 150, 155, 157, 198, 204, 227, 245, 246
administrative officers: Chief Administrative Officer (CAO), 101, 103, 104, 105; Chief Executive Officer (CEO), 65, 101, 170, 182, 183, 243, 248, 250; Chief Financial Officer (CFO), 101. *See also* president *and* deans
Africa, 113, 117, 123, 237, 245, 258, 259
ALFA-ACRO Project, 116. *See also* accreditation
ALFA-Tuning, 116
Argentina, 114, 161
Assessment of Higher Education Learning Outcomes (AHELO), 118
Association of Universities and Colleges of Canada (AUCC), 72, 78, 79, 81, 82, 89, 98, 99

Aston University, 39
Australia, 234, 241ff.
Austria, 5, 6
autarchy, 17
autonomy, 4, 5, 8, 11–17, 19, 20, 21, 35, 40, 41, 50, 54, 64, 84, 131, 147, 148, 150–156, 158, 173, 183, 184, 209, 210, 212, 214, 215, 219, 221, 222, 226, 227, 228, 230, 231, 236, 241, 245–249, 252, 253
Axworthy, Lloyd, 79, 80

Belarus, 11
Benemérita Universidad Autonoma de Puebla, 150
Birnbaum, Robert, 51, 67, 74, 134, 137
block plan, 98, 99
Bolivia, 114, 115
Bologna Process, 3, 5, 11, 116
Bologna University, 14
Bradley, Denise, 247, 248, 251, 252
branding, 32, 204
Brazil, 114, 115, 117
Bricall, Joseph, 16

Canada, 4–6, 48, 49, 52, 54, 56, 58, 64, 65, 67, 68, 71, 72, 77–83, 89, 90, 95, 96, 98–100, 102
Canada Foundation for Innovation, 80, 82
Canadian Association of University Teachers (CAUT), 53, 56, 67, 68
Canadian Federation for the Humanities and Social Sciences, 83

Carleton University, 54
Chile, 114, 115, 117, 143, 161
China, 209ff., 234, 245
Chrétien, Jean, 78, 79, 81, 82, 83, 88, 91, 92
Collegiate Learning Assessment, 118, 248
Colombia, 114, 115, 119, 122
commercialization, 4, 8, 9, 43, 237
Communist Party of China, 209
community colleges, 6
Confucius/Cofucianism, 211ff.
Consejo Nacional Educación Superior, 162
Consortium of Indonesian Universities-Pittsburgh, 227
corporatization, 7, 52, 64, 65, 197, 203, 204
curriculum, 3, 6, 13, 33, 37, 40, 50, 55, 96, 97–100, 104, 105, 126, 127, 128, 136, 141, 180, 189, 204, 205, 206, 225, 226, 230, 233–235, 238

deans, 29, 30, 31, 33, 36, 37, 68, 101, 130, 170, 172, 189, 190, 206
Delgado, Rafael Correa, 161
distance education, 30, 32, 33, 226, 228, 229, 232, 236–238
Duff-Berdahl Report, 47, 52, 53, 58, 67, 68
Durham College, 86, 87

economy, 17, 20, 48, 88, 110, 151, 163, 164, 218, 222; knowledge economy, 4, 7, 81, 163, 241, 242, 244, 253
Ecuador, 5, 161ff.
efficiency, 6, 8, 20, 26, 35, 88, 126, 127, 129, 131, 134, 135, 139, 141, 147, 148, 150, 155, 163, 169, 170, 172, 182, 184, 186, 188, 190–194, 228, 245
employers, 64, 118, 140, 235
England, 118, 245
entrepreneurial, 3, 9, 19, 20, 33, 36, 37, 41, 133, 149, 228, 230

Europe, 5, 11–14, 18, 20–22, 44, 56, 77, 111, 116, 214
European Union (EU), 3, 5, 14, 114, 118

Fachhochschulen, 6
faculty, 3, 4, 8, 9, 27–42, 59, 63–74, 96–99, 101–105, 117, 127, 128, 130–137, 139–142, 148, 157, 163, 170–174, 181, 183, 187, 189, 190, 193, 197, 198, 200–207, 218, 229–235, 237
faculty association, 52, 53, 55, 56, 58, 59, 64, 65, 68, 69, 90
flexibility, 13, 32, 55, 129, 210
Foucault, Michel, 110, 122
funding, 13, 129, 140; external/private, 3, 97, 138, 227, 230, 231, 235; public, 4, 5, 50, 51, 54, 55, 71, 79, 80, 81, 82, 84, 85, 127, 131, 138, 139, 152, 164, 170, 179, 180, 185, 187, 227, 229, 230, 244, 245, 250; research, 26, 27, 53, 56, 81, 188, 245; targeted/incentive-based, 7, 128, 172, 218, 244, 247, 250

Germany, 5, 6, 77, 78, 180, 214, 216
globalization, 6, 7, 10, 22, 25, 31, 43, 45, 109, 110, 111, 120, 123, 205, 223, 242, 243, 253, 255, 259
governance, 4, 6, 8, 12, 27–30, 33–37, 39, 40, 47–59, 63–75, 77, 83, 87, 95, 97–99, 101–104, 110, 111, 116, 118, 119, 121, 125–134, 137, 140–142, 147–153, 155–158, 162, 165, 169–171, 173, 180, 181, 183, 189, 190, 192, 209, 213, 215, 222, 227, 228, 231, 237, 258; collegial, 8, 68, 69, 71, 73, 101, 102, 105, 125, 130, 131, 132, 133, 141, 142; global, 110, 111, 119, 121; governing boards, 47, 50–59, 63–66, 68, 69, 73, 74, 81, 98, 100, 101–103, 156, 171, 180, 188, 189, 190, 192, 193, 203; professoriate in, 47, 65, 66; self-, 13, 17, 20, 36; senate, 8, 28, 31, 36, 37, 50, 51, 52,

INDEX 263

54–59, 63–69, 71, 73, 75, 101, 188; shared, 26, 29, 47, 132; students in, 66; university councils, 131, 149, 170, 189
government, 5–8, 27, 30, 47, 49, 50, 51, 55, 59, 64, 65, 66, 71, 77–90, 96, 100, 111, 117, 118, 120, 121, 127, 131–136, 139, 141, 147–158, 180, 181–191, 193, 194, 197–207, 209, 210, 214–217, 219, 220, 226, 227, 229, 230, 233, 234, 236, 237, 241, 243, 244, 246–253; global, 110; national/federal, 55, 78ff., 127, 128, 129, 135, 136, 139, 142, 148, 149, 150, 152–157, 162–170, 172–174, 179, 180, 181–191, 209, 241ff.; provincial/state, 5, 49, 51, 55, 56, 57, 58, 66, 78, 83ff., 96, 138, 243
graduate degree, 154, 170
graduate education, 25, 32, 132
Great Learning, 213, 216
Guelph University, 55

Healy, David, 56
Hirosaki University, 191
Hobbes, Thomas, 111
Hong Kong, 245
human capital, 25
human resources, 7, 233, 236–238
Humboldt, Wilhelm von, 6, 16. *See also* university models

Independent Administrative Agency (Japan), 181, 182, 190
Indonesia Open University, 237
industry, 4, 6–10, 20, 27, 32, 55–57, 86, 88, 99, 163, 174, 200, 201, 206, 207, 231, 235
institutional autonomy, 5, 11, 12, 13, 16, 18, 19, 20, 84, 183, 227
International Monetary Fund (IMF), 109, 114
internationalization, 9, 13, 27, 32–34, 198, 201, 202

Ireland, 118
isomorphism, 3, 138

Japan, 5, 6, 179ff., 198ff.

Kant, Immanuel, 15
knowledge, 4, 7, 15–18, 20, 25, 27, 40, 41, 73, 81, 113, 120, 127, 163, 166, 182, 201–204, 210–222, 237, 241, 242, 244, 251, 253; knowledge workers, 20, 41. *See also* economy, knowledge economy
Kyoto Institute of Technology, 207
Kyoto University, 197

Lakehead University, 54
land grant universities, 6
Latin America, 5, 107, 110, 113, 114, 115, 116, 121, 122, 151, 158, 161, 175, 214, 259
Law for the Coordination of Higher Education (Mexico), 148
Law on Educational Entities (Indonesia), 228
liberal education, 97, 216, 220

Magna Charta Universitatum (Europe), 14, 16, 22
managerial, 9, 12, 13, 40, 51, 53–57, 59, 69, 125, 132, 137, 156, 189, 193, 207, 245
managerialism, 8, 41, 53, 58, 59, 140, 141, 210
market, 4, 7, 9, 18, 19, 20, 25, 42, 47, 51, 55, 84–89, 102, 118, 119, 121, 129, 133, 136, 139, 140, 151, 154, 156, 162, 163, 181, 198, 218, 226, 230, 234, 237, 238, 242, 244, 245, 247
marketization, 7, 164, 181, 218
Martin, Paul, 78, 80, 81, 82, 83, 88, 91
Marxism, 218
McMaster University, 50
Mencius, 214, 216, 219

MERCOSUR, 115. *See also* North American Free Trade Agreement
Mexico, 5, 109, 114, 115, 117, 119, 122, 125–133, 135, 137, 139, 141, 143–145, 147, 150–153, 155–161, 174, 257, 258
Millennium Development Goals, 114
Ministry of Education (Japan), 180, 184, 186, 187, 191, 197, 201
modernization, 20, 128, 133, 150
Monaco, Fabio Roversi, 16

Nara Institute of Science and Technology, 191
National Permanent Planning System of Higher Education, 149
National University Corporation (NUC), 181–191, 194
National University Corporation Law (Japan), 183, 189
New Paradigm, 227
New Public Management, 121, 128, 129, 136, 142, 157, 181, 194
non-university institutions, 6
North American Free Trade Agreement (NAFTA), 115. *See also* MERCOSUR

Olivieri, Nancy, 56
Ontario, 5, 54–56, 59, 61, 75–77, 80, 81, 83, 84, 86–88, 90–92
Organization for Economic Co-operation and Development (OECD), 27, 113, 117, 118, 120, 179, 198, 242, 244, 245, 249, 251, 252

partnerships, with other universities, 86, 231, 232, 234, 236, 238; with non-university agencies, 9, 20, 27, 32, 33, 83, 163, 228, 231, 248
People's Republic of China, 218
perestroika, 12
performance indicators, 5, 51, 54, 65, 150, 154, 227, 244, 260

Plato, 211–213
politics, 15, 17, 47, 49, 59, 67, 73, 90, 133, 137, 151, 155, 213
polytechnics, 6, 86
Portugal, 118
Post-Secondary Education Choice and Excellence Act (Ontario), 86
power, 4, 5, 16, 17, 26, 28, 35, 39–41, 49, 51, 52, 57, 58, 64, 73, 86, 87, 89, 98, 101, 109, 110, 112, 116, 118, 121, 126, 127, 129, 132, 133, 141, 142, 149, 151–153, 155, 156, 168, 170, 173, 181–185, 188–193, 199, 202, 206, 209–211, 214, 215, 218, 234, 241, 243, 245, 248
President (rector), 8, 30–32, 37, 41, 48–50, 53–55, 57, 59, 60, 64–75, 79–82, 85–87, 89, 98, 100, 101, 103–105, 130–133, 135, 141, 161, 162, 164, 167, 168, 170–173, 182, 183, 188–190, 192, 193, 197, 198, 200, 202, 203, 206, 208, 230, 231, 235, 257, 258, 260
Prichard, Robert, 81
private universities, 26, 91, 136, 154, 162, 165, 166, 167, 168, 169, 170, 172, 173, 198, 199, 200, 207, 226, 243
privatization, 7, 20, 163
professors, 29, 31, 34, 35, 36, 38, 40, 41, 47, 49, 50, 51, 56, 71, 99, 102, 130, 132, 133, 141, 150, 152, 154, 157, 158, 169, 180, 203; clinical and adjunct professors, 35; evaluation, 52; sessional, 53, 72, 102, 105; tenure, 34, 35, 37, 41, 50, 59, 68, 70, 102, 103, 130, 132, 135, 136. *See also* teaching
Program for International Student Assessment, 117
public universities, 5, 26, 32, 39, 49, 74, 98, 128, 129, 131, 132, 137–140, 148–150, 152–158, 165, 166, 168–170, 172, 173, 199, 200, 225, 227, 228, 238

Qian, Sanqiang, 211
Qian, Weichang, 211
Qian, Xueshen, 211
Quality for Undergraduate Education (QUE), 227. *See also* accountability
Quebec, 48, 55, 57, 61, 78, 82, 91
Quest University Canada, 95, 96

ranking, 6, 9, 33, 37, 41, 51, 59, 116, 117, 119–121, 227, 236. *See also* world-class regimes, 111
research, 4, 6, 8, 9, 13–20, 26–32, 35, 36, 39, 40, 50, 51, 53, 56–58, 64, 69, 71, 72, 78, 81–84, 88–91, 96, 99, 100, 102, 103, 121, 126, 136, 141, 150, 152, 155, 157, 158, 161, 163, 165, 168, 172–174, 180, 183, 184, 186, 188, 192, 194, 197, 200, 203–209, 211, 212, 214, 218, 226, 227, 231, 235, 236, 238, 241, 243, 245, 246, 249, 252, 257, 258, 259, 260; industry co-operation, 4, 6, 8, 27, 56, 163, 174. *See also* funding, research
Ritsumeikan Asia Pacific University, 198, 208

Scholastic Aptitude Test, 34
Sea to Sky University Act (British Columbia), 97, 100
Sebelas Maret University, 236
Secretaría Nacional de Planificación y Desarrollo (Ecuador), 162
Séminaire Laval, 48
Singapore, 245
social capital, 152
Social Sciences and Humanities Research Council of Canada, 83
soft law, 111
South Africa, 245
state, the, 5, 12, 14–19, 49, 78, 125, 127–129, 137–140, 147, 148, 151, 158, 170, 180, 181, 209, 211, 213, 216, 217, 222; evaluative state, 128

Strangway, David, 82, 95–97, 100–102
student-instructor ratios, 64, 229
students, 3, 4, 7–9, 13, 26, 27, 29, 31, 33–35, 37, 42, 48–52, 54, 55, 58, 63, 64, 66, 67, 70–73, 79, 84, 85, 91, 96–101, 105, 115–118, 127, 128, 130–132, 135, 136, 138–141, 148, 152, 157, 163, 164, 169–172, 185, 187, 198–203, 205, 206, 208, 218, 220, 226, 228–235, 237, 243, 244, 247, 252, 259; access, 5, 18, 32, 39, 113, 127, 137, 141, 154, 163, 164, 171, 173, 199, 207, 225, 226, 228, 229, 232, 234, 237; activism, 52, 90, 237; enrollment, 5, 6, 26, 27, 28, 64, 67, 71, 98, 99, 115, 156, 199, 227, 229, 236, 243, 244; financial assistance, 79, 82, 84, 85, 89, 90, 138; international, 7, 27, 117, 198, 244; non-conventional students, 26; student government, 75. *See also* tuition
Sweden, 118

teaching, 4, 8, 13, 15, 17, 19, 29, 30, 33, 35, 36, 40, 42, 49, 50, 52, 53, 57, 58, 64, 71, 72, 96, 98, 102–105, 118, 137, 141, 154, 157, 173, 199–203, 205–207, 211, 230, 234, 241, 243, 246, 257
technical universities (*Technische Hochschulen*), 6, 86
Tertiary Education Quality and Standards Agency (Australia), 241, 242. *See also* accountability
Tertiary Education Quality and Standards Agency (TEQSA), 241, 242, 244, 246–253
Tiananmen Square, 218
transfer payment, 79, 80, 83, 87
Transforming Australia's Higher Education System (Australia), 241, 244
transparency, 50, 52, 53, 127, 129, 244. *See also* accountability

Tremblay-Pépin, Simon, 58
Trent University, 54, 83
trust, 66, 73, 103, 135, 148, 152, 155, 241, 249, 250, 251, 252
Tsinghua University, 216
tuition, 4, 7, 27, 35, 51, 52, 55, 63, 71, 73, 78, 79, 84, 85, 88–90, 100, 139, 164, 169, 180, 199, 200, 228–230

undergraduate, 27, 30, 32, 34, 52, 64, 72, 76, 85, 96, 97, 100, 104, 132, 170, 201, 203, 227, 231
UNESCO, 13, 112, 114, 167, 259
United Kingdom (UK), 6, 22, 39, 143, 180, 186, 205, 223, 244
United States, 5, 6, 48, 51, 52, 64, 98, 102, 115, 118, 180, 205, 234, 244, 248, 251
Universidad Autónoma de Ciudad Juárez, 150
Universidad de Guadalajara, 150
Universidad de Sonora, 150
Universidad Veracruzana, 150
Université du Québec à Montréal, 55, 57

university models: government-commissioned (land-grant), 6, 180; Humboldtian (German), 180, 214; private, 180
University of British Columbia (UBC), 82, 95, 96, 97, 143, 260
University of Ontario Institute of Technology (UOIT), 86–89, 91
University of Pittsburgh, 231
University of Sao Paulo, 117
University of Shanghai Jiao Tong, 116
University of Toronto (U of T), 50, 56
University of Waterloo, 83

Weber, Max, 130, 134, 212, 216
Wilfrid Laurier University, 59
work/workforce, 4, 7, 20, 41, 88, 201, 234
World Bank, 26, 36, 113, 114, 117, 118, 227, 228
world-class, 6, 117, 119, 120, 219, 230, 235, 238. *See also* ranking

York University, 54, 55

GPSR Compliance

The European Union's (EU) General Product Safety Regulation (GPSR) is a set of rules that requires consumer products to be safe and our obligations to ensure this.

If you have any concerns about our products, you can contact us on

ProductSafety@springernature.com

In case Publisher is established outside the EU, the EU authorized representative is:

Springer Nature Customer Service Center GmbH
Europaplatz 3
69115 Heidelberg, Germany

www.ingramcontent.com/pod-product-compliance
Lightning Source LLC
LaVergne TN
LVHW051914060526
838200LV00004B/140